KOREAN STUDIES OF THE HENRY M. JACKSON
SCHOOL OF INTERNATIONAL STUDIES

Clark W. Sorensen, Editor

WRONGFUL DEATHS

Selected Inquest Records from Nineteenth-Century Korea

COMPILED AND TRANSLATED BY

Sun Joo Kim

AND

Jungwon Kim

UNIVERSITY OF WASHINGTON PRESS
Seattle and London

This publication was supported in part by the Korea Studies Program of the University of Washington in cooperation with the Henry M. Jackson School of International Studies.

UNIVERSITY OF WASHINGTON PRESS
PO Box 50096, Seattle, WA 98145, USA
www.washington.edu/uwpress

LIBRARY OF CONGRESS CATALOGING-IN-PUBLICATION DATA
Kim, Sun Joo, 1962–
    Wrongful deaths : selected inquest records from nineteenth-century Korea / compiled and translated by Sun Joo Kim and Jungwon Kim.
        pages   cm. — (Korean studies of the Henry M. Jackson School of International Studies)
    Includes bibliographical references and index.
    ISBN 978-0-295-99312-6 (hardback : alkaline paper) ; 978-0-295-99313-3 (paperback : alkaline paper)
    1. Korea—History—Choson dynasty, 1392–1910—Sources. 2. Korea—Social conditions—1392-1910—Sources. 3. Wrongful death—Korea—History—19th century—Sources. 4. Court records—Korea. 5. Courts—Korea—History—19th century—Sources. 6. Law—Social aspects—Korea—History—19th century—Sources. 7. Social classes—Korea—History—19th century—Sources. I. Kim, Jungwon. II. Title.
    DS915.15.K57   2014
    951.9'02—dc23   2013037570

CONTENTS

ACKNOWLEDGMENTS

O UR VENTURE WITH INQUEST RECORDS FROM THE LATE CHOSŎN period began about ten years ago in a graduate seminar where we read the cases in the *Inquest Records of Chunghwa County* (Chunghwa-bu ogan), a rare book in the collection of the Harvard-Yenching Library. Jungwon quickly realized that inquest records are treasure troves in which the quotidian lives of ordinary people can be traced, and wrote her dissertation based primarily on this particular type of source. Meanwhile, we began to use a translation of Yang Hang-nyŏn's death (case 1), a product of the seminar, in our undergraduate classes, and also made it available to several colleagues who wished to adopt it as class reading. We received streams of enthusiastic responses from students and colleagues who were awed at how this inquest record, unlike conventional sources, revealed the everyday lives and thoughts of common people.

The decision to collaboratively translate and analyze a sample of eight cases occurred almost spontaneously during one of our long phone conversations about our work. The impetus for acting on our decision was a Collaborative Research Grant from the American Council of Learned Scholars for 2009 through 2011. Thanks to this generous grant, we were able to take research leaves from our universities and focus on this project. For Jungwon, an Academy of Korean Studies grant (AKS-2010-DZZ-2101) also partially supported her completion of the project. Though our work sites were several hundred miles apart, we carefully divided up the work and followed our plans closely, communicating via email and telephone as well as with face-to-face meetings in Cambridge and Seoul.

Though the entire work is a result of true collaboration, it was Jungwon who primarily translated cases 4, 6, and 7 and wrote introductions to them, while Sun Joo took charge of cases 2, 3, 5, and 8. We contributed equally to the introduction and case 1. At every step we discussed various translation strategies, worked on creating a uniform writing style and terminology list, and reviewed and provided feedback for each other's work. We went through several stages of revisions before finalizing the manuscript. Our collaborative work proved not only productive in its own right but also instrumental in advancing our individual scholarship.

Many people provided insightful questions and suggestions. First of all, we would like to officially acknowledge that this research was assisted by the Collaborative Research Fellowship Program of the American Council of Learned Societies from 2009 to 2011. We would also like to thank the two anonymous reviewers for the University of Washington Press who offered critical comments and advice. Our colleagues Carter Eckert, John Duncan, Eugene Park, Ronald Toby, and Nancy Abelmann supported our endeavor with great enthusiasm and trust. Dae Hong Kim, Myoun Hoi Do, Min Jung, Wenjiao Cai, Robert E. Hegel, Edward J. Baker, and Gina Kwon helped to decipher some difficult passages and translate Korean legal terms. We are particularly grateful to Dae Hong Kim, who reviewed parts of our translations and shared thoughtful comments during the revision process. We would also like to thank William Alford, Jasper Kim, and Jae-Woo Sim, all of whom showed a keen interest in our project. Conversations with Yonglin Jiang not only enriched our understanding of the use of the *Great Ming Code* in Ming and Qing China and Chosŏn Korea, but also sharpened our theoretical approach to interpreting Korean inquest records. Of course, any remaining errors in the translation are ours.

We jointly presented part of our work at the annual meeting of the American Historical Association in 2011 and the Association for Asian Studies in 2011. We thank Dana Rabin, Janet Thesis, David Eason, and the audiences at these conferences for sharing invaluable feedback with us. We also gave individual lectures on various parts of the project and are grateful for those opportunities to engage with colleagues: Sun Joo spoke at the Center for Korean Studies at the University of California at Berkeley, Binghamton University, and for the East Asian Legal Studies at the Harvard Law School, while Jungwon spoke at Columbia University and the Institute for Advanced Study in Princeton, New Jersey.

Although we had the privilege and pleasure of working together on this project, we were initially discouraged to learn that a number of major university presses that used to publish works on the premodern period have since discontinued such publications. We are extremely grateful that the Korean Studies series of the Henry M. Jackson School of International Studies, a University of Washington Press publication program, remains strong and that its editor, Clark W. Sorensen, embraced our manuscript with enthusiasm. We would like to thank all the staff at the Press, whose professionalism made the entire publication process seamless. Special gratitude also goes to the Kyu-janggak Archive at Seoul National University and to the Korean Christian Museum at Soongsil University, which granted permission to reproduce items from their collections in this book.

Over the last two decades, English scholarship in Korean Studies has seen phenomenal, albeit uneven, growth. Publications in the field of premodern and early modern Korea are still few in number. It is our genuine hope that this book will help spark increased interest on the part of students in traditional Korea, while also providing scholars in the broader field of social and legal history with access to the legal materials of early modern Korea.

TRANSLATORS' NOTES

A FULL INQUEST REPORT IS A LONG DOCUMENT. TO GIVE THE reader the gist of a full report, case 1 is translated in full without omitting a word. As readers will quickly learn, there are many repetitions, particularly in the inquest official's interrogation. This, however, almost always led to another round of more incisive and clarifying questions. These redundancies in the questions and testimonies are summarized in the other seven cases. To avoid confusion, these summaries and our own commentaries, which are intended to remove repetition and keep the reader oriented within a translation, are set in *italics*.

The traditional writing format was very different from modern Korean. We tried to preserve its formatting characteristics as much as possible, in terms of indenting, line spacing, and so forth, because the document format itself reveals certain characteristics of a society and its culture. For example, in the original texts, direct references to the king and his official pronouncements are raised one character space above the text, or begin after a blank space, or simply begin on the next line. References to an upper government authority or to his official pronouncements are often, if not always, preceded by a blank space. These practices are indicated in the translations by the use of ALL CAPITAL letters.

Both the subject as well as the object of a sentence are often omitted in literary Chinese and Korean writings. In translation, we supply these when they are clear without putting them in square brackets. However, when we need to provide substantial information to make the sentence comprehensible, we enclose our insertion in square brackets.

For transliteration, we use the McCune-Reischauer system for Korean and Pinyin for Chinese. Most administrative units are not translated but are transliterated and rendered from smallest unit to largest, in accordance with American practice, though the original text gives the units in the opposite order. Likewise, geographical names such as rivers and mountains are not usually translated but are transliterated, except in a few cases when a translated name helps the reader imagine the place to which it refers.

DATES, TIME, AND AGE

In traditional Korea, dates were recorded by a two-character name for the year in the sixty-year cycle, which is a combination of ten units of Heavenly stems (*ch'ŏn'gan*) and twelve units of Earthly branches (*chiji*), in accordance with the dating system developed in ancient China. Almost all inquest records also use this dating system. It is sometimes difficult to pinpoint exactly what year is being referred to because each name recurs every sixty years; for example, 1744, 1804, and 1864 are all *kapcha* years. Researchers, however, often have ways to figure out the exact year by analyzing the content of the document, as we were able to do in all the cases translated in this book.

In official records of Chosŏn Korea, dates were often recorded by reference to the reign period of the current Chinese emperor, followed by a corresponding name of the year in the sixty-year cycle, and then the lunar month and the day. For example, "Tongzhi i-nyŏn kyehae ku-wŏl sa-il" is given in this traditional order in translation as "1863.9.4," which we have followed with the corresponding date in the Western calendar in parentheses like this: (10/16/1863). The differences in the dates are due to the exigencies of the lunar calendar, discussed later in this section. Some official records go by the reign year of the Korean king's posthumous title rather than the Chinese emperor's reign title; for example, "Ch'ŏlchong sipsa-nyŏn ku-wŏl sa-il" would appear as "1863.9.4" in translation. In 1897, Chosŏn changed its official name to the Great Han Empire (Taehan Cheguk), and Emperor Kojong adopted his own reign title, "Kwangmu." From then until 1910, many official documents used the reign year of the Korean emperor for dating; thus "Kwangmu sam-nyŏn sibi-wŏl o-il" is "1899.12.5."

Like the solar calendar, the lunar calendar consists of one year divided into twelve months. However, each month has either twenty-nine or thirty days. An extra intercalary month (*yun*) is added approximately once every three years to resolve the problem of lagging behind the sun's movements, and to keep the dates and seasons in order.

In Chosŏn Korea, time of day was divided into twelve units (twelve Earthly branches) beginning with *cha-si*, which marks eleven at night to one o'clock in the morning; *ch'uk-si*, from one to three in the morning; and so on. In translation, we chose the middle hour; thus *cha-si* is "around midnight" and *ch'uk-si* is "around two in the morning."

Koreans in the traditional period followed the Chinese custom and counted a newborn baby as already being one year old upon birth. An individual then became a year older on New Year's Day rather than on his or her birthday. (Many older-generation Koreans in today's Korea still follow this practice.) Therefore, a baby born on the last day of the year is considered to be two years of age the following day. The character used to mark a person's age is either *nyŏn* or *se*, translated as "years in age" or "years old."

WEIGHTS AND MEASUREMENTS

Toe, mal, and *sŏm* are measuring units of grain and other goods. Although the exact amount of each unit varied according to locality and time, approximate amounts are as follows: 1 *sŏm* = either 15 or 20 *mal* = 1 picul of grain by volume = either 89.464 or 119.285 liters; 1 *mal* = 10 *toe* = 5.96 liters; and 1 *toe* = 10 *hop* = 0.596 liter.

    Ch'ŏk is a measuring unit of length. Several different *ch'ŏk* (rulers) were used during the Chosŏn dynasty. The lengths of these different *ch'ŏk*, before they were standardized by King Sejong in the fifteenth century, varied from 20.8 to 46.7 centimeters. According to the *Coroner's Guide for the Elimination of Grievances* (Muwŏllok, originally a publication of Yuan China [1271–1368]), it was the *kwan-ch'ŏk* (official ruler) that was recommended for inquests.[1] *Kwan-ch'ŏk* seems to refer to the *chu-ch'ŏk* (Zhou ruler), which was 20.795 centimeters during the fifteenth century and 20.48 to 21.6 centimeters in the late Chosŏn. The *chi-ch'ŏk* (land-measuring ruler) that appears in case 8 was presumably for measuring ground distance and may refer to the *yangjŏn-ch'ŏk* (land survey ruler), which was used for land survey and registration. There is evidence that one *yangjŏn-ch'ŏk* for first-grade land (there were several different grades of land fertility in the Chosŏn) during the fifteenth century was 99.296 centimeters long. In any case, 1 *ch'ŏk* is equivalent to 10 *ch'on*, and 1 *ch'on* is equivalent to 10 *p'un*.[2]

    A *li* is a longer unit of distance, equaling 2,100 *ch'ŏk*. Thus, according to late Chosŏn *zhou-ch'ŏk*, a *li* measured between 430.08 meters and 453.60 meters. A *kan* is a unit for measuring the size of a house; 1 *kan* refers to the width between two bearing poles, or 10 *ch'ŏk*. A *p'ok* is a unit of fabric by width. A *yang* is a monetary unit; 1 *yang* = 10 *chŏn* = 100 *p'un* or *mun*. The cash/grain commutation rate set by the government in the late Chosŏn was 3 *yang* per 1 *sŏm*, though the market rate had been fluctuating greatly. In P'yŏngan Province in 1811, one family could live for a month on 3 *yang* of cash.[3]

    Other measuring units introduced in each case that are not explained here are annotated in the translation itself.

NAMES

A number of appellations are used in inquest reports, and each carries delicate social and cultural implications that are difficult to translate into English. Here we shall try to define their meanings and historical uses as best as we can. Females are referred to in inquest records using only their surnames followed by an appellation. Upper-class women of Chosŏn Korea did have a given name, although these were not used in public. *Ssi* is in general used for a yangban (elite) woman; *choi*, which is the colloquial reading of *sosa*, was originally reserved for commoner women, though even yangban women were often referred to using the appellation *choi* in the late Chosŏn period. *Nyŏ* is another term used in inquest records, and it seems that *nyŏ* carried a somewhat derogatory implication, though not all the time. For example, in case 2, which occurred in the late eighteenth century, the victim, Ms. Pak, was a local yangban (*hyangban*) but was called either Pak *choi* or Pak *nyŏ*. We translate *ssi* as "Madam" and *choi* as "Ms." to differentiate between the two; for *nyŏ* we try to carry the context by translating Kim *nyŏ* in case 5, for example, as "that woman Kim" or "Ms. Kim." In Chosŏn (as well as in contemporary Korea), a married woman kept her maiden name after marriage.

In inquest records, males are referred to by their full names when appearing for the first time, then subsequently by either the full name, the given name only, or the surname followed by a certain appellation. Various appellations were used for men. *Pan* is reserved for a yangban, as seen in case 2 for Sin *pan*, which is translated as "Yangban Sin." *Ka* (or *ga*) literally means "surname," thus Yang-*ga* is rendered "Mr. Yang." *Han* seems to connote a derogatory sentiment, thus Yang-*han* is probably "that bastard Yang." In case 7, in which tanners, one of the lowest social status groups, have the appellation *han* throughout the document, we translate *han* as "brute" to convey its demeaning implication. A person who had a certain bureaucratic office or a state examination degree, even a preliminary examination degree such as *ch'osi*, is often recorded with his surname followed by his office or degree. Thus Kim Saengwŏn is an honorific way of referring to Mr. Kim who has a classics licentiate degree, while Yi Ch'ŏmji in case 3 is Mr. Yi who had a senior third (Sr. 3) rank military post.

All Korean names in the text are given in Korean order (surname followed by the given name, not separated by a comma). Korean and Chinese names in the bibliography also appear in this way, except for authors who publish in

English, whose last and first names appear in their own preferred spelling and separated by a comma.

ONLINE SOURCES

There are numerous useful online resources for researchers, and we relied upon these greatly, though without making a note of each and every reference. For the *Veritable Records of the Kings of the Chosŏn Dynasty* (Chosŏn wangjo sillok), we used the edition provided by the Kuksa P'yŏnch'an Wiwŏnhoe (National Institute of Korean History) at http://sillok.history.go.kr/main/main.jsp. All references to this record are noted according to the *sillok* of each king, followed by year.month.day (e.g., *Injo sillok*, 1633.1.8). For online dictionaries, *NAVER sajŏn* (Naver dictionaries) at http://dic.naver.com is most useful. The *Han'guk yŏktae inmul chonghap chŏngbo sisŭt'em* (Comprehensive information database of historical persons in Korean history) compiled by the Han'gukhak Chungang Yŏn'guwŏn (Academy of Korean Studies) at http://people.aks.ac.kr/index.aks provides basic information on historical persons of the Chosŏn dynasty, including information related to degree-holders of higher civil service examination (*munkwa*) as well as lower civil service examinations, such as those who passed a classics licentiate exam (*saengwŏn*) or a literary licentiate exam (*chinsa*), and to their immediate family members. More comprehensive information concerning those who passed the higher civil service examination and their family members is available at *The Wagner and Song Munkwa Roster of the Chosŏn Dynasty*, compiled and annotated by Edward W. Wagner and Song Chunho, and made available by Dongbang Media at www.koreaa2z.com/munkwa. For calendar conversions from lunar to solar and vice versa, we took advantage of the tool provided by the Astronomy and Space Science Information at http://astro.kasi.re.kr/Life/Convert SolarLunarForm.aspx?MenuID=115.

WRONGFUL
DEATHS

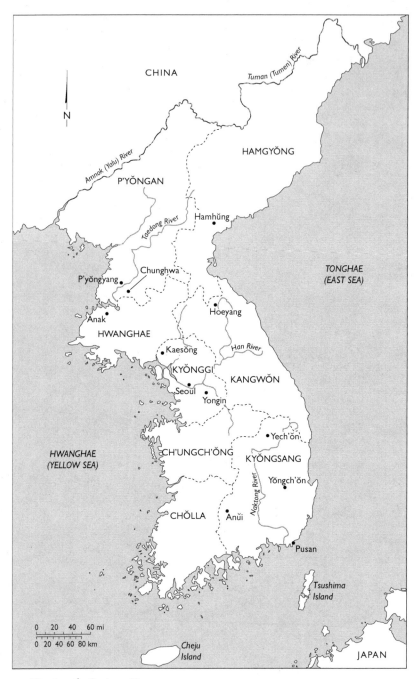

CHINA

Tuman (Tumen) River

HAMGYŎNG

Amnok (Yalu) River

P'YŎNGAN

Taedong River

Hamhŭng

Chunghwa

P'yŏngyang

Anak

HWANGHAE

Hoeyang

TONGHAE
(EAST SEA)

Kaesŏng

Han River

KYŎNGGI

KANGWŎN

Seoul

Yongin

HWANGHAE
(YELLOW SEA)

CH'UNGCH'ŎNG

Yech'ŏn

KYŎNGSANG

Naktong River

Yŏngch'ŏn

CHŎLLA

Anŭi

Pusan

Tsushima
Island

0   20   40   60 mi

0   20 40 60 80 km

Cheju
Island

JAPAN

Nineteenth-Century Korea

N

INTRODUCTION

Chosŏn Korea in Its Last Century

N INETEENTH-CENTURY CHOSŎN (1392–1910) IS AN AREA OF CON-
tention in Korean historiography, as Qing China and Tokugawa
Japan are in Chinese and Japanese historical studies. With the sudden demise of King Chŏngjo (r. 1776–1800), historians agree that nineteenth-
century Korea departed from the sociocultural renaissance mode of the
previous century under the strong leadership of kings Yŏngjo (r. 1724–76) and
Chŏngjo. The watershed event was the "opening" of the country to the West,
beginning with the Kanghwa Treaty with Japan in 1876, a convenient moment
that historians often use to divide Korean history between the premodern and
modern periods, although the same Yi royal house ruled the country until
1910, when Japan annexed Korea and made it its colony. The fact that Korea
became a colony after maintaining independent state systems for almost two
thousand years, with an unusually low number of dynastic turnovers during
that long time span, has vastly complicated Korean efforts to explain such a
humiliating historical anomaly.

The most conventional and traditional explanation employs the idea of the
dynastic cycle, according to which an initially robust dynastic system is des-
tined to decline, a process often accelerated by bureaucratic inefficiency and
corruption and resultant popular rebellions. In the case of Korea, historians
have found that the rise of in-law politics in the first half of the nineteenth
century, fueled by the enthronement of successive juvenile kings, brought
general disarray in numerous key dynastic institutions, including personnel
affairs and tax administrations. These institutional breakdowns prompted
bureaucratic abuses and exploitation, which led to the eruption of major
popular revolts, beginning with the Hong Kyŏng-nae Rebellion (1812). These
were followed by numerous tax-resistance movements, mostly in the southern

provinces (1862), and by the Tonghak revolts (1894–95), which were initially religiously motivated but soon turned into more complex popular movements that demanded various social and financial reforms and acquired certain nationalist tints in their later stages.

Before and after the opening of the country, Chosŏn rulers and elites made various attempts at institutional reform—both more traditionally oriented reforms initiated by Taewŏn'gun (1820–98), the father of the reigning King Kojong (r. 1863–1907) and the de facto ruler during the initial years of Kojong's rule, and more radical reforms with a modern outlook in the last few decades of the dynasty, mostly pursued by "enlightened" elites who had had the opportunity to learn about Western modernity after the opening of Korea. To some historians, the failure of these reform efforts was inherent in Chosŏn's institutional arrangements, which precluded any single group of political leaders from becoming powerful enough to lead the country toward a modern state at this crucial time when certain swift and epochal reforms were needed for Korea's survival.[1]

To others, Korea was not simply repeating similar dynastic cycles but constantly evolving and developing toward eventual modernity. Scholars of this line of thought, which is often called the internal development theory (*naejaejŏk palchŏn non*), see the seventeenth century onward as a period of dynamic social and economic growth in which sprouts of capitalism emerged and the hierarchical social status system collapsed. According to this view, the popular revolts in the nineteenth century were largely peasant wars against the impotent state and corrupt, exploitative ruling elites and overlords, a necessary historical stage that would lead to a modern, democratic polity. Side by side with this bottom-up movement toward modernity, top-down reforms, which had their roots in late Chosŏn intellectual movements seeking practical learning and institutional reforms, emerged and were poised to transform the country until it was on a par with other civilized modern states. The internal development theory therefore holds that Korea's annexation by Japan was due not to a lack of internal development but to the timing of world history, which led to a particular mode of imperialism (that of Japan) posing an insurmountable obstacle to Korea's spontaneous evolution toward modernization.[2]

Whereas these explications acknowledge the shock of colonization and blame either Korea's traditional system or Japan's brutal imperialist drive, recent scholarship explores more factual and microscopic aspects of nineteenth-century Korea in an effort to understand the time, space, and people in nuanced and detailed ways. By using unconventional primary sources, such as lineage and family archives, diaries, letters, petitions, and criminal records, it supplements earlier studies derived from official and widely recognized documents representing the voices of male elites, though it is not necessarily immune to the larger debates discussed earlier. For instance, a number of social historians have used diverse privately held documents that cover several centuries of the late Chosŏn, such as inheritance certificates, legal proceedings, and regulations and records produced by various local and village associations, to inform their view of the nineteenth century—especially the mid-nineteenth century, on the eve of the opening of the country—as a social crisis. By crisis they mean that the yangban ruling system had mostly broken down by this time because of the growth of non-yangban status groups and their encroachment on the privileges long monopolized by established yangban.[3]

From a slightly different angle, a group of economic historians who painstakingly collected and analyzed every piece of economic data available from both official and unofficial documents—including private diaries that multiple generations of a family kept, which recorded trivial matters such as rental rates and prices of major goods and services—came to the conclusion that the economy began to stagnate from the beginning of the nineteenth century on, and fell into a serious crisis around the middle of the century.[4] From this perspective, various reforms planned and implemented in the last few decades of the Chosŏn dynasty were nothing but futile.

In response to this general view of nineteenth-century Chosŏn as declining or failing, some studies have proposed somewhat different pictures, based on their close readings of frequently used sources and on their introduction of new sources. For example, in her analysis of the causes of the two popular rebellions in the nineteenth century, the Hong Kyŏng-nae Rebellion and the 1862 popular revolts, Sun Joo Kim has pointed out that the dynastic administration was capable of meeting these domestic challenges, and that local elites who were loyal to the dynasty were quite successful in holding on to their power and prestige despite various social and economic challenges that might have weakened their domination in society.[5] In her study of a local yangban association, she also found that although socioeconomic changes in the late Chosŏn did fuel the rise of "new" elites in local society, the established ruling elites held together tightly until the end of the dynasty.[6] Anders Karlsson's studies of dynastic relief systems in the nineteenth century also support the idea that viable dynastic institutions existed.[7]

Because of these diverse perspectives, it may be difficult for general readers to form a clear picture of nineteenth-century Korea. Not only is history subject to interpretation based on one's own predilections, but Korea's modern paths have been complicated by colonization, civil war, the cold war, and division in the twentieth century. An understanding of Korea's preceding centuries is anything but simple. Yet our intellectual motivation for writing this book emerges precisely from this complex historiography. It was the very vagueness of nineteenth-century Korea that alerted us to the possibility of exploring this period of vortex from hitherto unseen perspectives and through previously unheard voices, namely, by examining inquest records (*kŏman*).

THE SOURCES: *KŎMAN*

The primary sources of this volume are *kŏman*—inquest records or legal testimonies of late Chosŏn Korea (hereafter "inquest records"). *Kŏman* is an abbreviation of *kŏmsi munan*, meaning "a legal draft on examining a dead body." However, the *kŏman* sources are far more than simple records of examinations of corpses: in fact, the bulk of each *kŏman* source consists of people's testimonies. In addition, it is not easy to locate these sources as single documents titled "*Kŏman*" in Korean archives; rather, most of them carry a long title beginning with the specific area where the death or investigation occurred, and including other relevant information such as the name, gender, and social status of the victim. Moreover, various long and short versions of inquest records exist—from a full document with a thorough inquest report followed by an inquest form, testimonies, and a concluding statement, to abridged ones omitting some parts of the fuller reports. Whereas the fuller version of an inquest record either consists of a single-volume compilation with its own long title (as for cases 7 and 8) or comes as a collection of several cases (cases 1 and 5), shorter versions are found in volumes with more generic titles, such as *Selected Inquest Records* (Kŏman ch'o), which contains dozens of death cases reported within one region during a specific period (cases 3, 4, and 6). Also, depending on the bureaucratic level of the office where a report was prepared, some records contain only concluding statements by inquest officials, which serve more as settlement memoirs for incidents than as an archetypal inquest record (case 2).[8]

A full version of an inquest record compiled by the inquest official, then, is a long and repetitive document, beginning with an opening statement explaining how the county magistrate who acted as an inquest official embarked on his investigation, accompanied by a death report often made by the close relative of the deceased (*sich'in*), a brief deposition given by the complainant, and examination of the corpse, followed by a few rounds of interrogation of all persons involved in the death incident, including the accused (*chŏngbŏm*). This takes up the bulk of the document. The inquest record ends with the inquest official's concluding statement (*palsa*), in which he states his analysis both of the true cause of death (*sirin*) and of the death incident. Because the inquest officials frequently used allegories and parables or referred to stories from ancient Confucian classics and literature, the concluding statement is the most difficult part of the document for a modern reader to decode. The provincial governor's adjudication is often appended to the inquest record. Yet because there were many stages before final sentencing took place in a death case, and an inquest record does not carry any information beyond the county and provincial levels of investigation and judgment, we do not learn the final verdict against the accused.

It is unclear when the practice of compiling inquest records began during the Chosŏn, although the use of the manual *Coroner's Guide for the Elimination of Grievances* (Muwŏllok) in examining a death case had existed since the early dynasty. Some of the earliest known inquest records date to the latter part of the eighteenth century, but most extant inquest records, especially fuller versions, were produced during the nineteenth. While summaries of legal cases appear in official dynastic histories such as *Veritable Record of the Chosŏn Dynasty* (Sillok) and *Record of Daily Reflections* (Ilsŏngnok), pre-nineteenth-century original and full inquest records may have been lost or have been recorded in different formats. That said, it seems there was no explicit format for an inquest record prior to King Chŏngjo's reign, and that may be a reason for the concentration of extant inquest records from the nineteenth century. In 1779, in response to Chŏng Ho-in (1728–?) of the Ministry of Penal Affairs, who pointed out the complexity of the different investigation reports produced by each province, King Chŏngjo ordered that a standard inquest record be prepared and distributed throughout the eight provinces.[9] The standard format drafted at that time is similar to the format found in the full inquest records now extant, though the guideline suggests excluding the list of questions asked during the investigation and recording only the important statements made. The guideline also recommends that testimonies of joint interrogation under torture (*tongch'u*) for a doubtful case be kept succinct, rather than being recorded in detail.[10] About five years later, King Chŏngjo announced a slightly revised version of the 1779 inquest record, to provide an even more concrete format while retaining fundamental guidelines, such as not recording the list of questions and avoiding unnecessary redundancy.[11]

Several of the late-nineteenth-century cases we introduce in this volume nevertheless contain the magistrate's list of questions (cases 1, 5, and 8), which may indicate that, rather than one definite inquest record format, some divergent formats were still employed and produced until the end of the dynasty, although the essential framework was kept intact.

About six hundred reports categorized as *kŏman* are stored in the oldest archive in Korea, the Kyujanggak Archive. There are also several compilations of inquest records available at the National Library of Korea, containing short- to mid-length reports as well as numerous concluding statements. The Harvard-Yenching Library has several collections of inquest records, mostly compiled under the title of a county or a province. While most of these reports deal with death cases of the nineteenth and even first few years of the twentieth century, a few publications of the copious decisions on capital offences during King Chŏngjo's reign—namely, the *Treatise on the Ministry of Penal Affairs* (Ch'ugwanji), *Records of Royal Reviews* (Simnirok), and *New Writings on Circumspection in Judicial Decisions* (Hŭmhŭm sinsŏ)—are valuable resources for examining the legal reasoning of eighteenth-century Korea and thus supplement our knowledge of nineteenth-century Chosŏn judicial practices.[12] In selecting the eight cases introduced and translated in this book, we aimed to show the diversity of existing sources of inquest records in terms of format, length, compilation year, archive, location of the incident, type of crime or assault, and status and gender of the victim. The earliest case is from the late eighteenth century (case 2) and the latest from 1899 (case 8); the 1899 case is also the longest inquest record in this volume, comprising three full reports and six official pieces of correspondence and serving as a perfect example of the changes in legal terms and judicial procedures at the turn of the century.

The inquest records were written in a mixture of literary Chinese and "clerk's writing" (*idu*), a device of borrowing either the reading or the meaning of Chinese characters to express some part of colloquial Korean, particularly for some pronouns, particles, conjunctions, and verb endings. Toward the end of the nineteenth century, medieval Korean script replaced some clerk's writing used for particles and verb endings (cases 7 and 8). The use of clerk's writing is usually found in local and personal documents, such as various types of reports and certificates, investigation documents, and petitions. That a 233-*idu* vocabulary list is attached to the *Essential Knowledge for Scholar-Officials and Clerks* (Yusŏ p'ilchi)[13] as an appendix shows its importance in formulating and understanding all kinds of documents often used by the local courts. "Clerk's writing" in inquest records enabled the court recorder to inscribe oral testimony in colloquial form; literary Chinese, the official written language for Chosŏn Korea, was unable to attain this effect because Chinese and Korean are such two fundamentally different languages. The power of inquest records lies precisely in this intersection of colloquial speech, literary Chinese, and clerk's writing, which conveys the impression that we are hearing the voices of the people who testified in the trials, in the same way that modern courtroom transcripts do.

While they were being recorded by the brushes of local officials, it is important to note that the testimonies were simultaneously being edited to meet judicial guidelines, and some alteration of nuance inevitably occurred. As Robert E. Hegel and Mathew Sommer discuss in their studies of Qing legal documents, despite the strength of inquest records in delivering the contemporaneous voices of illiterate people in late Chosŏn Korea, these records are nevertheless textual products crafted from oral testimonies and were carefully molded by the priorities of the magistrates.[14] Though containing true narratives, they were deliberately organized and composed not only to filter out some "fictive elements" but also to avoid any vulgarity in the stories told by ordinary people; thus, it is impossible to know how much of the participants' genuine voices has been lost in the process of mediation between exactly what people said and what the magistrates recorded.

Indeed, although we have used these inquest records to explore the most intimate and intense real-life experiences of men and women, the theoretical approach to analyzing the many-layered voices in inquest records remains challenging. We have therefore constructed our conceptual framework based on other studies derived from legal archives, for example, those by historians of early modern Europe, such as Natalie Davis and Carlo Ginzburg. Davis delves into this paradoxical articulation between archival fictions and historical narration in her superb analysis of sixteenth-century letters of remission, and Ginzburg reveals how transformation of the popular notion of witchcraft was manipulated by the inquisitors' perception of it. These studies ultimately suggest that creative use of ostensibly trivial details in inquisitional or court records can enable researchers to reconstruct popular attitudes and practices.[15]

Therefore, we argue that the constraints found in these inquest records as products of the official consumption of court proceedings do not completely erase the voices of the people who appeared in the court, fashioned their narratives themselves, and may already have been familiar with how to recount to a magistrate what had actually happened. Although inquest records do not represent transparent real lives or absolute truth about incidents and can be understood only as constructions that may have had a calculated effect in court, they are still the most tangible sources we have that actually penetrate the prescribed hegemonic value of Confucianism and grasp the rich variety of attitudes and behaviors of ordinary people who lived under the apparent uniformity of a Confucian state. Most of all—given that for many years the only resources available for the study of Chosŏn society through legal archives were either legal codes (and other prospective legislation issued by the courts), drastically compressed summaries of legal cases, or petitions—no other primary source may transmit the intact statements and realities of people from every corner of Chosŏn society more vividly than inquest records do.[16]

LOCAL ADMINISTRATION

How did the Chosŏn state rule the country? How much of the state's power did the villagers come into direct contact with, and through what means? The structure of provincial and local administrations underwent a number of changes in the early half of the dynasty, but the main skeleton of local administration established during the seventeenth century did not change much for the rest of the dynasty. In the nineteenth century, before some administrative shuffling took place after the Kabo Reform in 1894, the entire country—except for Hansŏng-bu (Seoul Magistracy) and four yusubu (municipalities) nearby established for defense of the royal capital—was divided into eight provinces, each of which was governed by a provincial governor (kwanch'alsa or kamsa) of junior second (Jr. 2) rank who oversaw various administrative matters, including judicial administration in the province (see the frontispiece).[17] Provinces were further divided into administrative units called pu, taedohobu, mok, tohobu, kun, and hyŏn (we adopt the generic term "county" for these in translation, see table 1), to which an official of a rank ranging from junior second to junior sixth was centrally appointed. Despite the fact that the governing magistrates' official ranks could and did vary, there was no hierarchical order among different levels of counties; all magistrates reported directly to the provincial governor, while also reserving the right to communicate directly with the king. Although there were fixed terms of service, ranging from 600 to 1,800 days for magistracy, it was rare for a county magistrate to serve his full term; this frequent change of magistrates, one of the well-known institutional problems, caused administrative inefficiencies, though this particular problem was not confined to the late Chosŏn period.[18]

In each county, the magistrate, who exercised executive as well as judicial

TABLE 1 Provincial administration in nineteenth-century Chosŏn (before the Kabo Reform of 1894)

Administrative Unit	Title of the Post	Bureaucratic Rank	Number of Administrative Units
Hansŏng-bu (Seoul Magistracy)	P'anyun (Chief Magistrate of Seoul Magistracy)	Senior second	1
Yusubu (Municipality)	Yusu (Chief Magistrate of Municipality)	Junior second	4 (Kaesŏng, Kwangju, Kanghwa, and Suwŏn)
To (Province)	Kwanch'alsa or Kamsa (Provincial Governor)	Junior second	8
Pu (Special City)	Puyun (Magistrate of Special City)	Junior second	5 (Chŏnju, P'yŏngyang, Hamhŭng, Kyŏngju, and Ŭiju)
Taedohobu (Greater County)	Taedohobusa (Magistrate of Greater County)	Senior third	4 (Andong, Kangnŭng, Anbyŏn, and Yŏngbyŏn)
Mok (Special County)	Moksa (Magistrate of Special County)	Senior third	20
Tohobu (County)	Tohobusa or Pusa (Magistrate of County)	Junior third	44
Kun (Lesser County)	Kunsu (Magistrate of Lesser County)	Junior fourth	82
Hyŏn (Prefecture)	Hyŏllyŏng (Magistrate of Prefecture)	Junior fifth	34
Hyŏn (Lesser Prefecture)	Hyŏn'gam (Magistrate of Lesser Prefecture)	Junior sixth	141

power, received administrative support from three quasi-official organizations: the Bureau of Local Yangban (Hyangch'ŏng), Bureau of Public Administration (Chakch'ŏng), and Bureau of Military Administration (Much'ŏng). Local clerks (ajŏn or hyangni) in the Bureau of Public Administration carried out daily administrative duties, which were divided into six administrative areas in imitation of the six ministries in the central court: personnel, taxation, rites, military affairs, penal affairs, and public works. Although local clerks had shared genealogical roots with yangban ever since the late Koryŏ (918–1392) and early Chosŏn, their status had been drastically degraded beginning in the early Chosŏn through a number of legislative means, and by the late Chosŏn they were unsalaried hereditary service personnel.[19]

The personnel in the Bureau of Military Administration were a more complex mix of people. Although military service had been subordinated to the civil branch during the Chosŏn period, high-ranking military officers such as *chunggun* (chief military officers) in the bureaus of certain counties were supplied from the established group of local yangban and thus enjoyed the same prestige yangban did, while ordinary commoners filled the positions of the lower-level military officers who provided actual military and police services.

The Bureau of Local Yangban (Hyangch'ŏng), which oversaw the other two bureaus and also supported and advised the county magistrate, was originally a local yangban's institution representing their interests. The major local yangban lineages of each county had organized an exclusive, self-regulating association from the mid-Chosŏn period on, and this association intervened in county administration by sending its representatives to the Hyangch'ŏng as its director (*chwasu*), assistant director (*pyŏlgam*), and granary supervisor (*ch'anggam*). In some counties, the prestige of these quasi-bureaucratic posts (*hyangim*) at the Bureau of Local Yangban degenerated until those who held the positions were tantamount to local clerks, for they handled various administrative matters, taxation in particular, that the established yangban tended to avoid. However, in other counties, established yangban continued to hold these posts and fulfill these roles.[20]

A county was subdivided into districts (*myŏn* or *pang*), which were composed of several subdistricts (*li* or *ri*), which in turn comprised several villages and hamlets (*tong* or *ch'on*). There were a number of different titles for district administrator, such as *p'unghŏn* and *yakchŏng* (collectively called *myŏnim*); for subdistrict administrator, such as *chonwi*, *ijŏng*, and *ihŏn* (collectively called *iim*); and for village headmen or elders, such as *tumin*, *tongsu*, *tongjang*, and *chwajang*. These headmen played a role as liaisons between the county office and the people on various administrative matters. When a murder or a suspicious death took place, it was their responsibility to report it to the county office immediately, and to be present and testify during the inquest investigation.

JUDICIAL ADMINISTRATIVE STRUCTURE: INVESTIGATION AND CRIMINAL PROCEDURE

English scholarship on Korea's legal history is disappointingly meager. William Shaw's authoritative book, *Legal Norms in a Confucian State*, published almost thirty years ago, nonetheless provides a firm foundation for understanding the legal system and legal reasoning of Chosŏn Korea. Therefore, the following description of judicial institutions and criminal procedures is largely borrowed from this book, supplemented by more recent scholarship in the Korean language.[21] The Chosŏn court, while inheriting many institutions and legal codes from the preceding Koryŏ dynasty, carried out a number of Confucian reforms during the first several decades of the dynasty. The result was the collection of new administrative codes published as the *Great Code of Administration* (Kyŏngguk taejŏn) in 1485, which subsequently became the legal foundation of the dynasty. While keeping the structure laid out in the *Great Code of Administration*, numerous legal changes and royal orders were issued throughout the Chosŏn dynasty. These new codes and regulations were periodically collected and published as a vital reference for administrators, culminating in the 1865 publication of the *Comprehensive Collection of Dynastic Codes* (Taejŏn hoet'ong).

The *Great Ming Code* (Chinese: Da Ming lü; Korean: Taemyŏngnyul)[22] served as the basic criminal law of the dynasty from its beginning. Traces of the *Great Ming Code* can be still found in the 1905 *Comprehensive Collection of Penal Codes* (Hyŏngbŏp taejŏn) and disappeared only when the Japanese colonial government promulgated the *Chosŏn Penal Order* (Chosŏn hyŏngsaryŏng) in 1912.[23] Throughout the dynasty, however, the Chosŏn court adopted a number of crucial revisions of the *Great Ming Code* in order to address cultural and socioeconomic differences between Ming China (1368–1644) and Chosŏn Korea, as much as the late Ming's profound social changes such as commercialization and the arrival of the Manchu Qing dynasty (1644–1912) required flexible translation of the *Great Ming Code* in judicial rulings in China.[24] While the *Great Ming Code* was employed as a general criminal law without much revision during the first half of the dynasty, the increasing complexity posed by the war experiences of the late sixteenth and early seventeenth century, as well as subsequent socioeconomic changes, demanded that the Chosŏn state enact new statutes to address new challenges. The fact that copious volumes of special laws were published and compiled from the reign of King Sukchong (r. 1674–1720) onward shows how the state endeavored to respond to new and complex social problems, such as rampant gravesite litigations during the late Chosŏn (cases 2 and 8).

In judicial administration, there was no clear division among executive, legislative, and judicial branches of government in Chosŏn Korea, as in Ming China, and the criminal procedure was somewhat diffused because a number of different government offices exercised judicial authority. For example, provincial governors, county magistrates, and almost all the major central government offices—the State Council (Ŭijŏngbu), Border Defense Command (Pibyŏnsa), Royal Secretariat (Sŭngjŏngwŏn), Ministry of Penal Affairs (Hyŏngjo), Ministry of Military Affairs (Pyŏngjo), Capital Magistracy (Hansŏng-bu), and Office of the Inspector-General (Sahŏnbu)—could arrest and imprison criminal suspects as long as the case concerned matters under the purview of the office that was exercising authority. Yet judicial investigation, trial, and judgment were under the sole jurisdiction of a few offices, as follows.

The State Tribunal (Ŭigŭmbu) was a special judicial institution convened only on royal orders for the ad hoc consideration of political cases, accusations of treason or *lèse majesté* on the part of members of the official class, and crimes committed by royal relatives. The Capital Magistracy, which was responsible for all general administrative matters within its jurisdiction, also dealt with misappropriation of public funds and goods, daytime policing, physical violence, debt disputes, discord among relatives, robbery and adultery, inquest hearings, and others. The Ministry of Penal Affairs, which had jurisdiction over civil as well as criminal administration, was in charge of the review of death-penalty cases, legal education and research, criminal cases and penalties and the enforcement of prohibitive ordinances, and slave registration and slave-related litigation. The Ministry had a number of different offices that were served by 204 officials and functionaries at all levels in the mid-Chosŏn period, thus making it the largest of the six ministries.

In the local government, provincial governors and county magistrates oversaw penal administration. Provincial governors exercised initial jurisdiction over murder or other death-penalty cases and final judgment powers over crimes punishable with banishment (*yuhyŏng*) or less. County magistrates could pass final judgment in criminal cases for which the punishment was fifty or fewer blows with a light stick (*t'aehyŏng*), but were required to forward more serious cases to the provincial governor.[25] All criminal cases involving homicide, treason, and violation of the three cardinal values and five human relations (*samgang oryun*), and thus falling into the category of capital punishment, had to be reviewed by the king, who was to render final judgment in consultation with relevant high-ranking officials.[26] Only the king could decide on the death penalty.

In fact, every murder or doubtful death had to be reported to the local court and required an inquest investigation (*kŏmhŏm*) to determine the true cause of death (*sirin*) and the principal offender (*chŏngbŏm*). An inquest was initiated by a complaint petition (*palgwal* or *paekkwal*) filed by a close relative of the deceased (*sich'in*), or by a low-level local administrator in cases where a close relative was not identified or located (as in case 7). The county magistrate who received such a complaint had to immediately begin the inquest investigation by traveling to the site of the death, accompanied by a relevant staff of clerks and attendants, such as a coroner's assistant (*ojak*), medical specialist (*ŭisaeng*), legal clerks (*yulsaeng*), and military officers (*kun'gwan*). Upon arrival, the inquest official (*kŏmgwan*) carried out inquest investigations composed of two major activities—the physical examination of the body (*kŏmsi*), and the questioning of all the people connected to the case, including the close relative of the deceased, the principal offender, witnesses, and relevant subcounty-level administrators. Procedural emphasis was evidently placed on speed and a pattern of open confrontation: speed in order to obtain an accurate examination and determination of the true cause of the death before bodies were too far decomposed, and open confrontation in order to create psychological pressure on the persons involved in a murder, the murderer in particular, for an unequivocal resolution of the case.[27]

Before the physical examination of the body, a preliminary deposition was taken from the close relative of the deceased and others to initially set a ground for the case. Routine questions at this stage included personal information about the deceased, including age and occupation, previous illnesses and bodily marks, the exact circumstances of the incident, previous animosity between the victim and the suspect, and the sizes and disposition of murder weapons. Immediately after the preliminary deposition, the inquest official supervised the physical examination of the body, which strictly followed the detailed procedures and prescriptions of the *Coroner's Guide for the Elimination of Grievances* (Muwŏllok), originally a publication of Yuan China (1271–1368). Although Song China's *The Washing Away of Wrongs* (C: Xiyuan jilu; K: Sewŏllok) had become the most reliable reference on forensic science in China,[28] Korean officials relied on the *Coroner's Guide*, which had been annotated and even "translated" into vernacular Korean later in the dynasty, to aid easier reading and understanding of the original work, which was written in literary Chinese with many technical terms.[29]

The examination of the body began with observation of the corpse in its dry condition. After that, the inquest officials washed the corpse and used various "inquest materials" (*pŏmmul*), such as lees and vinegar, which were sprinkled over the body as aids to make injuries more visible.[30] Another essential inquest material was a silver hairpin, which was routinely used to determine whether or not the deceased had been poisoned. If the hairpin, which was put deep inside the corpse's throat, turned black, then the actual cause of the death would be "being poisoned" (*chungdok*).[31] The silver hairpin was also inserted into the anus, especially when someone was thought to have poisoned him- or herself and the poison might already have reached the intestines. In such a case inserting a silver hairpin into the throat could not prove anything.[32]

In keeping with the guidelines of the *Coroner's Guide for the Elimination of Grievances*, however, there was always flexibility in the process of conducting autopsy. In case 6, the inquest official did not carry out a silver hairpin test of the woman's anus when the test of her mouth turned out to be normal. In case 2, poisoning was ruled out as the cause of death because the silver hairpin, which turned black when inserted into the woman's body, regained its natural color when it was washed with a concoction of boiled water and pods of soap bean. The black stain on the silver hairpin would not have disappeared that easily if it had been caused by poison, according to the *Coroner's Guide*.[33]

The handling of the body must have been an anathema to many of the yangban officials serving as magistrates. The *Coroner's Guide* repeatedly emphasizes that the magistrate should examine the body in person rather than leaving the job to his staff and attendants.[34] In 1789, King Chŏngjo formally announced an edict punishing those magistrates who either delayed the investigation of a corpse or moved it to another region to avoid the autopsy.[35] The magistrate who played the role of coroner, however, did not actually touch or handle the corpse but examined it with a professional coroner's assistant called an *ojak* (C: *wuzuo*). An *ojak* was a slave, and was thus sometimes termed *ojak no* (slave coroner's assistant), though this was changed to *ojak saryŏng* (coroner's assistant) after the abolition of slavery in 1894 (as exemplified in case 8).

The *Coroner's Guide* also addresses the embarrassment of investigating a woman's body and states that, especially in inspecting its virginity, a female corpse must be examined by an old midwife instead of a male coroner's assistant, under observation by some female relatives or neighbors of the dead woman.[36] Although the *Coroner's Guide* is silent about different autopsy procedures based on a woman's social status, we know that in 1752 it was forbidden to perform an autopsy on a yangban woman.[37] Thus it is no wonder that in the present book we have only one case of a brief female autopsy, which was carried out on a non-yangban woman (case 6).

The primary purpose of the physical examination of the corpse was to identify the cause of death, which was the essential part of the investigation procedure to obtain concrete evidence. Together with confessions, detecting the true cause of death served to determine the principle offender as well as the appropriate level of punishment. Yet as the title *Coroner's Guide for the Elimination of Grievances* indicates, the ultimate objective of conducting a thorough examination of a dead body was to redress any wrongs done to the dead person and his or her family, thus maintaining social harmony by officially recognizing their grievances. According to the *Coroner's Guide*, each county office had to have on hand its own preprinted inquest form (*sijang*) with an identifying serial mark. There are some extant inquest records with such an inquest form attached (as in case 8, though there the form itself was not printed but handwritten on ruled paper). This form provided close guidance as to which parts of the body needed to be examined, and the examiner was supposed to call out loudly if there were any unusual bodily marks or injuries as he examined the corpse from head to toe, on the back (dorsal) as well as front (ventral) side. Every wound had to be measured as to its depth and width; the color of each part of the body was also regarded as crucial in determining its abnormality. All the details found during the examination were recorded and interpreted as a whole when the inquest official determined the true cause of death. The court produced three identical copies of the inquest form: one issued to the close relative of the deceased, one filed at the county office in charge of the inquest, and one attached to the inquest report forwarded to the provincial governor for review.

Though the *Coroner's Guide for the Elimination of Grievances* remained the basic manual for autopsy procedures throughout the dynasty, it underwent several changes and additions to meet specific circumstances in Chosŏn society. For example, in addition to using a silver hairpin to determine death by poison, the *Coroner's Guide* suggests a test using a chicken as a sort of litmus paper. To do this, the examiner first inserts a cooked rice ball into the mouth of the corpse and covers it with a paper. About an hour later, the rice ball is fed to a chicken. If the chicken dies, this proves that the person died of poisoning.[38] Yet the use of a chicken was banned in 1764 because such chickens were sold to people to eat even after being used to test for poison.[39] Moreover, whereas the *Coroner's Guide* outlines and encourages the examination of a corpse already buried or encoffined as a critical way to investigate the actual cause of death, in 1765 King Yŏngjo banned autopsies on bodies that had been buried for a long time.[40] This was reversed in 1777 by King Chŏngjo, when officials memorialized about allowing an autopsy for a buried corpse. Retaining the essence of the previous edict as well as that of the *Coroner's Guide*, however, King Chŏngjo decreed that an autopsy of a previously buried body was allowable only when there had been a secret burial after a homicide.[41]

Following the physical examination of the body, a new set of depositions was taken from everyone concerned, including witnesses. The late Chosŏn criminal court classified witnesses as belonging to one of three categories: *kanjŭng*, an eyewitness who was present at the spot of the crime or familiar with the victim's state of mind; *kallyŏn*, an "involved witness" who endeavored to mitigate the situation; and *saryŏn*, a "related witness" who merely observed the event after the criminal act took place.[42] For example, in case 3 the slave Yi Pong-dol committed suicide by throwing himself into a deep pond. One of Yi's relatives who saw he was upset and witnessed him talking about killing himself was recorded as an eyewitness. A neighbor who dived into the water and tried to save him was recorded as an involved witness, while a bystander who witnessed the rescue operation was recorded as a related witness. These terms of art were regularly used in Korean legal case descriptions in the late Chosŏn and the distinctions among the three different types of witnesses seems to have been very clear to officials.

Testimonies taken at the court did not always fit together. In case of discrepancies among testimonies, second, third, and sometimes fourth and fifth depositions were conducted, until some acceptable and coherent level of detail about the incident was attained. The face-to-face confrontation of conflicting witnesses (*taejil*) was an essential technique in questioning and uncovering the "truth" within confusing testimonies. After the process of interrogation and cross-examination was complete, the inquest official made his judgment as to the true cause of death and the identity of the principal offender. Most inquest records end with the inquest official's "concluding statement" (*palsa*), which consists of a summary statement of the case and the judgment, complete with the evidence and reasoning that led to his conclusion. The entire package—of inquest report with attachments of the inquest form and drawings of the murder site, weapons, tools, or suicide notes if available (see case 8 for an example of this type of drawing)—was then sent to the provincial governor with a recommendation for a second inquest investigation (*pokkŏm*). The second inquest was conducted by an available magistrate of a neighboring county, and the procedure was identical to the first inquest. The purpose was to obtain an independent investigation as a check against the accuracy and thoroughness of the first inquest investigation. It was not unusual for the second investigation to come to a conclusion different from the first, which then called for a third round. In cases where the defendant did not confess his or her crime or there were still doubts, the inquest officials, with the permission of the provincial governor, carried out repeated interrogations of the defendant under torture (*tongch'u*), held three times a month as a form of joint interrogation by inquest officials. When no confession was achieved, continued torture sometimes led to the accused dying in prison. This procedure of interrogating the defendant under torture was regarded as a crucial method in obtaining a confession, the final proof of criminality. When investigations were completed, the provincial governor carefully reviewed all reports and forwarded them to the Ministry of Penal Affairs along with his own view on and recommendation for the case.

The king was the supreme judge who handed down the final sentence for cases involving doubtful deaths during the Chosŏn dynasty, though he consulted his officials present during the special royal review (*simni*). As shown in case 2, some doubtful cases, in which the principal offender or the cause of death could not be determined, were under repeated royal review and follow-up investigations for a number of years. As discussed in more detail in case 2, *Records of Royal Reviews* (Simnirok), the collection of royal reviews during the reign of King Chŏngjo, provides a variety of perspectives on eighteenth-century Chosŏn society and culture, although it tends to highlight the royal judgments on each case because it presents only a case summary along with a given royal judgment in its entirety.[43] It seems that King Chŏngjo had a great interest in rectifying various procedures of investigation and autopsy, for the *Records of Royal Reviews* was compiled during his reign and he even ordered that any adultery-related homicide should be reported to the king from the outset of an investigation.[44] In contrast to the *Records of Royal Reviews* summaries, however, the inquest records—especially the full versions translated in cases 1, 5, 7, and 8—supply much more dynamic and complete life stories.

The Kabo reforms of 1894 through 1896 brought some important changes to criminal laws and institutions.[45] A series of laws introduced new systems of punishments while abolishing most of the traditional five punishments (though beating with a light stick still remained). Along with abolition of the social status system and slavery, criminal legal institutions adopted the principle of equal rights for everyone before the law. In addition, the judicial branch became independent of other branches of government and a modern-style court system was created. The Ministry of Justice (Pŏmmu Amun), established in 1894, whose name was changed to Pŏppu next year, was to exercise independent judicial power and lead various institutional changes. Yet legal reforms met several difficulties and could not be carried out as designed. For example, there was no adequate educational and training infrastructure to produce a large number of legal experts, including judges and prosecutors to replace traditional practitioners of law such as provincial governors and county magistrates. Therefore, it was only in 1907, when magistrates were excluded from conducting inquest investigations, that this task was transferred to the police when the trial itself took place in the local court. The principle of independence of jurisdiction also declined because of the revival of authority of the monarch as the final arbiter of heavy punishments. Cardinal Confucian values were still taken as the essential guideline for judicial affairs, and thus special treatment of high-ranking officials and other privileged status groups returned. Despite such limits in legal reforms, some changed legal structures and procedures can be observed in case 8, whose inquest investigations took place between 1899 and 1901.

LAW AND SOCIETY IN THE NINETEENTH CENTURY, AS INSCRIBED IN INQUEST RECORDS

Inquest records were introduced to Korean academia in the late 1990s, but have thus far been underused for detailed study of the sociolegal history of Korea. As we come to understand the nature of inquest record materials produced by the systematic judicial process and dynamic human interactions, however, many facets of nineteenth-century Korean life are revealed that are simply not found in other conventional and official documents. Numerous stories, straight from the lips of men and women in these investigation reports, demonstrate how ordinary people consistently interacted with and redefined sociocultural categories, both in the context of a crisis and through everyday practices.

Scholars have shown that litigation and legal testimonies on various subjects were not unusual in late Chosŏn society.[46] As in any early modern society, legal codes and procedures were fully understood by local people, who then employed them to secure their own interests. During the reign of King Chŏngjo alone, for example, about four thousand petitions were filed and recorded in the *Record of Daily Reflections* (Ilsŏngnok), one of the court records that focused on daily activities of the monarch.⁴⁷ While the majority of these concerned disputes over personal property, such as land and slaves, many of them sought to restore ancestors' moral and scholarly reputations or addressed adoption issues. Although Chosŏn society was highly stratified and segregated by gender, it is clear that people, including women and even slaves, actively utilized the existing legal channels to resolve various conflicts and rectify their grievances. It is certainly a remarkable aspect of the Chosŏn legal system that the state recognized everyone as an independent legal subject, regardless of gender or status.⁴⁸

Moreover, trials at the magistrate's office were generally open to the public, who were thereby able to gain valuable knowledge about law, judicial procedure, and punishment. On the one hand, audiences listened to interrogations of people involved—from principal offenders and victims' families to neighbors—and learned how they sometimes twisted testimonies in order to protect their positions. On the other hand, they witnessed the severity of the law practiced on the scene, such as court officers with the instruments of punishment and torture, if that proved to be needed to extract a confession. All such indirect or direct interactions and experiences in court gave ordinary people a legal perspective. In the meantime, magistrates hearing cases were well aware of perverse statements and usually tried to ferret out the truth. Therefore, a careful and critical reading of each inquest record proves to be an extremely valuable source of information about the everyday life of ordinary people in nineteenth-century Korea.

The eight cases selected and examined in this volume introduce various groups of people who are rarely, if ever, spotlighted in any historical materials and who have otherwise disappeared from the records of the past. Although we did not intentionally seek out cases involving the most marginalized groups in Chosŏn society, countless main actors in death cases were people of lower status, perhaps because they had few ways to solve their problems short of going to court. The testimonies of these non-elite people, whether speaking for themselves or for dead family members, suggest the potential for accommodation, negotiation, and reproduction between ideas and actual practices in nineteenth-century Korea. Despite the status gap, it is evident that some non-elites did not hesitate to confront a yangban's abuse, not only between people of the same gender (non-yangban man versus yangban man, as in case 3) but even between a non-yangban woman and a yangban man (case 6). Clashes within the same status group were not uncommon either, for the sake of securing personal or familial interests, especially among yangban groups whose positions in a locality may have been weakened by a series of new socioeconomic challenges in the nineteenth century (case 8). And in contrast to the typical image of secluded Chosŏn woman, many women are seen actively defending their personal integrity and their position in a family and community, not to mention participating in economic transactions (cases 2, 4, 5, and 6). Finally, though female chastity and sexual virtue were an integral part of maintaining Confucian sociofamily order, adultery was not an incident unfamiliar to men or to women (cases 1 and 7).

While it is difficult to propose that the handful of cases translated here confirms upward social mobility or the breakdown of the status system, they do certainly complicate our picture of nineteenth-century Korea and clearly reveal diverse human interactions that transgress the usual Confucian boundaries of gender, law, and especially social status. People witnessed a great deal of change throughout the century, from domestic instability as exemplified by major popular movements such as the Hong Kyŏng-nae Rebellion (1812), numerous tax resistance movements (1862), and the Tonghak Rebellions (1894–95), to radical reforms by the Taewŏn'gun in the mid-century and more "modern" reforms in its last decade, to foreign encroachment in the latter part of the century. In addition, nineteenth-century Korea has been typically described as a drastic departure from the previous century, which flourished socially and culturally under the strong leadership of kings Yŏngjo and Chŏngjo. Yet the lives of people do not seem to have undergone sudden sweeping changes. In the meantime, the legal procedures and testimonies preserved in inquest records illustrate in minute detail the dynamic intersection of state and society in reaction to the changing social and economic circumstances in nineteenth-century Korea. Throughout such legal testimony, defendants as well as witnesses express a variety of responses to the conflicts as active agents, interpreting the sociocultural norms of their place and time according to their personal circumstances and needs. By divulging various cracks within families and communities, the cases in this volume thus offer readers a profound departure from the conventional picture of nineteenth-century Chosŏn society, and ultimately illuminate the complex constellations of constraint and opportunity that shaped the lives of the people whose voices we hear in these depositions, on both the individual and institutional levels.

AN ADULTEROUS WIDOWER
MEETS A VIOLENT DEATH

Yang Hang-nyŏn (P'yŏngyang, P'yŏngan Province, 1866)

ADULTERY, THE ROOT CAUSE OF MURDER IN THIS CASE, IS ONE of the most common sources of violence and misery throughout human history and has been regarded as a crime in many societies in which marriage and patriarchy are the social and moral foundation. During the Chosŏn dynasty, both adulterous men and women were punished by law following Ming codes. According to an article in the *Great Ming Code*:

> In all cases where a wife or concubine commits adultery with another, if [her own husband] himself catches the adulterer and the adulterous wife at the place of adultery and immediately kills them, he shall not be punished. If he only kills the adulterous lover, the adulterous wife shall be punished in accordance with the Code [Art. 390] and be remarried or sold by her husband.[1]

The relevant punishments prescribed in the *Great Ming Code* for all cases of fornication with consent were eighty strokes of beating with a heavy stick; a woman who had a husband received ten additional strokes.[2] Chosŏn legal practitioners introduced their own adjustments that eventually deviated from the original Ming statutes. For example, the level of punishment differed in accordance with the offender's status: capital punishment was encoded for an adulteress of yangban status from the early sixteenth century onward, while an adulterous commoner woman in the late Chosŏn was often enslaved. There were also cases where an adulterous man, especially one of lower status who had had illicit sex with a yangban woman, was severely punished, even with the death penalty.[3] However, to reinforce the principle of female chastity, late

Chosŏn elites made much more strenuous efforts to regulate women's sexual behavior rather than men's. Legal scholars have noted inequalities for members of different social status groups and genders, as revealed in legal statutes and practices in Chosŏn Korea, as one of the country's prevalent legal characteristics.[4]

In the same vein, it had become acceptable by law for a husband to kill an adulterer on the basis of hearsay or suspicion alone, most likely in an effort to more strictly control women's sexual behavior and make women even more subject to the patriarchal family order than ever before. This change moved away from the original article 308 of the *Great Ming Code*, which stated that the only unpunishable crime was the husband's immediate killing (*tŭngsi salsa*) of the adulterous couple when they were caught in the act by the husband himself (*kanso ch'inhoek*).[5] Case 1 fits nicely into this tendency in the late Chosŏn period. The principal offender, Mr. Hong, originally confessed that he had killed the victim, Mr. Yang, after he learned that Yang had sexually harassed his wife during his absence. In his third deposition during the first inquest investigation, however, he changed his story to sound as though he had caught the two in the act of committing adultery and killed the adulterer Yang right there. Whereas the first inquest official naturally reasoned that the case fell under article 308—catching the adulterer in the act and immediately killing him—the second inquest official's concluding statement implies that Yang was murdered only after Hong's wife complained to him about Yang's harassment of her (so that it was not very clear whether or not adultery had taken place).

To the provincial governor, however, it did not matter whether or not Hong caught the adulterer in the act and immediately killed him. In his reasoning, the killing took place not because of a single incident on that tragic night but because the incident fanned the flames of jealousy in Hong following many previous episodes of flirtation and suspicious behavior between his wife and Yang. Therefore, the provincial governor concluded without much hesitation that Hong's killing of Yang—whether or not it took place on the spot—did not constitute a crime, although his act of indiscriminate stabbing and premeditated arson to hide his killing did. For that crime only, Hong was sentenced to "one round of beating" (*ŏmhyŏng ilch'a*).[6] Ms. Kim, Hong's wife, was also sentenced to one round of beating for her lewd conduct. From the existing record, it is not clear whether or not she was subsequently enslaved; her fate was to be determined solely by her husband.

The phrase "requital for a life" (*sangmyŏng*) appears in every inquest report, for the close relative of the victim always finishes his or her opening testimony with an appeal to redress the grievance suffered by the deceased with the sacrifice of another life—that of the perpetrator. It seems to have been assumed that punishing the perpetrator would relieve the grief and resentment of the survivors. It is apparent that people of all walks of life in the late Chosŏn commonly accepted this notion. Yet as William Shaw observed in his review of late eighteenth-century death review cases, "nothing indicates that the principle was applied mechanistically."[7] In fact, as Shaw found, "the establishment of full culpability in the legal sense took precedence over the task of providing requital for the death of the victim," and it was uncommon for defendants in capital cases to receive a death sentence.[8] Similarly, Hong, the defendant in this case, as well as other principal offenders in other murder cases translated in this book, does not seem to have received capital punishment. The provincial governor found that Hong's killing of the adulterer was not a punishable crime. In this case, Yang, the dead man, was the culprit, not Hong, so the plea for requital for a life by Yang's family was not applicable.

While it is true that Hong's testimony varied over time, he confessed to killing Yang in his very first deposition. Why might he have confessed this? Perhaps Hong was a reasonable person who realized that, under the circumstances, he could not hide the fact that he had killed Yang. Yet, as the investigators noted, there were no eyewitnesses to the incident—either the murder or the arson—so Hong could have denied any involvement. One of the investigative tactics that Korean courts adopted, in emulation of Chinese practices, was to conduct the inquest hearing by gathering every relevant person in the case, including the defendant, the accuser, witnesses, neighbors, administrators, and officers from the county office. As Brian E. McKnight has argued, such a setting may well have put tremendous psychological pressure on the defendant, which may in turn have moved the defendant as well as all participants "to acts and statements which under normal circumstances they would have avoided," including, in this case, Hong's confession of his crime.[9]

This inquest report concerning the death of Yang is one of seven reports in the *Inquest Records of Chunghwa County* (Chunghwa-bu ogan). All seven death incidents took place between 1866 and 1867, with the magistrate of Chunghwa County (Chunghwa Tohobu) acting as either the first or second inquest official.[10] This case is one of two from this particular collection selected and translated for this book, the other being case 5. Yang's death took place in P'yŏngyang Special City (P'yŏngyang-bu), which was also the provincial governor's administrative seat during the Chosŏn dynasty. Administratively, the provincial governor of

P'yŏngan Province held the concurrent post of magistrate of P'yŏngyang Special City. Because the provincial governor himself could not be the first inquest official for a death case that took place in P'yŏngyang, the magistrate of Chunghwa, a county south of P'yŏngyang, took the job. According to the *Records of the Royal Secretariat* (Sŭngjŏngwŏn ilgi), the magistrate of Chunghwa at the time was Han Yong-sŏn and the provincial governor was Pak Kyu-su (1807–76). Apparently, Han was a model magistrate and received an upgrade of his rank on 1865.11.28 (1/14/1866). He served a second term as the Chunghwa magistrate because of his good service to the people and subsequent recommendation by Provincial Governor Pak.[11] From these facts, it is very likely that this particular collection of inquest records was compiled in order to commemorate Han's years as the Chunghwa magistrate. Pak Kyu-su, provincial governor at the time, is well known in Korean history as the person at the center of the burning of the American merchant ship *General Sherman*, which sailed up the Taedong River to P'yŏngyang, demanding open trade without respecting Chosŏn's adamant policy against such trade with Westerners. This particular incident took place in August 1866, only a few months before the present case.

INQUEST REPORT (*MUNAN*) OF THE FIRST INQUEST INVESTIGATION (*CH'OGŎM*) INTO THE CASE OF THE DECEASED, YANG HANG-NYŎN [HAK-RYŎN], FROM YI SUBDISTRICT, NAECH'ŎN DISTRICT, IN P'YŎNGYANG SPECIAL CITY

Root cause (*kŭnyu*) of death: Adultery (*kanŭm*)
True cause of death (*sirin*): Stabbed to death (*p'ija*)

The brevetted magistrate of Chunghwa County conducted the investigation of the body as the first inquest official.[12]

In the DIRECTIVE[13] (*kamgyŏl*) issued by the provincial governor that arrived around six in the evening (*yu-si*) on the sixth day of the month, it is written: "I appointed the deputy commander (*chunggun*) [of the P'yŏngyang Military Commander's Office]—a concurrently held post—as the first inquest official for the case of the deceased, Yang Hang-nyŏn of Yi Subdistrict, Naech'ŏn District, in P'yŏngyang Special City, and ordered him carry out the investigation right away. However, he immediately replied that he could not conduct the investigation because the ROYAL ORDER prohibited military commanders from serving as such. For this reason I appoint the magistrate [of Chunghwa] as the first inquest official (*ch'ogŏmgwan*). [I order you] to go to

P'yŏngyang as soon as you receive this directive and conduct the investigation in accordance with proper procedures."

I, the Chunghwa magistrate, accordingly rushed to depart in the company of appropriate assistants. After traveling north for about 25 *li* from the Chunghwa county office to the Taejŏng Post Station in P'yŏngyang, the day had already grown dark. Thus, we spent the night there. We took to the road again at the break of dawn the next day, the seventh. After traveling north for about 26 *li*, we arrived in Yi Subdistrict, Naech'ŏn District, where the corpse of the deceased Yang Hang-nyŏn lay. The inquest investigation with [relevant] people in attendance was then carried out.

On 1866.12.7 (1/12/1867), Yang Hak-pŏm, the close relative of the deceased (*sich'in*), no military obligation (*muyŏk*), fifty-four years in age, and registered in the household register.

[Magistrate:] "I, by the DIRECTIVE of the provincial governor, am about to open an investigation into the death of Yang Hang-nyŏn. How are you related to the deceased? When, where, under what circumstances, and with whom did he fight? Which part of [Yang Hang-nyŏn's] body was injured? When did he die? How old was the deceased? Did he have any military duties? Describe the clothes worn by the deceased and whether he had any notable scars on his body when he was alive. Also, who were the eyewitnesses (*kanjŭng*) when the fighting began? Was the weapon used in the criminal acts set aside? All must be told truthfully without fail." In such a way, I interrogated Yang Hak-pŏm.

[Yang Hak-pŏm:] "The dead Yang Hang-nyŏn is my younger brother. He was an old widower who made a living by making and selling reed floormats. He lived in Yi Subdistrict. I also make reed floormats and live in Sam Subdistrict, which is a bit away [from the Yi Subdistrict].[14] Because I have been busy making ends meet, we did not see each other often. On the morning of the sixth of this month, Hong Chin-o, who was a close neighbor of my brother's, came to me and said, "Your brother's house burned down in a fire last night and your brother burned to death." I could not suppress my surprise and rushed to my brother's house. Indeed, the house was already burned and destroyed. When I entered and looked at the room, my brother was lying there. But his face had open wounds with blood all over the place, and it was apparent that he had not died from the fire but had been murdered by someone. And that is why I reported it to the authorities. My brother was fifty-one years old and did not hold any military obligations. While alive he did not have any marks on his body. [At the time of death] he wore a cotton jacket and a pair of cotton pants. Since I did not see the fight, I do not know who the witnesses were, nor was I able to collect the murder weapon. My brother, who was healthy, was seriously injured and suddenly died overnight. Please, I beg for requital for a life (*sangmyŏng*) by bringing the murderer to swift justice."

On the same day, the slave coroner's assistant (*ojak no*) Yun-sam, thirty-six years in age and registered in the household register. [He took an oath saying:] "Now, upon the examination of the body of Yang Hang-nyŏn, if I do not record the correct measurements and subsequently such a wrongful deed is disclosed, I shall submit myself for punishment."

On the same day, I examined the body of Yang Hang-nyŏn, which lay in a thatched-roof house facing west, which was 2 *kan* in size with a kitchen 1 *kan* in size. Because of the fire, the house was severely damaged. One room with a thatched [roof] was also damaged. The lower front part [of the room] was covered by a reed screen. After removing the screen, there was a door to the room and two narrow windows. The door was completely destroyed. The measurements of the four corners of the room were: 2 *ch'ŏk* to the eastern wall, 6 *ch'ŏk* to the southern wall, 2 *ch'ŏk* 4 *ch'on* to the western wall, and 2 *ch'on* to the northern wall. The body was first covered with a mat, under that was a purple-blue cotton coat, then [under that] was a 5 *p'ok* wide cotton bedspread. When [all] were removed, a blue wooden pillow was supporting the head, and it was covered with bloodstains. It was a male body. The age seemed to be fifty-one or fifty-two. The head was to the west; the feet were to the east. The body lay facing the ceiling on a reed mat. The dress was like this: one torn cotton jacket and one torn cotton trouser. All were taken off and placed next to the body. He was wearing one sock. I could not conduct the examination [of the body] because the room was too small. Thus the body was moved outside to a windless area and put on a wooden board. I had the slave coroner's assistant turn the body to wash it and also measure the body, which was 5 *ch'ŏk* tall. The tied hair was loosened and measured to be 1 *ch'ŏk* 2 *ch'on* in length.

The ventral side of the body [was as follows]: The face color was red and white. Both the mouth and the eyes were open. Both hands were clenched softly in fists. Both legs were straight. The crown of the head, fontanel, left and right head, cranium, and the left forehead all looked normal. The right forehead had a knife wound that measured 5 *p'un* in length and 1 *p'un* in depth. Both temples and the right eyebrow looked normal. On the corner of the right eyebrow there was a spot where the skin was broken and exposed. When measured, the circumference was 2 *ch'on* 2 *p'un* and the depth was 2 *p'un*. Right in between the two eyebrows there was also a knife slash, which was 1 *ch'on* 8 *p'un* in length. The width of the slash was 1 *p'un* on the upper part, 4 *p'un* on the middle part, and 1 *p'un* on the lower part. The depth was 2 *p'un*. The two eyes were closed and looked normal. When the eyelids were opened, the pupils looked normal. Right below the right eye was a knife slash that was 9 *p'un* long, 1 *p'un* wide, and 6 *p'un* deep. The cheeks, both ears, ear flaps, ear lobes, ear holes, the bridge and tip of the nose, nostrils, and philtrum all looked normal. The inside of the upper lip was torn, and the inside of the lower lip had traces of biting. One upper front tooth was broken, but [the root] was still there. All bottom teeth looked normal. The tongue did not protrude from the mouth. There was a scar on the left side of the jaw, which looked like a piece of red bean. The throat, esophagus, depressed area above the shoulder blades, shoulder blades, armpits, upper arms, inside of the elbows, wrists, palms, fingers, fingertips, underneath the fingernails, chest, both breasts, between the chest and belly, upper belly, ribs, sides under arms, lower belly, groin, penis and scrotum, thighs, and right knee all looked normal. The left edge of the left knee had an old moxibustion scar, which was shaped like an acorn. Both shins, ankles, tops of the feet, toes, and toenails were all normal.

The dorsal side of the body [was as follows]: The occipital, neck hairline, roots of the ears, backs of the neck and shoulders, elbows, palms, backs of the hands, fingers, fingernails, spine and area along the spine, back ribs and back sides under the arms, waist, buttocks, anus, thighs, crooks of the knees, calves, ankle bones, heels, soles, toes, toe tips, and underneath the toenails all looked normal.

The silver hairpin inserted inside the mouth and anus did not change color.[15] At the same time, when examining the head of the body, the mouth and eyes were open, while both hands were in loose fists, etc. All these conditions fit into the article of "murder" (*p'iin salsa*) in the *Coroner's Guide for the Elimination of Grievances*. Therefore, I record the true cause of death as "stabbed to death."

On the same day, Hong Chin-o, the principal offender (*chŏngbŏm*), a scout soldier (*tangbogun*), forty-three years in age, and registered.

[Magistrate:] "According to the testimony from the close relative of the deceased Yang Hak-pŏm, during the inquiry into the criminal case concerning the deceased Yang Hang-nyŏn, you came to tell Yang Hak-pŏm in the early morning of the sixth day of this month that his brother's house had burned down the previous night and his brother had died in the fire. When

Yang went to his brother's house, the latter's face looked as though it had been assaulted and was covered in blood. He therefore suspected that the cause of his brother's death was not the fire, and reported it to the authorities. Since you and the deceased lived within one and the same fence, you breathed the same air and must have helped each other when in need. It would have been clear to you that someone had murdered him when his face was covered in blood. You must have had a reason to state that the brother had died in a fire when you delivered your message. Do not dare to conceal or hide anything in this court and state the conditions of the incident truthfully." In such a way, I interrogated Hong Chin-o.

[Hong Chin-o:] "My father lives in Yongsan District, and I live separately in Naech'ŏn District. My fourteen-year-old daughter was about to be married, and all the wedding preparations and procedures were to be undertaken at my father's. With the intention of returning home on the sixth, I took my daughter and left for my father's house on the fifth. The groom's family had earlier promised to prepare the wedding chest. However, the groom's side suddenly sent 3 *yang* and asked us to purchase the chest with it. So I came back home that night to buy the chest. Then my wife said, 'Mr. Yang, next door, seeing that I was alone, barged in and harassed me. How could this happen?' I became very upset and could not let this go, so I went straight to Yang's house. Mr. Yang was lying in his room, so I stabbed his face with a knife and started a fire to cover my tracks. There is nothing more to testify. Please take this into consideration."

On the same day, Kim Hyŏng-un, a related witness (*saryŏn*), village elder (*chwajang*), sixty-one years in age, and registered.[16]

[Magistrate:] "On hearing the confession of Hong Chin-o during the inquiry into the criminal case concerning the deceased Yang Hang-nyŏn, on the night of the fifth of this month, after Yang Hang-nyŏn was found dead [as a result of] the fire in his house, you sent Hong Chin-o to Hang-nyŏn's brother Hak-pŏm's house to deliver the message [about the incident]. As the village elder, no village matters could have escaped your attention. As for the fire at Hang-nyŏn's house, you saw it with your own eyes. In addition, you were the one who had someone else [Hong Chin-o] deliver about the news of Hang-nyŏn's death. Thus you are the most crucial witness in this incident; who else could it be? Now you are under inquiry in this court; tell us straightforwardly how the fire started and the true cause of Hang-nyŏn's death, without hiding anything." In such a way, I interrogated Kim Hyŏng-un.

[Kim Hyŏng-un:] "On the night of the fifth of this month, I was at home, deep asleep. Right after the rooster crowed, I heard cries about a fire. So I went outside immediately and saw that Yang Hang-nyŏn's house, which was right next to Hong Chin-o's, was on fire. After the village heads and I all got together and put out the fire, I inquired as to the whereabouts of the owner of the house. Hong Chin-o went inside the room to investigate and said that Hang-nyŏn was already dead. Thus, I had Chin-o go inform Hang-nyŏn's brother Hak-pŏm about what had happened. By this time, day was already breaking. Hak-pŏm arrived and saw his brother's body. He was startled and said that it seemed his brother had died wrongfully and that he had to report this to the authorities. We yangban village heads (*pansu*) did not know what had really happened overnight. But because the front eaves of the dead person's house were right inside the courtyard of Hong Chin-o, and because the fire first started from the corner of Chin-o's yard, we thought there must have been something going on [with Hong]. Thus we placed Chin-o into custody. Before noon, county military officers came and took both Chin-o and me, saying that this must be dealt with as a criminal case. There is nothing more to testify. Please take this into consideration."

On the same day, Sŏ Yu-dŏk, a related witness, no military duty, sixty-seven years in age, and registered.

[Magistrate:] According to the testimony of Hong Chin-o during the inquiry into the criminal case concerning the deceased Yang Hang-nyŏn, on the night of the fifth of this month, the house of his next-door neighbor, the deceased, accidentally caught on fire and the owner of the house, Hang-nyŏn, died. The village elders Kim Hyŏng-un, Sŏ Yu-dŏk, and others gathered at the site and had him [Hong Chin-o] convey Hang-nyŏn's death to Hang-nyŏn's brother [Hak-pŏm]. You were one of those who gathered there and had him deliver the message. You must have seen and known in detail the cause of Yang Hang-nyŏn's death. Now you are under inquiry by this court; you must tell truthfully what happened." In such a way, I interrogated Sŏ Yu-dŏk.

[Sŏ Yu-dŏk:] During the night of the fifth, when the rooster was about to crow, there was a loud commotion. I went outside the gate and saw that there was a fire raging at Yang Hang-nyŏn's house. All the villagers gathered to put out the fire, but the owner of the house, Hang-nyŏn, was nowhere to be seen. Thus we had Hong Chin-o search around. After going inside the room, Chin-o said that Hang-nyŏn was already dead. After sending Chin-o to the dead man's brother, Hak-pŏm, I came back home. There is nothing more to testify. Please take this into consideration."

On the same day, close neighbors (chŏllin): Cho Hyŏng-suk, no military duty, seventy-two years in age; Sin Kyŏng-sŏp, no military duty, twenty-three years in age; and O Ch'ang-jo, no military duty, seventy-four years in age; all are registered.

[Magistrate:] "Since the incident of Yang Hang-nyŏn's death occurred in your neighborhood, you must know the beginning and the end. Under this investigation, each of you should testify everything [you know] truthfully." In such a way, I interrogated them.

Cho Hyŏng-suk: "Since I am old and have a hearing problem, I often stay at home. On the night of the fifth, there was a lot of noise in the middle of the night, so I went outside to see. For some reason, Yang Hang-nyŏn's house was on fire. Since the fire seemed to have already been put out by the yangban village headman, the village elder, the village headman, the subdistrict administrator, and others, I went straight home. The morning of the next day, the sixth, there were rumors that Yang Hang-nyŏn, the owner of the house burnt the night before, had died. So I learned that. Military officers arrested me, saying that there was a criminal matter, and so I am here."

Sin Kyŏng-sŏp: "I was sleeping at home on the night of the fifth. After the rooster crowed, there were sudden cries of fire, so I hastily put on some clothes and ran outside to see [what was going on]. Villager Yang Hang-nyŏn's house was on fire, and all the village leaders had gathered to put it out. The village leaders said that although the fire was out, the owner of the house was dead, so they should exercise caution about the matter. They sent a person to deliver [the message of Hang-nyŏn's death] to his brother Yang Hak-pŏm. They then went to the house of a yangban village elder to put together a report of the incident in writing for the authorities. That was what I understood. I went home because I couldn't stand the chill of the early morning air. On the evening of the sixth, military officers came to arrest me, saying that there was a criminal matter. So I am here."

O Ch'ang-jo: "My sons are all blind and sick, and they live within the walls of the county seat. Because I live a bit away from the village where the incident took place, and also because I cannot hear well, I did not know there was a criminal matter in the village. Around noon on the sixth, I received a message that my son was severely ill. As his father, I was deeply concerned and heading toward my son's house at the county seat to nurse him. On my way, I was arrested by military officers for being a close neighbor [of the dead man]. Yet, I do not know anything about the incident at all." Take each of these testimonies into consideration.

On the same day, O Tae-ryŏn, the district administrator (*p'unghŏn*), seventy years in age, and registered.

[Magistrate:] "The criminal case concerning the deceased Yang Hang-nyŏn occurred in your district. You are the administrator of this district and there is nothing that you have not observed. Therefore, you must have intimate knowledge about this particular case. In this court, you shall truthfully report everything you heard and saw." In such a way, I interrogated O Tae-ryŏn.

[O Tae-ryŏn:] "I live in a village about 7 *li* away from where the incident took place. On the morning of the sixth, when I was having breakfast, I received a handwritten report from Sŏ Yong-gŭn, a village headman (*tumin*) of Yi Subdistrict. The report said that there had been a fire in the villager Yang Hang-nyŏn's house and that he had died. So I came to know of the incident and subsequently relayed the report to the county office. Later I also heard that Hang-nyŏn had been killed [by someone]. There is nothing more to testify. Please take this into consideration."

On the same day, Yi Chŏng-gon, subdistrict administrator (*ihŏn*), thirty years in age, and registered.

[Magistrate:] "The criminal case concerning the deceased Yang Hang-nyŏn occurred in your subdistrict. You are the administrator of this village and there is nothing that you have not observed. Therefore, you must have intimate knowledge about this particular case. In this court, you shall truthfully report everything you know in detail." In such a way, I interrogated Yi Chŏng-gon.

[Yi Chŏng-gon:] "Although my house is in the same subdistrict where the incident took place, it is a bit away from there. When I was having breakfast on the sixth of this month, Kim Hag-in, a liaison of the district, came and told me that there had been a fire in a house in Namsu Village in my subdistrict and that a person had been killed. [He also told me that] the elders of the village requested the presence of the subdistrict administrator. So, I hurried to the [crime] scene and carefully asked the village elder and village administrator how the incident had occurred. They answered that on the night of the fifth, after exterminating the fire at Yang Hang-nyŏn's house and then entering his room, [they found] the owner of the house, Hang-nyŏn, already dead. Therefore, I went to see for myself, and I found that the head of the deceased was covered in blood and there was no doubt that the cause of death was not from the fire. I sought out Hong Chin-o, who shared the same courtyard [as the dead man], and questioned him. Hong said, 'I was away at my father's house, located in Yongsan District, to prepare for my daughter's upcoming wedding. I came back home late at night to buy a wedding chest. The incident took place during that night, so I do not know how it happened.' This is all I have heard and seen. Please take this into consideration."

On the same day, Sŏ Yong-gŭn, a yangban village headman, seventy-three years in age, and registered.

[Magistrate:] "The criminal case concerning the deceased Yang Hang-nyŏn occurred in your village. You are the yangban headman of this village and there is nothing that you have not observed. Therefore, you must have heard and known about this particular case. In this court, you shall truthfully report everything you know in detail." In such a way, I interrogated Sŏ Yong-gŭn.

[Sŏ Yong-gŭn:] "I was sleeping at home on the night of the fifth of this month. Around the time the rooster was due to crow, I went out to the court-yard to urinate and [noticed] there was a bright fire. So I went there, inside the village. The house of some reed-mat maker, Mr. Yang, whose first name I do not even know, had caught on fire. After I ordered all the villagers to put out the fire, I then went back home. At dawn the next day, the sixth, the village elder Kim Hyŏng-un came to tell me that a dead person was in the house [that had been] on fire. When I heard that a person had been found dead in the house, I could not rest, so I went to the house myself and carefully examined the dead person. It was the owner of the house, Yang Hang-nyŏn, who was indeed dead. Therefore, I sent Hong Chin-o to the deceased's brother Hak-pŏm's house to let him know about the incident. Please take this into consideration."

On the same day, Yi Kun-sŏ, subdistrict administrator (*chipkang*), fifty-five years in age, registered.

[Magistrate:] "The criminal matter concerning the deceased Yang Hang-nyŏn occurred in your subdistrict. You are the administrator of this subdistrict and there is nothing that escapes your attention. When the fire broke out at Hang-nyŏn's house that day, you must have gone to see it. You must have seen and known about this incident from the beginning to the end. Tell us all you know truthfully." In such a way, I interrogated Yi Kun-sŏ.

[Yi Kun-sŏ:] "Upon hearing loud noises on the night of the fifth after the rooster crowed, I went outside my gate and saw that Yang Hang-nyŏn's house was engulfed in fire. The village elder was directing people to rush and carry water over [to put out fire], so I did not have a moment to pay attention to anything but carrying water. After the fire was out, [the village elder] had me write a report to inform the district administrator (*myŏnim*) of the death of Yang Hang-nyŏn. After informing the district personnel, I in turn filed a report with the county office. I only entered the county seat to deliver the district's report, and I do not have any clear knowledge about the cause of the crime. Please take this into consideration."

On the same day, Yang Hak-pŏm, the close relative of the deceased, second deposition (*kaengch'u*).

[Magistrate:] "In your first testimony, you said: On the sixth, Hong Chin-o came and told you about the fire at your younger brother's house and the death of your brother caused by the fire. When you rushed to go see it, your brother's face had open wounds with blood all over the place. So you thought that he had not died from the fire but had been murdered by someone. If you thought your brother had been killed by someone, out of rage you must have first asked Hong Chin-o about it then and there, and you must have also asked the subdistrict administrator (*iim*) about the incident. Tell us what kinds of conversations went on at the time, and whether your brother had any animosity against anyone when alive. Tell the truth about everything." In such a way, I interrogated Yang Hak-pŏm.

[Yang Hak-pŏm:] "I stated everything in the previous testimony. After hearing from Hong Chin-o that my brother had died in a fire, I hurried there to go see it. From the multiple wounds on his face, I realized that he had definitely been murdered. Thus it was clear that Mr. Hong's saying that my brother had burned to death was a lie. It was not that I did not want to follow up on Mr. Hong's remark. Yet at the time, out of a revengeful mind, I only wanted to report this to the court as soon as possible. So I did not go as far as to confront Mr. Hong. My younger brother was a poor longtime widower who mainly stayed at home. He just made reed floormats; how could he have caused anyone to resent him? Since the offender Mr. Hong has already admitted to the crime, please avenge the death swiftly so that [my brother's] deep grudge from the netherworld shall be resolved. Please take this into consideration."

On the same day, Hong Chin-o, the principal offender, second deposition.

[Magistrate:] "In your earlier testimony, you said: When you returned home from your father's place that night, your wife told you that Mr. Yang from the front house had barged in and harassed her, seeing that she was alone. You became very upset and could not let this go. So, you went straight to Mr. Yang's house and stabbed him to death. In order to cover your tracks, you set fire to his house. There is no need to repeat the interrogation because you have already confessed. Yet, when the bastard Yang harassed your wife on that night, your wife had already scolded him and fought back. As a husband, you must have felt very enraged. But why did you not report the matter to the authorities and instead go directly to kill him? You must have already accumulated some resentment against him. Now, under this re-investigation, truthfully describe your criminal actions and report the root causes of Yang Hang-nyŏn's death." In such a way, I interrogated Hong Chin-o.

[Hong Chin-o:] "My testimony is no different from the previous one. On that night, although my wife said that she had scolded and driven away the bastard Yang, in my mind I felt that he must have raped my wife. I could not repress my boiling rage, so I went to Yang's house holding a knife. Mr. Yang was lying on his back sleeping, so I climbed atop his belly and stabbed his face and then I set fire to his house. But I did not hold any old grudges against Mr. Yang before this. Please take this into consideration."

On the same day, Kim Hyŏng-un, a related witness, second deposition.

[Magistrate:] "In your previous testimony, you said: On the night of the fifth of this month, after extinguishing the fire at Yang Hang-nyŏn's house and searching for the owner of the house, [you found out that the owner] was already dead. You had Hong Chin-o inform the deceased's older brother Hak-pŏm [about what had happened]. Hak-pŏm came and saw that his brother was dead, and went to the county seat to report the incident to the authorities. Although you did not know what exactly happened that night, the front eaves of the dead person's house face Hong Chin-o's courtyard and the fire started from the front eaves of the house. This created suspicion of Chin-o, and thus you put him under confinement. Now, you and the dead person lived in the same village, so you must know his usual whereabouts very well. In addition, you are the one who sent the death report and who placed Chin-o in custody. Everything came from your close supervision. If there is one most qualified witness in this case, who else could it be but you? A man's life is extremely valuable; criminal investigation is extremely strict. Now you are under a second interrogation; tell us directly and truthfully, not like before, [when] you stated things unclearly." In such a way, I interrogated Kim Hyŏng-un.

[Kim Hyŏng-un:] "On that night, while I was deep in sleep, I suddenly heard alarms about a fire. So I rushed outside to see. There was a great fire that seemed to have started from the front eaves of the dead man's house. After I got the villagers to gather and put the fire out, I searched for Mr. Yang everywhere but he was nowhere to be found. I told Mr. Hong to go into the room to look around. Mr. Hong said that Hang-nyŏn was dead in his room. I had Mr. Hong go to the dead man's brother Hak-pŏm to inform him. When Hak-pŏm subsequently arrived, he and I both went into the room to see Hang-nyŏn. His face had traces of blood all over it. Hak-pŏm said, 'My brother had a violent death and I must report it to the authorities right away.' I thought that there was reason to be suspicious of Mr. Hong since Mr. Hong and the dead man shared the same yard. So I had Mr. Hong confined inside the village. The dead man was an artisan making reed floormats and did not go in and out of the village much, so there is not much to remember him by. There is nothing more to testify. Please take this into consideration."

On the same day, Sŏ Yu-dŏk, a related witness, second deposition.

[Magistrate:] "In your former testimony, you said: On the fifth day of this month when Yang Hang-nyŏn's house was on fire, you had Hong Chin-o search for Hang-nyŏn, the owner of the house, because he was nowhere to be seen. Upon Chin-o's report, after checking the room, saying that Hang-nyŏn was in the room but already dead, you sent Chin-o to Hang-nyŏn's brother's place to inform [him of Hang-nyŏn's death]. Then you said you returned home. You were wondering where the owner of the house was and had a person examine [the house]. If someone were in the room, there must have been much concern that that person might have become unconscious because of smoke inhalation. If that had been the case, you would have quickly entered the room to save that person without wasting time. When the fire broke out, it burned and destroyed the grass roof of the house. But if it did not destroy the floor of the room, how could one burn to death? You sent the message as though Mr. Yang had been scorched to death, only listening to Mr. Hong's account of his death. Your words are ambiguous and there are many negligent traces. At this second interrogation, you should confess everything truthfully, unlike the previous time." In such a way, I interrogated Sŏ Yu-dŏk.

[Sŏ Yu-dŏk:] "I have already told everything to the court. On that night, after the fire was extinguished, when we were looking for the owner of the house, neighbors said that Mr. Yang was dead. From the beginning, I did not closely examine the dead body and just went home. So how could I have known if Mr. Yang was dead from the fire or had been killed? There is nothing more to testify. Please take this into consideration."

On the same day, Hong Chin-o, the principal offender, third deposition.

[Magistrate:] "On the said night, having heard your wife's story of Mr. Yang's harassment and taking it as that of forceful rape, you concealed a knife and went to Yang's house. Seeing that he was asleep in his room, you sat on top of his belly and stabbed his face. Now, your wife said that she had not suffered any violent rape, although she had been verbally abused. Why, then, did you have so little difficulty committing such an atrocious act? Aren't you hiding something? If not, you came to commit this crime of killing him because you must have had other causes to harbor hate [for Mr. Yang] and seek retribution. It is as clear as seeing a light that you are attempting to transfer blame to others. Now, upon this repeated interrogation, tell the truth without adding or subtracting an iota, unlike the way you testified before." In such a way I interrogated Hong Chin-o.

[Hong Chin-o:] "I already said most of what was in my mind in the previous testimonies. My wife and I met and have lived together ever since we were youths in our pigtails.[17] There was a special bond and we shared a great deal of affection between us. Meanwhile, we raised a grown son, and now even our daughter is about to be wed. So even when there was some unpleasantness, we tried to forgive and bury the past. That is why, in fear of exposing my wife's lewd act, I could not reveal the truth, and tried to hide it in my first and second testimonies. But how can it not come out under such repeated interrogations? On that day, I went to my father's home in Yongsan District to prepare my daughter's wedding. I returned from my father's house to buy the wedding chest at night. It was when the rooster was about to crow and the lights were already out. I opened the door and entered my room. When I woke up my wife, she said, 'You went to your father's house for the wedding preparations. Why have you already returned in the middle of the night?' When I looked around carefully, I could tell that there was someone else in the room. I looked closely, while yelling, and indeed there was a naked man lying underneath the blanket. His belt was laid next to him, so I took the belt and tied his hands. After I lit the lamp I could see his face, and it was none other than my next-door neighbor, Yang Hang-nyŏn. I always kept a knife by the lamp, so I grabbed it and stabbed the man's face repeatedly until he died. I also wanted to kill my wife, but I thought about our poor children and could not do it. After calming down a bit, I took Mr. Yang's corpse to his own house, placed a wooden pillow under his head, and covered him with his blanket. I set the house on fire to cover my tracks. At first I did not kill my wife because of my children, but now my only regret is that I did not kill her. There is nothing more to testify. Please take this into consideration."

On the same day, Hong Chin-o, the principal offender, fourth deposition.

[Magistrate:] "In your second testimony, you said: After hearing that your wife had suffered shame, you secretly took a knife and went straight to Mr. Yang's house. After climbing on his stomach, you stabbed his face. In your third testimony, you said: Upon returning from your father's house that night, you felt that someone else was there besides your wife. After turning on the lamp to see, you found that it was Yang Hang-nyŏn. Therefore, you took his belt and tied both of his hands, and with the knife that you usually kept by the lamp, you killed him by repeatedly stabbing his face. Now, you have changed your testimony in the midst of this solemn investigation, causing havoc in the court. That itself is extremely malicious. How is it that there were no traces of blood on the floor or floormats of your room? Whether you killed him in your room or in his room, you stabbed Hang-nyŏn for sure. Now, which hand did you use, and how many times did you stab him? Where did you hide the murder weapon and the bloodstained clothing of the victim, as well as the belt? Answer each of these questions truthfully without retracting your words." In such a way, I interrogated Hong Chin-o.

[Hong Chin-o:] "I already confessed everything in the last testimony. On the day when I stabbed and killed the bastard Yang, there was blood that soaked into the reed floormats. But thinking that it could be seen as evidence, I rolled the mat up and took it to Yang's house and burned it along with the rest. As for the bloodstains on the floor, I scraped the area with a hoe. When I committed the heinous crime, I had my knife in my right hand and stabbed his face. I do not know how many times I stabbed him, but it seemed like five to six times. The knife and the belt were thrown into the fire and must be burnt by now. After moving the body to his house, I placed the clothing by the corpse. So, the earlier testimony that I grabbed a knife and went straight to Yang's house and killed him was a lie that I made up. Please take this into consideration."

On the same day, Song Chi-hyŏp, head clerk (hojang), thirty-nine years in age; Kim Yun-o, court recorder (kigwan), sixty-one years in age; Han Che-hyŏp, clerk at the Bureau of Penal Affairs (hyŏngni), twenty years in age; Hong

Hae-bung, herbalist (*ŭisaeng*), thirty-five years in age; Hong Chae-u, legal clerk (*yulsaeng*), thirty-five years in age; Kim Ch'i-muk, head officer (*changgyo*), fifty-nine years in age; Ch'oe Chun-ak, assistant director (*hyangso*) of the Bureau of Local Yangban, forty-eight years in age; Yun-sam, slave coroner's assistant; Yang Hak-pŏm, the deceased's close relative; Hong Chin-o, the principal offender; Kim Hyŏng-un and Sŏ Yu-dŏk, related witnesses; Cho Hyŏng-suk, Sin Kyŏng-sŏp, and O Ch'ang-jo, close neighbors; O Tae-ryŏn, district administrator; Yi Chŏng-gon, subdistrict administrator; Sŏ Yong-gon, yangban village headman; and Yi Kun-sŏ, subdistrict administrator; all registered.

When the first inquest investigation of the body of the deceased Yang Hang-nyŏn was conducted, all of us attended as persons relevant to the investigation. We did not add or delete anything to the record of the proceedings in uncovering this evil crime. There is nothing more to testify. Please take this into consideration.

On the same day, the watchmen (*sujikkun*) [were]: Hyŏn Sa-ch'ŏl, no military duty, forty-eight years in age; Pak Sŏk-hwan, no military duty, forty-five years in age; and Chŏng Nan-yŏl, no military duty, forty-five years in age; all registered.

After the first inquest investigation of the body of the deceased Yang Hang-nyŏn, we had the order of guarding [the body]. If there were any unforeseen problems, we would be responsible for them.

ADDENDUM (*PYŎLJI*)

On the same day, Ms. Kim, the wife of the principal offender, a commoner (*yangnyŏ*). In her testimony, she said: "My father-in-law lives in Yongsan District. My husband and I came to live in Naech'ŏn area in the ninth month of last year. Our daughter, fourteen years in age, was getting married, but all preparations were to be done at my father-in-law's place. When it was time for the groom's ceremony to bring a pair of wild geese to the bride's house (*chŏnan*), we sent our daughter to my father-in-law's to perform the ritual. With the plan of returning on the sixth day, my husband led my daughter to my father-in-law's house on the fifth and I was left alone in the house. In the middle of the night, Yang Hang-nyŏn, who shared the same yard with us, abruptly appeared and harassed me. Since I am only a weak woman, I had no choice but to bed with him. Right then, my husband unexpectedly returned. After grabbing Mr. Yang and stabbing him to death, my husband took him to his house and also set fire to the house. I do not have anything more to add. Please take this into consideration."

. . . .

CONCLUDING STATEMENT (PALSA)
[OF THE FIRST INQUEST INVESTIGATION]

Each person's testimonies are as recorded.[18] In general, when it comes to the difficulty of criminal hearings, nothing can be compared to a murder case. Testimonies can change greatly during the process of inquests, and a lie can instantly become the truth. If a hearing is conducted without deep reflections into the law, truths cannot be uncovered even with the fairest of intentions. Whether a person is going to live or die is determined by such. All methods should be used to uncover the underlying and detailed causes, so that the offender cannot hide [facts] and injustice is rectified. Since the fundamental cause of this case lies in licentiousness, there is no one to pry the information from. Furthermore, because the incident occurred in the middle of the night, [I] was doubtful that there would be any reliable witnesses. Therefore, I probed into all suspicious points.

The deceased Yang Hang-nyŏn's body [was tested with] inquest instruments (pŏmmul), washed [with the prescribed concoction], and rubbed by hands; there were no particularly suspicious injuries on his upper or lower body. There were several crisscross wounds around the eyebrow. When checking by inserting fingers inside the injuries, there was no bone damage. There was a knife wound under the right eye; the depth of the wound was 6 p'un when measuring with a dry twig. A person could have arrived at death with that wound alone; how much more so since there were two such wounds. But the depth and shallowness and the lightness and heaviness of the lacerations must be distinguished. The cuts around the eyebrow were a bit wide but shallow. In contrast, the lacerations under the eye were deep and serious. If the deeper lacerations are surmised to be the cause of death, this not only coincides with the confession of the criminal but also seems logical. The face of the deceased was full of knife marks, and it would be difficult to match the injuries with the murder weapon. Because injured areas broke open and bled heavily, there is no need to discuss where the offender began and ended his attack. In examining the head of the body, the mouth and eyes were agape and the hands were clenched in loose fists that correspond to the category of "murder" (p'iin salsa) in the Coroner's Guide for the Elimination of Grievances.[19] Therefore, I file with the [Chunghwa] county office that the true cause of death was "stabbed to death" and fill out all entries in three preprinted inquest forms (*sijang*) with the *un* serial mark: one copy is to be sent to the county office; one given to the relative of the deceased; and the other attached [to the rest of the inquest report] and sent to the PROVINCIAL GOVERNOR'S OFFICE.[20]

Most murders derive from one of three things: lust, greed, or vengeance.[21] The deceased lived in front of the criminal. He was always impoverished, and, as a maker of reed floormats, there cannot have been any monetary dealings, nor did he have any occasion to form enemies with other people. That leaves lust, and that is the primary fit for this case. Already advanced in age, the deceased must have lamented his destitute bachelordom. His mind did not age, as though there were a wild butterfly fluttering inside him. Living in the same yard was close enough for one to feel the other's breath. In going in and out, each other's faces became quite familiar, and in living together for days and months, the man and the woman became friendly. Incidentally, he noticed that the husband had left home [for the wedding matter], and he seized the opportunity to realize his passion by sharing the same pillow [as Ms. Kim]. But even before his lustful dream was fully realized, everything toppled into chaos. How pitiful; the feeble man was crushed under vicious hands. Like an alarmed mouse chased by a cat or a scared pheasant snatched by a hawk, he was tied up and stabbed. After moving the body, as if all that were not enough, the offender even burned the house down. The cause was particularly cruel; when imagining the scene of the crime, it is unspeakably horrendous.

No witness has stepped forward; therefore, the court relies on the self-confession of the culprit. Although there is a constant fear of misjudgment, in deeply reexamining the incident, this case is no other than being caught and killed in the act of adultery.[22] The deceased deserved to die and must not have resentment. The killer killed the one who should die, and the killing was driven by rage. Yet, examining the case, the indiscriminate stabbing and the premeditated arson are all cruel and vicious acts. How could he avoid pertinent punishment for such a crime?

Hong Chin-o is recorded as the principal offender. Because of procedural difficulty (*yuae*), I carried out only one interrogation without torture (*p'yŏngmun*) of Ms. Kim, and her testimony was attached as an addendum.[23] Ms. Kim is over forty years in age, with grown children. Even if she had sexual drive, she should have cleansed away her lustful mind. Instead, she had an illicit relationship, which ended up causing a homicide. It is most appropriate that she receives a heavy punishment to serve as an admonition to others. Yang Hak-pŏm, being the older brother of the deceased, is recorded as the close relative of the dead man. Since there were no real witnesses as the incident took place at night, the column for living witnesses (*kanjŭng*) is left blank. Village elders Kim Hyŏng-un and Sŏ Yu-dŏk, after extinguishing the fire, had another person deliver the death report; so they are all recorded as related witnesses. Since Cho Hyŏng-suk, Sin Kyŏng-sŏp, and O Ch'ang-jo were living relatively close to the murder site, they are recorded as close neighbors. Kim Hag-in, a servant for the district, attended court but could not testify because of illness. The murder weapon, a knife, was thrown into the fire by the culprit, so it can neither be sketched nor sent along to the PROVINCIAL GOVERNOR'S OFFICE. The corpse was put back in the original place. As for preserving the corpse with ashes (*hoebong*) and securing it with seals (*in'gi*), I commissioned the village administrator to take charge [of this]. I also had him guard [the corpse]. All the people who were interrogated are in the custody of the county office and standing by for the second inquest investigation (*pokkŏm*). I request that the magistrate of Sangwŏn Lesser County be called in to take charge of the second inquest investigation. This magistrate [of Chunghwa] is temporarily staying at the official hostel [of P'yŏngyang] in order to assume the position of escort (*siwigwan*) on the eleventh, when the successful candidates for the provincial examination (*togwa*) will be announced. I respectfully submit this report.

· ·

CONCLUDING STATEMENT OF THE SECOND INQUEST INVESTIGATION

There are numerous incidents of murder involving stabbings due to adultery. Some are caught at the scene and some are dealt with through bribes. Hot tempers determine a person's life. As for this case, even if the husband did not witness the scene of [Yang's] violating his wife, he heard from his wife about what had happened. How could hearing about the incident be any different than witnessing it with his own eyes? At that point he became so infuriated [that] he hacked Yang with the phantom hatchet. The poor Yang Hang-nyŏn was a widower for many years and called down his own disaster. He spent nights [alone] in an empty room and disaster struck. The accuser eventually withdrew his demand for revenge, and everyone shut their mouths [and did not want to testify against Hong]. If it were not for the culprit's first testimony, how could one know who the killer was?

I carried out the examination of the body in the presence of all relevant people in accordance with the law. Some slashes on the face were red, while others were blue. All were stab wounds. The lacerations' widths and depths were not the same, with the deepest being the cut below the right eye. When examining the head, the mouth and the eyes were open, and both hands were slightly clenched. All of these fit the article of "murder" in the *Coroner's Guide for the Elimination of Grievances*. Therefore, the true cause of death is recorded as "stabbed to death" in the county [i.e., Sangwŏn Lesser County], and three preprinted inquest forms with the *chin* serial mark have been filled out. One is to be kept in this office, one [given] to the deceased's close relative, and one attached and sent to the PROVINCIAL GOVERNOR'S OFFICE.

Alas! Hong Chin-o and Yang Hang-nyŏn lived sharing a fence and did not hold any special ill will toward each other. However, when Mr. Yang was frequently coming and going across the yard, there were many suspicious behaviors. Mr. Hong as a husband became resentful and jealous. When the husband unexpectedly returned on that night, the thickheaded wife said something strange. Having had prior suspicions that were now newly fanned, Mr. Hong ran straight to Yang's house, searched and got hold of a knife, and stabbed Yang again and again. He only thought of stabbing Yang, but the victim died with one [fatal] stab. However, what kind of awful personality would be driven to set fire to the house to hide the remains of his cruelty? Having released his poisonous anger, the culprit was now composed enough to tell Yang's older brother that Yang died in the fire. When considering everything from beginning to end, how can a person reach such extremes?

Hong Chin-o is recorded as the principal offender, but this case is different from killing a person in the midst of a brawl. There seems to be some room for clemency after taking into consideration the circumstances under the law. Ms. Kim, the wife of the principal offender, having committed adultery, dared to tell her husband words not to be spoken in order to hide the traces of her own filthy act, which consequently resulted in such a grave disaster. The calamity of this crime derives solely from the fact that her husband was the principal offender. Because of the procedural difficulty in questioning Ms. Kim, she was interrogated only once without torture and her testimony is attached as an addendum. For her own lewdness, she shall receive a heavy punishment.

. . . .

In the adjudication (*chesa*) from the Provincial Governor's Office, it is written:[24] The inquest form has been filed. The named Yang Hang-nyŏn was only an impoverished old widower who made reed floormats. He possessed nothing that could cause any calamities. Moreover, living in the same courtyard where his room faced toward Mr. Hong's, he did not incur any animosity and resentment. So why did Hong Chin-o stab and kill Yang with a knife? [According to Hong's first confession,] this was a case of catching adulterers in the act. That woman Kim also testified in her separate interrogation that Yang was killed at the scene of violating her. What, then, made this stupid Chin-o not immediately gather neighbors and clarify the incident of adultery right there? Moreover, why did he not tell the truth at the inception of the investigation, rather than saying that he could not contain his rage and stabbed Mr. Yang after hearing his wife saying that Yang had attempted to forcefully enter his wife's room? In his succeeding [testimony], he stated that despite his wife saying she had rebuked Yang and sent him away, [he thought that his wife] had been raped. Being unable to contain his fury, he grabbed a knife and stabbed Yang, he said. It was only upon the third deposition that he confessed to killing Yang at the scene of adultery and removing the body to Yang's house. Aren't these alterations to the testimony a ploy to avoid heavy punishment and lessen his sentence? Even so, in logically following the details, there must have been some cause for suspicion prior to the incident. He may have heard something suspicious about that night. That day was his daughter's wedding and his returning home was to purchase a wedding chest; all makes sense. But when revisiting the whole story, it cannot be the case that the incident suddenly happened. There must have been plenty of lewd scenes that had been previously paraded before his eyes. As a result, uncontrollable rage erupted in his heart so fiercely that he could not restrain his hands and feet from committing violence. It was only out of fear that his murderous trail might be uncovered that he set fire to the house, without even considering that the neighbors could extinguish it. And without thinking that the corpse remained intact, he ran and informed Yang's brother that Yang had burned to death. In the beginning, he committed the crime out of anger, but in the end he lost his mind in his fear. It is not difficult to assess that the murder was committed at the scene of adultery.

Hong Chin-o and Ms. Kim shall both be prosecuted under the *Great Ming Code*. There is no need to sentence Hong Chin-o to any punishment. One round of beating shall be applied to that woman Kim, and then she shall be sent back to her husband. The whole crime that Hong Chin-o committed— killing the adulterous man and even setting the fire to burn the body—is cruel and vicious, and should be dealt with punishment. After one round of beating to set an example for others, he shall be released. Let the body be released for a burial, and release all others under custody.

In the first round of deposition of the witnesses Kim Hyŏng-un and Sŏ

Yu-dŏk, the query saying "You [Kim and Sŏ] sent Hong Chin-o to deliver the message" was stated as though Hong Chin-o had testified in such a way, whereas in fact Hong had not in his first testimony. This is a grave investigative error. In the last part of the second inquest investigation's concluding statement, there was no record of district and subdistrict administrators, and this is out of line with proper procedures. In the first inquest investigation's concluding statement, the character kwang (狂) was written as kwang (枉), and ki (歧) was written as ki (岐). This all demonstrates a slighting of the importance of court proceedings; the clerks at the Bureau of Penal Affairs in charge of both investigations shall be censured by informing the first inquest official and [other] local officials.

A FAMILY ACTIVIST CONFRONTS A LOCAL MAGNATE

Ms. Pak (Yongin, Kyŏnggi Province, Late Eighteenth Century)

GRAVESITE LITIGATION (*SANSONG*) INVOLVING ILLEGAL BURI-als (*t'ujang*) was an increasingly common social problem in the late Chosŏn period, with conflicts over gravesites often flaring up as both verbal and physical confrontations that sometimes resulted in death.[1] Rural conflicts over gravesites were grounded in at least three aspects—geomantic beliefs, economic benefits, and filial piety, which Chosŏn Confucian society upheld as a cardinal ethical value—all of which were closely intertwined. While locating and placing an ancestor's tomb at a propitious site for the sake of the dead ancestor was the obligation of a filial son, a more mundane moti-vation was popular belief in geomantic blessings supposedly emanating from auspicious gravesites. According to the doctrine of geomancy (K: *p'ungsu*; C: *fengshui*), subterranean energy flowing beneath the surface of the earth affects human affairs both positively and negatively. Whereas disturbing the circulation of this energy can upset the harmony of human society, the wise utilization of its vital spots could result in the prosperity of a dynasty, lin-eage, family, or town. In the late Chosŏn, the geomantic idea took hold that a propitious burial site for an ancestor was critically linked to the well-being and prosperity of his descendants. Though geomantic theories are extremely complex, an ideal burial site needs to be near a strong flow of earth energy, a place where the loins of the azure dragon of the east and the white tiger of the west are locked together in intercourse. The site must also be protected from high winds by a black tortoise mountain to the north and possess a good open view toward the protective hill of a red phoenix to the south. The slow flow of water from eastern and western hills meeting in front of the spot before moving away from the horseshoe-shaped lair of the dragon is another critical element.[2] Though numerous such sites were identified all over the Korean peninsula, fierce competition to locate the most beneficial ones emerged as more and more people came to subscribe to geomantic beliefs in the late Chosŏn.

In addition to abstract blessings that would bring prosperity and scholarly and bureaucratic success for many future generations, the owner of a gravesite came to have exclusive rights to the land surrounding the tomb, and also to the resources, such as firewood, lumber, and soil, that were produced there.[3] Although all forests and mountains were in principle common property for everyone to share in Chosŏn Korea, yangban elite in the late Chosŏn expanded their occupation of forestland and mountains by placing their ancestors' tombs there. Once a family had secured forestland and mountains as a family graveyard, its members came to have exclusive usufruct over the space, and other people could neither place a tomb nor gather any resources there. The holders of the usufruct eventually exercised the ownership right and sold forest resources and even the land itself. Thus, gravesite litigation involved not only the violation of another family's graveyard by placing an illegal burial there, but also conflicts over uses of forest products and the sale and ownership of the land.

The *Great Code of Administration* (Kyŏngguk taejŏn), the fifteenth-century state code, originally granted the right to occupy the land surrounding a grave only to ranked officials.[4] Subsequently, the royal edict of 1676 expanded the grantees to yangban without official ranks, and the royal edict of 1718 expanded it to all commoners.[5] The fact that the *Supplement to the Great Code* (Sok taejŏn), which was compiled in 1744, began to contain regulations concerning gravesite litigations reflects the increasing occurrences of such legal matters derived from the expansion of gravesite protection and occupation rights.[6]

Another cause for increased gravesite litigations in the late Chosŏn was that the laws regulating grave protection and forest usage rights were not clearly laid out. For example, the spatial perimeter that a grave would create was unclear, and this naturally led to disputes over ownership of certain pieces of land and the legality of another family placing a new tomb nearby.[7] Although gravesite litigations were often conflicts among yangban elites, non-yangban populations were also active in challenging the yangban who invaded their ancestral graveyards. In addition, they frequently trespassed on forestland owned by yangban in order to collect firewood and lumber, both for their own use and to sell on the market as increasing demand made it a lucrative business.[8] There were a number of reasons for this increased demand for firewood in the late Chosŏn period. The general population increase may well have generated more demand for cooking. In addition, heating rooms through a duct under the floor had become more popular in the late Chosŏn, and this must have resulted in exponential growth in the need for fuel for heating.[9] Major industries requiring firewood included ceramics, metallurgy, and salt production, whose demands probably increased with general population growth.

When someone violated another's gravesite and placed his or her own ancestor's tomb there, it was most likely out of the very selfish desire to rob the imagined blessings as well as to claim land rights. The violated family, when it discovered the illegal burial in its family graveyard, took the incident very seriously, for it meant not only an unthinkable assault on the buried ancestor, but also the loss of the family's imagined good fortune for the present and future, and the land rights themselves. The afflicted party, therefore, mobilized every possible private and legal tool to remove the illegal burial and resolve the issue.

The present death case of Ms. Pak began with the illegal burial of the wife of Kim Wŏn-ch'ŏl near the gravesite of Ms. Pak's husband. Ms. Pak, a widow who did not have any children and who had also lost her own father, acted on her own and filed complaints with the authorities to undo the injustice. Chosŏn women, though ideally confined to the inner realm and not involved in "public" matters, did have the right to submit appeals to the authorities on various matters. Numerous documents show that women were the agents of legal proceedings, especially those concerning property rights and on behalf of wrongfully accused husbands.[10] Ms. Pak's petition received multiple favorable resolutions issued by local officials, but the offender, Kim Wŏn-ch'ŏl, relying on his family's power and authority in the area, did not comply with the government's order to remove his wife's burial. Ms. Pak, frustrated and enraged by Wŏn-ch'ŏl's adamant attitude, dug up the illegal burial with her own hands, which eventually invited physical assault by Wŏn-ch'ŏl and his family. Ms. Pak died three days after the attack.

Apparently, powerful families in local areas intentionally violated other families' gravesites as a way to take over forestland, and often resisted removing an illegally placed tomb even after they had lost a suit.[11] One of the reasons the violator was able to resist the legal judgment was that there was no guideline specifying the use of official force to remove the illegal burial. Since there was no legal mandate enforcing the judgment of removal of the illegal burial, powerful families simply kept the tomb there and waited for time to pass until the complainant gave up. In this incident, the infuriated complainant, Ms. Pak, took the matter into her own hands and destroyed the illegal burial—an act that was in itself illegal.[12] But her death took the case to a different level of investigation and judgment. Arbitrary exercise of power, over a powerless woman in particular—combined with the offending family's plot to manipulate the cause of her death to make it look as though she had committed suicide by drinking poison—was regarded as an unforgivable crime, and the death penalty for the accused was ensured, at least in principle. Yet, as many of the royal reviews of late eighteenth-century murder cases in the *Records of Royal Reviews* (Simnirok) show, capital punishment was rare.[13] Likewise, the reigning king ordered another thorough investigation just to make sure that there were no different opinions and facts, as the translated case document shows.

The present case is one of twelve from various counties compiled in the book *Inquest Records* (Kŏman).[14] None of the cases in this collection carries a "full" inquest report. Some consist only of a royal judgment (*p'anbu*); in others, the royal judgment is preceded by a combination of concluding statements of the first and/or second inquest, adjudication of the provincial governor, and comments by the Ministry of Penal Affairs. A few cases even include a report made by the special investigator or by a secret royal inspector (*amhaeng ŏsa*). These characteristics of the collection resemble those of the *Records of Royal Reviews*, a collection of records of special royal hearings (*simni*) for more than one thousand cases held between 1776 and 1800, which overlaps with King Chŏngjo's reign. In fact, all twelve cases recorded in the *Inquest Records* are found in the *Records of Royal Reviews*. The *Inquest Records* was probably a draft for the *Records of Royal Reviews*, given the fact that it contains material not included in the *Records of Royal Reviews*.[15] However, the *Records of Royal Reviews* usually provides much richer information that is missing in the *Inquest Records*, including when the recorded incidents were first filed with the authorities.[16]

The present case was filed with the Yongin county office in the eighth month of 1783 and presented for a royal review in the fifth month of 1784, according to the *Records of Royal Reviews*.[17] The *Records of Royal Reviews* also reveals the surprisingly complicated nature of this case. Subsequent proceedings involved two petitions by "striking the gong" (*kyŏkchaeng*) by the principal offender's son in 1784, and eleven royal reviews, the last one in the fifth month of 1798—making the case unresolved and under review for fifteen years.[18] Considering that the average length of a trial was 41.8 months, from the case's filing date to the final royal judgment, the fact that this case was not resolved for sixteen years signifies the extraordinary difficulty it generated in rendering the firm final judgment.[19] The royal judgments for this case recorded in the *Records of Royal Reviews* can be divided into two groups: the first four (1784–85), and the rest (1797–98). The translated royal judgment here is in fact the fourth one, in the seventh month of 1785, and the fact that the case was reviewed again after a lapse of twelve years means that the principal offender Kim had probably been in prison during that time.

Apparently the true cause of Ms. Pak's death—whether she was beaten to death or whether she committed suicide by drinking poison—was the key question. During the first inquest, the silver hairpin inserted into her body to test for the presence of poison inside her system apparently turned black, but it regained its natural color when it was washed with pods of soap bean. This alone did not confirm Ms. Pak's suicide by drinking poison, for the stain on the hairpin should not have disappeared that easily if caused by poison.[20] Two women, meanwhile, came forward and made written testimonies in favor of the principal offender by saying that Ms. Pak, who was seventy years old at the time, tried to kill herself by harming her body first, and eventually by drinking poison, after she was battered and insulted by the Kims. Court officials and the king regarded such belated testimonies as untrustworthy. Yet, with conflicting testimonies and arguments, as well as physical evidence that left some doubt in determining the true cause of death, the case did not see a firm resolution even in the last royal judgment, which demanded another report from the provincial governor after seeking more evidence and reasoning. The fundamental quandary in this long-held case was that the requital for the life of Ms. Pak must be carried out, yet no death sentence could be rendered unless there was solid evidence against the accused because a wrongful sentence and death would only incur a greater grudge on the part of the dead.

YONGIN: KIM WŎN-CH'ŎL BEAT MS. PAK TO DEATH

In the concluding statement of the provincial governor: All maternal as well as paternal relatives of the criminal Kim Wŏn-ch'ŏl resided in the same village.[21] The deceased Ms. Pak was a widow without any child, and also in mourning for her father. Wŏn-ch'ŏl always flouted her. Upon his wife's death, he carried out an illegal burial of her corpse near the incoming dragon vein (*naeryong*) of the gravesite of Ms. Pak's husband.[22] Ms. Pak made the effort of going over the mountains and across rivers, and proceeded to submit appeals to the relevant county as well as provincial offices. She subsequently received numerous judgments that obliged Wŏn-ch'ŏl to remove his wife's grave. Yet Wŏn-ch'ŏl resisted for more than a year and did not take action. The way he resorted to his power to illegally occupy another's gravesite is extremely deplorable. Moreover, he did not move the grave even after the issuance of an official decision; this is certainly a habit of ignoring laws without shame. Ms. Pak was enraged and acted on her own to the extent that she grabbed a hoe and went straight to tear down the mound and remove the grave with her own hands. Although that was not womanly behavior, the fact that she reached that point lets us realize the extreme degree of Wŏn-ch'ŏl's arrogance. Both Wŏn-ch'ŏl and Ms. Pak are local yangban (*hyangban*). As for the mountain cemetery, there are differences between the owner and the guest. As for men and women, there are separations between the inner and outer realms. But Wŏn-ch'ŏl, together with his brothers and many male and female slaves, chased [Ms. Pak] to the top of the mountain cemetery and tied her up. They must have beaten her and dragged her to the hillside. Within three days, she died. Although he said that he had only tied her up but not hit her, there were numerous injuries, all in a critical state. Wŏn-ch'ŏl's two brothers and slaves not only followed him but obeyed his orders. It was Wŏn-ch'ŏl who tied her up. When he restrained and bound her, and also grabbed her hair to tie her up, he must have been angry and hit her wildly. With such force, he must have caused injuries all over her body. How could he dare to present confusion [at the court] in an effort to escape the charge? Furthermore, when Pak Kyŏm-ch'oe came to [the site of the incident] by horse, immediately after he heard that his sister had been beaten, Wŏn-ch'ŏl and others had already tied her up, pushed, kicked, dragged, and pulled her. As if she were a corpse, she could not speak a word. Pak Kyŏm-ch'oe did witness her like that with his own eyes. In addition, Ms. Pak, before her death, told her [brother][23] that Wŏn-ch'ŏl had tied her up, kicked her, and hit her back and chest violently with the handle of the hoe. Therefore, there is no doubt that Wŏn-ch'ŏl is the principal offender in this criminal case.

Among numerous wounds, the bruises on both the right and left breast and the right side of the back are the most severe and located in the most critical spots. There are also traces of tying around her elbows, and they are really severe. When imagining the scene of that day, the fact that Ms. Pak did not die on the spot [put this case under the category of] "the period of responsibility for crimes" (*kohan*).[24] Wŏn-ch'ŏl's illegal burial, followed by his arrest and battery of Ms. Pak—there is not a single excuse for clemency for what he had done. His maternal uncle[25] coaxed Chŏm-hwa[26] and fabricated a story that Ms. Pak drank bittern [and died of it]. This story was a plot to confuse the court and to escape prosecution. His lie has been exposed and there is no way to cover up his crime. In this kind of crime, confession must be taken for requital for a life. I shall send down a strict order to the inquest official, who should carry out interrogation in no time to attain his confession.

As for Kim Hyŏng-ch'ŏl, he accompanied and assisted his brother Wŏn-ch'ŏl for his brother's sake, and it is clear that he himself also beat her. On that same evening, [he] tied up Ms. Pak again and all his acts were extremely deplorable. However, his older brother has already been accused as the principal offender and it is inappropriate to hold him in prison passing a year. In addition, he has received four rounds of punishments and these would indeed be enough punishments for his crime. Therefore, your subject, the provincial governor, issued an order to release him. As for [Kim] I-ch'ŏl, his crime is on a par with [that of] his brother. In his participation in tying her again, what he did was no different from his older brother. However, when Ms. Pak, having been tied up and beaten, managed to escape and was on her way back home, I-ch'ŏl suddenly appeared and kicked and struck her, and caused her to fall off a horse which stunned her. The death of Ms. Pak must have derived from injuries [caused by this assault]. There is no way to avoid the application of the law concerning accomplices (*sujong chi yul*). It is exceptionally lamentable that he has not been arrested because he ran far away. Your subject, the provincial governor, sent out an order to relevant counties and garrisons to make a special effort to search for and arrest him. Former magistrate Ŏ Sa-p'il is the maternal uncle [of the accused].[27] He must have wanted to harbor [I-ch'ŏl], and that is not unusual in terms of personal sentiment. Yet it is extremely impertinent to hide a criminal. In addition, he secretly provoked his female slave to disseminate the rumor that [Ms. Pak] drank bittern to die. Furthermore, he stood up and criticized [inquest officials] at the time of inquest. How dare a person, who had served at the court, behave in such a way at the solemn criminal court! I fear we should censure him for the sake of this country's cardinal principles.

In the ROYAL JUDGMENT:[28] As for the criminal Kim Wŏn-ch'ol in the murder case of Yongin Prefecture, the royal law of "requital for a life" in a homicide case is very strict. Although I would like to let him live, there is no way. As a local magnate, he killed a vulnerable yangban woman. His scheme was extremely cunning; his dark trick and brutal acts were so cruel. Even people on the road would have spontaneously shed tears [of grief and rage] had they heard of his brandishing a sickle [to harm Ms. Pak].[29] His sly plot to concoct the story that she drank bittern has been revealed. Every act of his arouses great indignation. The discussion of his crimes by the Ministry of Penal Affairs has nothing out of line. Yet a criminal case must take the utmost care. Because people disagree [on certain things], order the new provincial governor himself to take charge of a detailed investigation and to submit his opinion. This is not to harm the meaning of legal prudence (*hŭmhyul chi ŭi*). Inform the provincial governor of this decision.

A DEFIANT SLAVE CHALLENGES HIS MASTER WITH DEATH

Yi Pong-dol (Anŭi, Kyŏngsang Province, 1842)

T HE DEATH OF YI PONG-DOL, THE SON OF A SLAVE AND THUS AN uneducable "fool" in the Chosŏn elite's view, was "in vain." His disrespectful speech and behavior upset a village yangban. The offended yangban invaded Pong-dol's home after failing to catch him and broke jars containing precious preserved sauces, a critical source of nutrition for Korean people all year long. Pong-dol, in despair and frustration, committed suicide by throwing himself into a deep pond. This case reveals a widespread social problem: violation of the distinctions of status between noble and lowborn (*ch'ŏnmin*) and between master and slave, as manifested in insolent speech or behavior by people of the non-elite class. The Chosŏn elite's sensitivity over the blurring of social status lines was acute throughout the dynasty because they believed that status distinctions were the foundation of society and that laxity in such matters meant institutional instability. Criminal incidents resulting from people crossing long-established social status lines seem to have increased in the eighteenth and nineteenth centuries, and scholars such as William Shaw have interpreted the phenomenon as "a by-product of economic changes" that enabled non-elites to purchase yangban titles and to imitate the yangban lifestyle while some local yangban fell into poverty and could not maintain their decorum and way of life.[1]

The Yi family in this suicide case seems to fit this formula. The victim, Yi Pong-dol, as already noted, was the son of a slave who was owned by relatives of the assailant, Sin P'il-ho, a man from a well-established yangban family in the area. Pong-dol's wife was a slave owned by the assailant, and his sister Ms. Yi was a private slave. Yet their eldest brother, Yi Pong-un, had the yangban title *ch'ŏmji*, a senior third military post that was often sold for grain contributions in the late Chosŏn. Pong-un also owned a bean field of unknown size. Considering the fact that this family of slave status had a surname, that Pong-un held a yangban title probably by purchase, and that they enjoyed some economic means, the Yi brothers and sisters were most likely descendants of the son of a yangban (or a commoner) by his slave concubine.[2] Yangban Sin's economic condition seems to have been modest, if not impoverished. He was in mourning for his mother but did not have the wherewithal to prepare all the needed daily ritual offerings. The audacity of Yi Pong-dol in accusing Yangban Sin of violating Yi's usufruct of the fish farm that Yi had built may well represent this complicated situation in the village, where status and economic wealth did not always go hand in hand. However, contemptuous attitudes of the non-elite class toward yangban elites did not necessarily represent the dissolution of the social status system but fluid boundaries between social status groups. Tensions and conflicts among different social status groups did exist, often erupting into fights and even resulting in deaths; yet it seems that the existing law still functioned, in strong favor of the ruling class, to maintain social distinctions and inequalities. The legal reasoning in this case also clearly proves that it was Pong-dol who violated propriety, and thus Yangban Sin was not liable for Pong-dol's death.

This does not mean that non-elites did not have any legal rights to sue elites when they felt that their rights had been infringed, as shown in this case, in which Ms. Yi made a report of her brother's "unjust" death to the authorities. Disappointingly to the victim's family, the assailant was found not guilty of Pong-dol's death, though he was punished for his excessive behavior of breaking Pong-dol's sauce jars. In fact, the state was keen to regulate oppressive yangban who exercised abusive power over villagers in the countryside. From the state's perspective, domineering and unruly yangban were anathema because they competed with the state in controlling local resources, both human and natural, and often disrupted the peace and stability in local society by exploiting and provoking people.[3] Cases 2 and 6 are such examples of a powerful yangban invading the rights of a fellow yangban woman and a non-yangban woman. Case 8 also involves private punishment imposed by a powerful local lineage.

The present case is one of forty-two preserved in the *Selected Inquest Records* (Kŏman ch'o); all forty-two death incidents in this collection took place between the fourth and twelfth months of 1842 in Kyŏngsang Province.[4] Case 4 is also selected from this collection. Each case record primarily consists of a summary of testimonies from the first inquest and the adjudication of the provincial governor. From this, it appears that the book may have been compiled by the provincial governor's office for its own record keeping or in preparation to report to the Ministry of Penal Affairs. The provincial governor at the time was Yi Kyŏng-jae (1800–73) of the Hansan Yi descent group, who had accepted a number of important bureaucratic appointments after passing the higher civil service examination in 1822. Later he served as the chief state councilor, the highest position in the Chosŏn bureaucracy.

ANŬI

The accused (*p'igo*): Sin P'il-ho
The deceased: Yi Pong-dol
True cause of the death: Suicide by drowning (*chaik*)

In the official report (*ch'ŏpchŏng*) submitted by Min Ch'i-sŏ,[5] magistrate of Anŭi Lesser Prefecture (Anŭi *hyŏn'gam*) and the first inquest official: On the twenty-seventh day of this month, Ms. Yi from Sŏmal Village, Kohyŏn District of this county, submitted a complaint saying, "My older brother Pong-dol had some altercation with Sin P'il-ho, a yangban from Cheha Village in Pukha District, and he drowned himself to death around noon the day before." Therefore, I [Min Ch'i-sŏ] conducted the first inquest investigation on 1842.4.27 (6/5/1842). The deceased was a man of about fifty-four or fifty-five years in age. On the ventral side of the body, the upper belly was bloated and there was an open wound on the right lower belly. It was yellow and 2 *ch'on* 9 *p'un* in length. There were two traces of abrasions on his elbows, in the shape of a bean.[6] On the dorsal side of the body, the right side of the spine has pockmarks that look like scattered millet. Both backs of the shoulders were yellow, and looked normal. There were feces from his bowel. When tested with a silver hairpin, there was no change of color. The true cause of the death must be suicide by drowning.

In the testimony of Ms. Yi, a close relative of the deceased: "On the twenty-sixth day of this month, I went to help out with some sowing work at my eldest brother Pong-un's bean field. Around lunchtime in the field, Yu Si-jong, who was living right by Choch'u Rock in Cheha Village, came to deliver a message to Pong-un, saying, 'Yi Ch'ŏmji,[7] your younger brother Pong-dol threw himself into the Choch'u Pond.' I was shocked and rushed to see him, together with my eldest brother Pong-un. Before we arrived, many villagers had gathered and had already pulled him out of the water. They were talking to each other about the incident [earlier that day]. My brother [Pong-dol] removed the fishing net that Yangban Sin (Sin *pan*)[8] had placed into the fish farm in the Chŏn Stream. Yangban Sin then got upset and went to my brother's house and broke the sauce jars. My brother, after seeing these broken jars, proceeded to the top of Choch'u Rock located in front of the village and threw himself into the pond. My eldest brother Pong-un wanted to file a report with the authorities at once, but Yangban Sin and others stopped him from doing so in many ways. Thus, I report this to you in secret like this."

In the testimony of Yi Pong-un, a close relative of the deceased: "When I was sowing beans in my bean field, I received a message [about my brother's death] from Yu Si-jong, who lives by Choch'u Rock, so I rushed there to see what had happened. My brother Pong-dol had already drowned in the deep water and been dead for a while. I was shocked and felt suspicious that a healthy person had died like this, so I investigated what had happened. Pong-dol had built a fish farm in the Chŏn Stream so that he could catch fish any time. On that day, Pong-dol removed the fishing net that Yangban Sin had placed earlier in the fish farm that he had built. When Yangban Sin scolded him for removing the net, Pong-dol said in reply, 'A yangban catches fish; a commoner should not?' Because Pong-dol's speech was so rude, Yangban Sin felt very offended and went to Pong-dol's house and broke the sauce jars. When Pong-dol returned home and saw those broken jars, he suddenly went to Choch'u Pond and ended up drowning himself to death. If Yangban Sin did not cause the trouble, would Pong-dol have drowned himself?"

In the testimony of Yu Si-jong, a related witness (*saryŏn*): "I live alone right by Choch'u Rock. Then I heard my daughter saying that Yi Pong-dol had drowned to death. Therefore, I indeed rushed to let his brother Pong-un know about this."

In the testimony of Ko Pok-chi, an involved witness (*kallyŏn*):[9] "I heard that a person had drowned to death at Choch'u Pond, and so hurriedly went there to see what had happened. All people there said, 'This pond is so deep. Once drowned, he cannot be pulled out.' I am kind of good at swimming, so I dived into the water. Yet I was not able to locate the body. Yangban Sin's second nephew then hooked Pong-dol's clothes with a sickle with a long bamboo handle and pulled him toward the margin of the pond. So I, together with Yu Si-jong, dragged him out of the water."

In the testimony of Kim Il-un, an eyewitness (*kanjŭng*): "I am Yi Pong-dol's cousin by a maternal aunt. That day, on my way back home after having worked at the field, I arrived in front of Pong-dol's house. Pong-dol said to me, 'I built a fish farm in Chŏn Stream. Because Yangban Sin set his fishing gear in the farm, I took it out. Then Yangban Sin got upset and scolded me. While I fled somewhere else to avoid him, Yangban Sin unexpectedly went to my house and broke our jars. How can I live [like this]? I want to drown myself to death.' When I strongly stopped him from doing it, he then said that his family members had gone to his eldest brother's place to help with sowing [beans in the field] and that he would go there to get some lunch. I believed his words and returned home. Before long, I heard the news that Pong-dol had drowned to death, so I hastily went to the pond. He was indeed dead. He drowned himself because of such a trivial thing and he died for no purpose."

In the testimony of Ch'oe Pong-nip, a close neighbor: "I am Pong-dol's cousin by an aunt. That day, on my way back home after having worked at the field, I arrived at the water's edge in front of the village. Pong-dol having drowned to death, many villagers got together to pull him out of the water. I inquired what had happened, and they said that Pong-dol threw himself into the water after having an argument with Yangban Sin about Sin's fishing net."

In the testimony of Sin P'il-ho, the accused: "I was in mourning for my mother. I had difficulty in obtaining side dishes for every morning and evening offering, and [that is why] I set my fishing gear in the fish farm in the Chŏn Stream. Although Pong-dol made the excuse that I had set my fishing gear in his fish farm, he blurted out such offensive words, grabbed my jacket, and pushed my back to the water, so that my clothes got wet. Pong-dol's wife is a hereditary slave of my household. Pong-dol himself is also the son of a slave owned by my relatives. So the incident was a matter related to propriety (punŭi). He was so ill-mannered that I could not overcome my anger and broke his jars. Pong-dol said, 'In such a lean year, when salt is so precious, you destroyed all our preserved sauces. I am going to kill myself. I will see how you manage to live after my death.' Then, he went to Choch'u Pond and threw himself into the water and died. I did not commit any crime and I have nothing to fear."

In the concluding statement: The entire altercation started with the trivial incident of removing fishing gear, but resulted in broken jars of preserved sauces. This foolish Pong-dol ended up throwing himself into a deep pond to his death. It is a useless death.

In the adjudication of the provincial governor: Send the inquest form as a reference for the second inquest investigation.[10]

In the report of Ch'oe U-hyŏng (1805–78),[11] magistrate of Tansŏng Lesser Prefecture and the second inquest official: The true cause of death and the testimonies by all related people are the same [as in the first inquest].

In the adjudication of the provincial governor: I received the inquest reports.[12] The primary matter of this incident—who set up fishing gear first—is such a trivial thing. However, a slave grabbed Yangban Sin's jacket and pushed his back, and his violation of propriety was absolutely extreme. Pong-dol's unruliness in his everyday life can be discerned. The ways in which Yangban Sin followed up and scolded Pong-dol are very understandable. This does not constitute a crime, and there is no doubt that it did not create the cause for Pong-dol's disastrous death. How could such a robust man harbor a suicidal thought? It originated from the fact that his sauce jars were destroyed by someone else. He naturally felt resentful, but he was not rational. He was stubborn and not friendly. Such a personality suddenly exploded into anger. Gazing at that huge rock, he huffed and puffed and went there. He looked down at the deep water and abruptly threw himself into it. In the end, his healthy body turned into a ghost in an instant. Thinking of the circumstances, it is very pitiable. Speaking of his death, it is largely futile and absurd. There is nowhere for the resentful soul to go. From the beginning, there is no way to discuss whether this constitutes a criminal case.

In speaking of Sin P'il-ho, although there is no ground to accuse him of any crime, he cannot avoid [the responsibility] for aggravating the whole matter [of Pong-dol's suicide]. As a man of a well-established yangban family, he must have embodied proper ways. It would have been enough to severely scold Pong-dol's misbehavior. But he chased down Pong-dol, then went to his empty house and destroyed those precious preserved sauces, which in turn drove Pong-dol mad and [caused him] to commit suicide. In addition, if he had heard [Pong-dol's] mention of drowning himself, why didn't he stop him with all his heart? From the beginning to the end, he was excessive and unreasonable. He must be punished for not being judicious in his behavior. Send down an order to punish him with one round of beating.[13]

As for Kim Il-un, he is Pong-dol's cousin by a maternal aunt. His feeling of caring [for Pong-dol] must be different from others. When Pong-dol proceeded to the water—and Yangban Sin also ordered him to go take a look—how come he was so casual and didn't go save Pong-dol? He cannot be simply dismissed as a fool and not punished. Punish him by flogging forty times and release him and all others. Release the body for a burial as well.

Even if this is not a criminal case that incurs requital for a life, the inquest is a serious matter in general. In the first inquest report, [it records] Yu Si-jong as "a related witness (*saryŏn*)" and Ko Pok-chi as "an involved witness (*kallyŏn*)," whereas both of them appear as "eyewitnesses (*kanjŭng*)" in the second inquest report. The fact is that the first inquest report is at fault. In the first inquest report, a close relative of the deceased is recorded as "a private female slave Ms. Yi" (*sabi Yi choi*). If identified as a private female slave, how can she have the title "Ms." (*choi*)? Furthermore, the eyewitness Il-un and the close neighbor Pong-sam have been identified as private male slaves (*sano*), but both are recorded with their surnames (*sŏng*). It is in the law that both public and private slaves (*kongsano*) are not addressed with their surnames. In the second inquest record, a close relative of the deceased in the first deposition is written as "Ing-sim, a private female slave," while in the second deposition, it is suddenly written as "Ms. Yi." As in the first inquest report, the second inquest report repeats the same mistake of recording Il-un and Pong-sam with their surnames while identifying them as private male slaves. A second nephew of Yangban Sin who appears in the first as well as second inquest reports must have been interrogated, but both courts did not do so. Why are the investigative records of a criminal case so lax? Both clerks at the Bureau of Penal Affairs [who served for those inquests] shall be apprehended and punished with twenty strokes of beating with a heavy stick (*chang*). Deliver this order to the first inquest official and have him carry it out.

TWO WIDOWS FIGHT

Madam Chang and Ms. Ŭn (Yech'ŏn,
Kyŏngsang Province, 1842)

N CHOSŎN SOCIETY, WIDOWS, ALONG WITH FILIAL CHILDREN AND
royal subjects, were the group most frequently honored by the Confucian
state, as long as they remained faithful to their deceased husbands and
did not remarry. A number of biographies of chaste widows, mostly written by male Confucian literati, testify to the fact that widows' virtuous acts
were recognized by the state as well as by society, particularly during the
latter half of the dynasty.[1] As heroines of the chastity discourse at that time,
many widows appear in such literature as sincerely committed to the ideal of
widow fidelity.

In contrast, records of the lives of ordinary widows who were not being
recognized for their chastity are scarce, and accounts of their widowhood are
almost nonexistent in the historiography of the Chosŏn dynasty. The only
time a widow appears to have been a main actor was when she made a decision about remarriage. Because the *Great Code of Administration* (Kyŏngguk
taejŏn), the fifteenth-century Chosŏn legal code, decreed that sons and grandsons of remarried women were barred from sitting for the civil service examination, widows with sons naturally had to be careful about the remarriage
option since it could directly influence their sons' future careers.[2] Contrary
to the common understanding, however, remarriage was never prohibited in
the form of an absolute law during the Chosŏn dynasty. In addition, though
the civil service examination, which was the primary route to holding official positions throughout the Chosŏn, was theoretically open to non-yangban
commoners, it was virtually impossible for them to afford exam preparation,
which required enormous economic resources as well as time. Therefore, this
famous legal provision making sons of remarried women ineligible for gov-

ernmental positions seems to have mainly affected yangban children, leaving non-yangban widows quite free of such legal repercussions. In other words, financially secure yangban women tended not to remarry for the sake of their sons' professional prospects, while the majority of lower-status women chose to do so for economic and practical reasons.

Women's widowhood during the Chosŏn has to date been a subject of scholarly discussion only in terms of their relations with male children, as though everything else about their identities and lives were nonexistent. How was the widow's position perceived by family (both in-law and natal) and local community? Did people really have different expectations of yangban versus non-yangban widows? How did a widow manage to survive economically if her family could not provide the quiet "inner quarters" life? What were her relations with neighbors, both female and male? In what ways could a widow solve problems when she had conflicts with various members of her local community?

The legal case translated here (together with case 2) may illuminate these questions, because it gives us a rare glimpse into the lives of widows in the real world. Whereas the biographies of chaste widows are sites where the lives of a limited number of dead widows were painted by male literati to fit the Confucian imagination of virtuous women, legal testimonies of widows transmit their voices from all walks of life. Although it is clear that the societal perspective toward widows at that time was filled with the idea of widow fidelity, meeting such expectations was an expensive option generally unavailable to widows from the lower classes or without stable economic means. These widows could not withdraw from the world into the private life of chaste widowhood after the deaths of their husbands.

Two widows are in conflict in this case of 1842: a yangban widow, Madam Chang, and a non-yangban widow, Ms. Ŭn.[3] Though of different social statuses, both were leading extremely impoverished lives. After having been widowed when young, Madam Chang resided in the rented room of a neighbor's house with her young son. Ms. Ŭn, widowed more than ten years before the events described here, lived in a dilapidated house. Eking out a living under bitter conditions, the two women competed over a small house owned by a neighboring man, Mr. Yi. The conflict arose when the house was eventually sold to Madam Chang, who then became the target of Ms. Ŭn's vicious gossip. Madam Chang, after several confrontations with Ms. Ŭn about how baseless her story of Madam Chang's adulterous conduct was, became frustrated and chose suicide as a last resort in her determination to prove her innocence. Her resolution to restore her integrity was clear, in that she asked her son to seek revenge on her behalf in case she should die.

As a series of testimonies by the villagers elucidates, the essence of the conflict between the two widows was gossip. Gossip was perhaps the most common weapon deployed, along with cursing and slander, in interpersonal disputes. Ms. Ŭn attacked her adversary, Madam Chang, in the area where Madam Chang was most vulnerable—her sexual reputation.[4] Everyone brought to the court acknowledges Ms. Ŭn's malevolent behavior—her jealousy over Madam Chang's purchase of the house, her endless cursing, and even the fact that she hung up animal bones to support her stories. In rebuttal, the offender, Ms. Ŭn, reveals that a rumor about Madam Chang's adulterous relations had already circulated in the town. In Chosŏn society, safeguarding honor or reputation was of the utmost importance in preserving the community standing of both an individual and his or her family. This point is reflected in the law that states, "In all cases of cursing others [i.e., humiliating others with bad or lewd language], the offenders shall be punished by ten strokes of beating with a light stick."[5] In a small local village, where almost everyone was connected through marriage and family relations, whether directly or indirectly,[6] honor was "a priceless possession and quality, one that when damaged is beyond repair."[7] In such a culture of reputation and disrepute, any gossip about (yangban) women could be taken as dishonoring.

Knowing that Ms. Ŭn's testimony could not only weaken the court case but ruin the Chang family reputation, regardless of how baseless her accusations were, Madam Chang's family tried to establish Madam Chang's fidelity and reputation from the very outset. Their strong assertions of her virtue established Madam Chang as morally upright, throwing into stark relief how profoundly this faithful lady had been wronged by Ms. Ŭn. Individual and family honor may have been less crucial to non-elites, but people such as Ms. Ŭn nevertheless understood how they could use it to negotiate various interests.

Although both Madam Chang and Ms. Ŭn chose not to remarry, they still had to face the actual world. Widows, regardless of their social status, had to participate in economic transactions such as buying and selling homes to and from men. They filed complaints with Chosŏn's judicial system against male neighbors over a wide variety of insults, frauds, and community conflicts as a way of securing their interests. Trapped between the ideal of a quiet, secluded widowhood and the reality of having to engage in economic transactions if they were to eat and otherwise survive, the real status of a widow was the most marginalized, complicated, and vulnerable of anyone in Chosŏn society.

The two widows in the case presented here made different choices to solve their predicament: while the victim, Madam Chang, chose death to clear her name, the offender, Ms. Ŭn, tried to turn to legal means for a solution to her struggles. Being brought to court as the accused, Ms. Ŭn was able to tell her version of the contested events to a magistrate. This clearly illustrates that these two widows cared just as much as men did about their precise standing within the local social hierarchy, and that they were highly sensitive to any challenge to their integrity. Widows' active mingling with others in a variety of settings, from the marketplace to the courtroom, leads us to reconsider the typical widow identity in Chosŏn society, which had been powerfully prescribed by the Confucian state but which in fact often varied profoundly from the stereotypical Confucian imagination about secluded widowhood.

YECH'ŎN

The accused: Ms. Ŭn
The deceased: Madam Chang
True cause of death: Suicide by hanging (chaaek)

In the official report, submitted by Kim Ki-hyŏn,[8] magistrate of Yech'ŏn Lesser County (Yech'ŏn kunsu): On 1842.5.29 (7/7/1842), at around four in the afternoon (sin-si), a young student (tongmong), Sin Kab-yŏn, who lives in Mojŏng Subdistrict, Tong District in this county, filed a complaint, saying, "My mother [Madam Chang] was slandered one day in the second month of the previous year by Ms. Ŭn, who lives in the same village, and committed suicide by hanging herself on yun 3.6 (4/26/1841).[9] Please shed light on the truth and resolve her indignation."

On 1842.6.2 (7/9/1842), in the testimony of a young student, Sin Kab-yŏn, the close relative [i.e., son] of the deceased: "When I was young, I lost my father and relied on my widowed mother. We lived by renting a small room from Kim Nak-ki. In the second month of last year, Yi Hyŏng-sŏk was selling his house so we bought it by paying 5 yang. Ms. Ŭn resented that my mother bought the house first. She endlessly humiliated my mother by making up groundless stories. In addition, in the intercalary third month, Ms. Ŭn hung animal bones from a tree near our house and in a very loud voice said, 'These are the bones of a child that Widow Chang threw away after giving birth.' She repeated this story to whomever she met. My mother could not overcome her mortification and rage, and went to Ms. Ŭn's house. They fought with each other all day. My mother returned and said to me, 'It is going to be difficult to clarify the truth of this mortification, so I will eventually die. After my death, you must avenge [me].'

"Around dawn the next morning, I did not see my mother right by my side when I woke up. Rushing along a path to my uncle's house, I suddenly saw my mother hanging by her neck from a jujube tree in front of Ms. Ŭn's house, from a rope made by twisting wicker bark. She was already dead. I urgently called my uncle and released her body. We heaved the corpse [down] and went to Ms. Ŭn's house. We tied up Ms. Ŭn and had the village administrator (*tongim*) watch her. Then my uncle and I were about to report [my mother's death] to the county office. Meanwhile, Ms. Ŭn's brother-in-law, Yi Hyŏng-sŏk, freed his sister-in-law and let her escape. I heard the news about Ms. Ŭn's escape on my way and, judging that it would not help to go to the county office, returned. Since that woman [Ms. Ŭn] just came back [to the village], I take it upon myself to file this complaint; please shed light on the truth and avenge my mother's [death]."

In the testimony of Sin Chong-su, the close relative [i.e., brother-in-law] of the deceased: "My sister-in-law purchased the house, and Ms. Ŭn cease-lessly made up terrible stories. My sister-in-law wanted to get to the root of the stories by grabbing and grilling Ms. Ŭn. Since Ms. Ŭn confessed to making up the stories, she was forgiven for her sins by having to put filth in her [own] mouth. After that, she hung animal bones at the entrance of the village and said they were the bones of my sister in-law's baby. My sister-in-law became enraged and killed herself. We wanted to immediately report the incident to the county office, but we only harbored our resentment because she fled. She just returned, so we now file this complaint."

In the testimony of Yi Hyŏng-sŏk, an involved witness: "Widow Chang is a maternal second aunt, and Widow Ŭn is the wife of my cousin. Widow Chang lived in a small rental room. When I tried to sell my concubine's house, Widow Chang borrowed the money and purchased the house. My cousin's wife [Ms. Ŭn], saying that the house that she had originally planned on buying had been snatched [up by Widow Chang], hurled vicious words at Widow Chang. She hung some animal bones at the entrance of the village, saying that they were the bones of a baby that Widow Chang gave birth to and threw away. Widow Chang could not overcome her mortification and rage and ended up killing herself. The close relatives of the deceased bound Ms. Ŭn and had the village administrator watch over her. Ms. Ŭn's son surreptitiously went through the wall of the room [and got in] and untied her and let her escape; I have done nothing related to her flight."

In the testimony of Kim Ku-sim, a village head: "Since I am old on top of being sick, I do not know the workings inside the village very well. Madam Chang became a widow in her youth and lived renting a small room from someone. She bought the house of Yangban Yi's concubine in the second month of last year. Thereupon, Widow Ms. Ŭn became envious of the fact that Widow Chang purchased the house, and [they] fought and slandered each other for more than ten days. In the end, when animal bones were hung at the entrance of the village and endless stories were made up, Widow Chang, not being able to overcome her rage, hanged herself and died. The relatives of the deceased bound Ms. Ŭn and intended to eventually file the complaint at the county office, but Ms. Ŭn cunningly fled. So Widow Chang's brother-in-law Yangban Sin [i.e., Sin Chong-su] burned that house down and took the land. Ms. Ŭn came back this spring and tried to get the land back. Since she filed an appeal on this matter with the government, Sin Chong-su, knowing that it was a crime not to have had reported [Widow Chang's death], filed a complaint on her death."

In the testimony of Kim Chong-ch'ŏl, a district administrator: "[Because I only] became district administrator this spring, I was ignorant of all the complicated reasons behind Madam Chang's death and did not know the situation well. In the fifth month of this year, I received an order [from the Provincial Governor's Office] in response to Ms. Ŭn's appeal to get her homestead back. I summoned Yangban Sin and asked about the situation. Sin replied that Ms. Ŭn endlessly harassed his sister-in-law by spreading words about his sister-in-law's obscene behavior, and his sister-in-law finally committed suicide. [He continued to report that] after Ms. Ŭn had fled, he could not stand looking at the woman's land and house and burned them. [He said that] the land was merely a few furrows on the mountainside, and he arbitrarily sold it to a villager at the price of 7 chŏn. Therefore, I returned the land to her, but I do not know the details of what happened last year."

In the testimony of Ms. Ŭn, the accused: "I was widowed over ten years ago and lived in a house that was almost falling apart. In the second month of last year, when Yi Hyŏng-sŏk, my cousin-in-law, said he would sell his concubine's house, I told him I wanted to buy the house. However, it was slyly sold to Widow Chang, and I was very angry and bitter. In the first month of last year, when there was a rumor of Widow Chang committing obscene acts, her brother-in-law [Sin Chong-su] broke the windows and pulled out the kitchen cauldron and broke that [too], and eventually wanted to chase her away from the family. Because I felt bitter about Widow Chang's stealing the house, I did not keep quiet about that confidential matter [about Widow Chang's adulter-ous behavior] and ended up mentioning the matter to my cousin-in-law [Yi Hyŏng-sŏk]. Widow Chang's brother-in-law [Sin Chong-su] blamed Widow Chang by saying, 'Our Sin family will not be able to show our faces.' Upon that, he also tied me up and beat me. Widow Chang confronted me and cried, saying, 'My brother-in-law is abusing me like this,' and so on. Therefore, I tried to comfort her in many ways. In the intercalary third month, Widow Chang committed suicide by hanging, and the relatives of the deceased came and blamed me for her death. They moved Widow Chang's corpse to my house. They bound me and laid me beside her body. I wanted to end my life with a knife, not being able to repress my bitterness and indignation. How-ever, Sin Chong-han lured me by showing his willingness to help me flee, so I was away hiding temporarily. In the fifth month of last year, when I returned to the village, Widow Chang's brother-in-law and others dug up the body of [Widow Chang] that had already been buried, and tried to bury me alive, tied alongside her in a hole. My cousin-in-law Yi Hyŏng-sŏk unraveled the rope and took me out of the hole. I wanted to report to the county office right away, but I did not because my cousin-in-law and the Sin family people came and pleaded with me not to do so. Yet I found that my house had already been burned down and was gone, so I had no place to stay and thus I temporarily moved to Malli Village. Since returning to my home village this spring, I have repeatedly filed a petition at the county office in order to get my land back. For whatever reasons, the Sin family all of a sudden filed a complaint at the county office, so whose resentment comes first and last in such an unexpected move? As for animal bones, I accidentally found them when I was in the fields in the third month of last year. I mumbled something to myself—thinking about the incident in which I was limitlessly beaten for making up the story about Widow Chang's adultery—that if these bones were the remains of a baby that Widow Chang had had and thrown away, I could have proved Widow Chang's adulterous acts. However, I [only] mumbled it to myself under the fence. Yet because Sin's house shares my house's fence, someone may have heard what I mumbled thoughtlessly on my own. I hung the bones at the entrance of the village next day and that was all. There was no such thing as that I had to eat filth [as a punishment for my wrongdoing]; that is absolutely groundless."

In the testimony of Sin Chong-han, a related witness: "I have been sick and suffer from illness in the eyes, so it has already been four years since I have been outside my home. Ms. Ŭn slandered and persecuted my second cousin's wife and drove her to suicide with groundless words. My illness is such that

I cannot even offer a mourning cry; how could I urge Ms. Ŭn to escape? No words or actions of Ms. Ŭn are good at all."

In the second testimony of Sin Chong-su, the relative [i.e., brother-in-law] of the deceased: "The obscene abuses from Ms. Ŭn made a faithful lady arrive at the point of suicide. Now she even conjures up a story about [my] breaking the windows and the cauldron to cause more havoc. Ms. Ŭn was tied up for only a moment but then fled. So it was too late for me to avenge [Widow Chang]. Malli Village is a mere 3 *li* away from here, so how could she have lived in peace over there? She did not show even her shadow once she had fled. Now she has returned. As for her house, it was more like a tiny earthen shed. There was nothing to hurt, even if demolished. It was indeed burned down. The fields were nothing more than a few furrows on the hill, so I asked a village administrator to sell [them]. The sale price of 7 *chŏn* was used to defray expenses for village meetings. As for her eating filth, I did see that. How could she dare to roll her eyes to deny that?"

In the second testimony of Yi Hyŏng-sŏk, an involved witness: "Widow Ŭn and Widow Chang are both cousins to me [by marriage], so how could I possibly support or criticize one over the other? It is just that the wife of my cousin [i.e., Ms. Ŭn] had a bad personality and tended to cause trouble all the time. She unexpectedly slandered and disgraced Widow Chang, and drove her to commit suicide. [Ms. Ŭn's] son released her from being pinioned, and [she] did not even show her shadow [after running away]. In the fifth month of last year, when I went to the county seat, I encountered Ms. Ŭn. She had barely escaped from being bound by many members of the Sin family. I felt so ashamed, but [nevertheless] had her escape. The story that [the Sin family] tried to bury Ms. Ŭn alive is groundless and there was no such incident. The story of her moving into Malli Village also does not make any sense at all. I did not witness that she confessed to have slandered Widow Chang and ate filth [as punishment], but heard about it. As for breaking windows and taking away the cauldron, I had neither heard nor seen [anything about that]. Widow Chang and Yangban Sin had always been friendly and enjoyed good relations. How could such perverse incidents [of breaking windows and cauldrons] have happened? About hanging animal bones on a tree, our village is surrounded by gorges, and I have often seen broken bones and skins of animals. Ms. Ŭn must have picked these up and hung them up on a tree and falsely insulted Chang."

In the second testimony of Ms. Ŭn, the accused: "The incident about the animal remains was out of my thoughtlessness about its repercussions. I exaggerated things without any grounds. I am extremely sorry. However, the incident of breaking windows and taking out the cauldron was truly not a false report. And there was no such thing as my feeding myself filth."

In the concluding statement: Widow Chang, essentially a chaste woman, decided to take her own life in her dejected heart after hearing such atrocious and dirty accusations. When thinking of her fate, how can we not lament? As for Ms. Ŭn, although she carried the title of yangban,[10] her usual conduct and personal character did not befit those of a [yangban] lady. She was resentful of Widow Chang's purchase of the house and spread groundless rumors, culminating in driving a flawless jade to crush itself [i.e., making Madam Chang commit suicide].[11] Therefore [this court] registers Ms. Ŭn as the defendant.

In the adjudication of the provincial governor: The second inquest official shall be selected and appointed.[12]

In the official report submitted by Sŏng Kyo-muk,[13] the second inquest official and magistrate of Yonggung Lesser Prefecture: Each and every testimony does not differ from the first inquest report.

In the adjudication of the provincial governor: The inquest investigation reports have been filed.[14] Truly, this is a case of a widow groundlessly slandering a widow and it is totally foolish and lamentable. One is virtuous while the other is twisted; there is a fundamental danger of the two becoming mixed up. It was only the purchase of a house for 5 yang.[15] How can that be such a big event? How flippantly Ms. Ŭn talked and slandered Madam Chang. Among the atrocious slanders of mankind, what can be worse than talk of adultery? Beautiful virtues of the inner quarters have unfortunately been damaged. Alas, this Madam Chang had maintained extremely virtuous ways for over ten years, but they were tainted and crumbled overnight. [It was as if] the stone wall of the past had already fallen, but her bitterness had not reached Heaven. Overcoming the current predicament was difficult, but she was so enraged that she did not care about her life. She chose death to forget the shame. She took a 3-ch'ŏk-long rope and silently carried out her determination in the middle of the night. How sad it is for the complete orphan [Sin Kab-yŏn] in deep sleep! Madam Chang's last breath lasted only a very short time; yet her warm hands were still hanging onto her resentment. We can deduce that the death of Madam Chang did not coincide with that of her husband [many years ago] only because of protecting her remaining child. There are no grades [in the award of] the commemorative arch for faithful women, and I, a passerby, lament [this] with a sigh [because Madam Chang's chastity deserves to receive much higher recognition than an ordinary commemorative arch].

Ms. Ŭn is a truly pathetic sort of person who made up baseless stories. She had already swallowed the excrement and apologized. Why on earth did she, audaciously and full of evil intention, hang bones to slander Madam Chang again? When Zhou officials considered punishments, fabricating rumors was the worst crime. In the imperial law of Ming China, there is no greater offense than persecution of [others] to the point of death.

I report that Ms. Ŭn was sentenced to one round of beating[16] and put into prison. Sin Kab-yŏn failed to report the death of his mother, who had died an untimely death over a year before. He seems to have forgotten about avenging his mother's death. Although his crime should be seriously punished, this can be attributed to mere child's foolishness, so his crime will not be questioned. As for Sin Chong-su, how could he ever overlook revenging his virtuous sister-in-law's wrongful death? In addition, would burning down Ms. Ŭn's house be lawful? His dealing with all these matters lost justice. He shall be sentenced to fifty strokes of beating with a heavy stick and released. Yi Hyŏng-sŏk stopped the Sin family from reporting the incident to the government and untied and freed Ms. Ŭn. He shall be sentenced to ten strokes of beating with a heavy stick and then released along with other people. As for the animal bones, send down an order to the first inquest official to bury them.

A HEARTLESS WET NURSE
ABUSES AN INFANT

Mun Chong-ji (Chunghwa, P'yŏngan Province, 1866)

N THE "SONG OF SIM CH'ŎNG" (SIM CH'ŎNG KA), THE IMPOVERISHED Blindman Sim begs breast milk for his infant daughter whose mother has died because of complications during birth; the baby survives only thanks to the sympathetic village mothers who let her suckle their breasts. It is apparent from such tales that the premodern environment was precarious for the survival of motherless infants.[1] Mun Chong-ji, the fourteen-month-old victim in this inquest record, was abandoned by his mother when he was just seven months old. He eventually died, though not because of a lack of breast milk—his father, Mun Yu-mok, had hired Ms. Kim, who happened to still be lactating following the loss of her own baby daughter. The usual first and second inquests found the true cause of death to be strangulation by Ms. Kim, who came to hate nursing the baby because of the father's endless nagging. Yet the fact that the baby did not immediately die but rather nine days after the incident left room for further investigation after the first and second inquests.

Yi Sŭng-gyŏng (1815–?) may have been chosen as the special investigator in this case because of his extensive legal knowledge. His job was to reconcile the contentious testimonies that had been given and draw a correct conclusion about the case.[2] After carefully dissecting the sequence of events and all relevant circumstances, Yi concluded that the true cause of death was that "nursing did not work" (*changyang pulhyo*) after the baby had been strangled. Basically, the strangulation had not been severe enough to cause instant or eventual death, and the baby died because he did not receive proper care afterward. Yi nevertheless judged that the perpetrator did choke the baby with murderous intent, and thus that the case fell into the category of homicide.

The provincial governor was critical of the special investigator's somewhat sophisticated discussion of how strangulation did or did not lead to death and his conclusion that the root cause of death was not strangulation. Instead, the provincial governor focused on Ms. Kim's murderous intent in her act of strangulation. We only know that she received one round of beating sentenced by the provincial governor, though the special investigator recommended a punishment of banishment, according to a brief summary of the case provided at the beginning of the inquest report. The delicate legal reasoning and incomplete nature of the testimonies recorded in the text raise much curiosity about the final decision on the case at the king's court, which is unfortunately unavailable.

We need to give credit to investigators in terms of their efforts to ascertain the true cause of death. The terminology they used here in describing how the skirt's sash, the murder weapon, choked the baby is a case in point.[3] The physical evidence was crucial in determining whether the baby's death was a result of accidental choking by the baby's own doing or strangulation by the baby's wet nurse. The *Coroner's Guide for the Elimination of Grievances* has two rather lengthy sections on "suicide by hanging" (*chaaek*) and "strangled to death" (*nŭksa*) in order to assist investigators in differentiating between the two. Although there is no way that the baby could have committed suicide by hanging, the first inquest official declares that the scars around the baby's neck were not derived from "a binding coil knot" (*chŏnyo*), which, according to the *Coroner's Guide*, was used for hanging oneself. This particular method of hanging involved the person binding his neck twice with a rope, climbing up onto something, tying the rope over a beam or a tree branch, and letting his body swing until dead. As a result, the deceased would have two sets of scars: a higher rope mark passing behind the ear and along the hairline, and a lower one encircling the neck evenly.[4] The first inquest official's finding does not match this description, signaling the possibility of death by strangulation: "There were scars on the area under the jaw and above throat that were bright red or blue. They were horizontal and crossing toward below the ears and under the hairline. They looked somewhat sparse, like insect bites or nail marks." Indeed, in his report the first inquest official concludes, "when examining the head of the body, the mouth and eyes were open, and both hands were open. All these conditions fit into the category of 'strangled to death' in the *Coroner's Guide for the Elimination of Grievances*. Therefore, I record that the true cause of death was strangled to death." Yet, one can question whether the physical evidence—the mouth and eyes were open, and both hands were open—was the result of strangulation that had taken place nine days before. It seems that the inquest official had determined the true cause of death more on the basis of oral testimonies at court, but then wrote his report as if the physical evidence was the main factor.

The initial testimonies by the wet nurse and witnesses contain inconsistencies and illogical stories, and the investigator's grilling of the defendant and witnesses to reveal the facts stands out in this as well as in other inquest records. Ms. Kim, for example, in her first deposition, uses the term *chŏnyo* (more precisely, this is the term recorded by the court official who converted Ms. Kim's oral testimony in vernacular Korean into literary Chinese), and argues the sash of the skirt that she used to cover the baby got tangled around the baby's neck because of the baby's violent movements during her absence, and thus the harm done to the child was an accident. But Ms. Cho, an eyewitness to the incident, differs from Ms. Kim on this. Ms. Cho was sure from the beginning that Ms. Kim choked the baby, saying that "the skirt's sash was wrapped around the baby's neck and its one end was tucked in." These contradictory testimonies gave the magistrate a reason to continue to press Ms. Kim, who in her third deposition finally confesses that she strangled the baby out of accumulated rage against his father and also because she was provoked by baby's constant crying, though she adds that she must have lost her mind at the time.

Aside from the nature of the case, a number of quotidian aspects of ordinary people's lives, though only preliminary, come to life as we read the case file. The most apparent points concern women in villages. Ms. Kim, who is at the center of this case, commoditized her breast milk to buy a home and make a living. She was even offered a better deal from another family who wanted to buy her breast milk. She was married to Ko Kyŏng-o, whose occupation is unknown, and her husband's older brother, Kyŏng-sam, who had suffered a stroke and was incapable of working, also lived with them. Ms. Kim was an active breadwinner, if not the sole source of income, for this household.

Throughout the document, Ms. Kim is portrayed as a heartless woman who killed the baby she was nursing. There is also another seemingly heartless woman, the infant's birth mother, who ran away. We do not know why this mother gave up the baby and fled. Given the fact that Mun Yu-mok, the baby's father, was sixty years old, the age difference between husband and wife may well have been significant. From the document, it is apparent that Mun Yu-mok was a person who antagonized his baby's wet nurse to the point of driving her to strangle his baby. From this, it is not too difficult to imagine that the baby's birth mother may have suffered from her husband's maltreatment and decided to flee. Note that Ms. Kim was only twenty-one years old; her husband may have been in his thirties, given that his older brother was forty-two years old, and thus the age difference for this couple was also significant.[5]

Another woman who is vocal in the case is Ms. Cho, who is a niece of the Ko brothers; her own father Cho Kyŏng-sin and the Ko brothers are half-brothers (by different fathers). That is, the Ko's mother married at least twice and produced children from those marriages. Ms. Cho's testimony was instrumental in drawing out Ms. Kim's confession, but her attitude toward her uncle Ko Kyŏng-sam, who had problems with speech and movement because of his illness, became a target of disapproval from the investigators. In her second deposition, Ms. Cho said that Kyŏng-sam was a person who, because of his longtime illness, was "barely able to talk coherently and think clearly," so she ignored him and did not ask how the baby was choked. This utterance and attitude upset the inquest officials, and the special investigator even commented that Ms. Cho was a thoughtless woman. From the perspective of the male elites who presided over this case, all these women were ill-mannered, stupid, and thoughtless, and had behaved outside the patriarchal norms prescribed by Confucianism. Yet these women were legitimate and dynamic members of a village community who exercised their agency both positively and negatively—whether as a vital economic actor, a crucial eyewitness, or a runaway wife.

INQUEST REPORT (MUNAN) OF THE DECEASED BABY MUN CHONG-JI FROM SAO VILLAGE, IL SUBDISTRICT, HADO DISTRICT, IN CHUNGHWA COUNTY

As for this criminal case, Ms. Kim, the wet nurse of Mun Chong-ji, has been designated the principal offender (chŏngbŏm) by both the first and the second inquest investigations (ch'ogŏm pokkŏm). Yet, because the conviction of that woman Kim (Kim nyŏ) could incur injustice in the end, the Provincial Governor's Office (Sunyŏng) appointed a special investigator (haengsagwan) and had him get to the bottom of the situation. The special investigator once again determined and recorded that woman Kim as the defendant (p'igo), and recommended the sentence of banishment. At the time, the special investigator was Yi Sŭng-gyŏng, magistrate of Sunan Prefecture.[6]

The brevetted magistrate of Chunghwa County (Chunghwa Tohobu) conducted the investigation of the body as the first inquest official. Around two in the afternoon (misi) on the seventh day of this month, I came to receive the oral report of Mun Yu-mok, who resided in Sao Village, Il Subdistrict, Hado District in this county. In the report, he said: "I have a two-year-old son. After his mother ran away, there was no way to nurse him. Therefore, I hired Ms. Kim, the wife of Ko Kyŏng-o, from the same subdistrict, as a wet nurse and had her raise him. I learned that the very woman Kim—whatever thinking she had I do not know—nearly strangled the baby to death, so I hurried myself to go see what had happened. The baby was not able to cry and eventually expired. I could not overcome my shock, and came to report to the authorities to arrest that woman. I tried everything to save the baby for many days, but in the end the baby did not suckle the breast and ended up dead. Please open an investigation for the sake of requital for a life."

I, the Chunghwa magistrate, immediately departed in the company of appropriate assistants and arrived in Sao Village in Hado District, about 1 li west of the county office, where the dead baby boy lay. The inquest investigation with all relevant people in attendance was then carried out.

On 1866.5.7 (6/19/1866), Mun Yu-mok, the close relative [i.e., father] of the deceased, no military obligation, sixty years in age, and registered in the household register.

[Magistrate:] "I, on account of your complaint, am about to open an investigation into the deceased boy Mun Chong-ji. In which month and date and for what reasons was your son Mun Chong-ji assaulted on which parts of his body? When did he die? Report everything one by one: the clothes worn [by the deceased]; whether he had any notable scars on his body; eyewitnesses of the incident; and whether the weapon used in the wicked acts was set aside." In such a way, I interrogated Mun Yu-mok.

[Mun Yu-mok:] "I am simply an impoverished person. I manage to live by hiring myself out here and there. On 1865.3.21 (4/16/1865), my wife and I had a boy and we raised him together. In the ninth month that year, however, my wife ran away in the middle of the night because of a bit of enmity between us, which was driven by some unpleasant family matters. I had no idea where she went, but the baby had to be brought up. In the beginning I settled with a wet nurse from a different village. Yet her breast milk was not enough and the baby was not healthy. Therefore, from around the second month of this year, I hired Ms. Kim, the wife of Ko Kyŏng-o from the county seat, as the wet nurse and had her raise the baby. I was hired by the family of Sŭng-mun, a public slave (*kwanno*), and lived there. On that day, I led my employer's horse and went to Yop'o Market in order to trade sea products. I ran back home on the same day and then went to see my baby. Because the baby could not swallow milk and had bloody marks around his neck, I asked Ms. Kim what had happened. Then Ms. Kim in reply told me that they were flea bites. Thus, I thought so. However, according to Sŭng-mun's words, Ms. Kim hated the baby's whining and had choked his neck with the sash of her skirt. Ko Kyŏng-sam, an older brother of Ms. Kim's husband, scolded and beat her while Ms. Cho, Ms. Kim's niece-in-law, loosened [the sash from around] the baby's neck. After hearing this, I got very upset and I submitted a complaint to the authorities to arrest that woman on the second day of this month. On the seventh day, my son finally died. How can the death not be derived from Ms. Kim's strangling the baby? As for the baby's clothing, he wore a cotton summer jacket. Eyewitnesses are Ko Kyŏng-sam and Ms. Cho. Bodily scars are: a pockmark from smallpox on the left armpit; a pockmark from smallpox a little behind the left side of the head; a pockmark from smallpox a little below the left breast; and another pockmark from smallpox a little to the left and between the chest and belly. As for the murder weapon, I was told it was a sash of a skirt. But I was not able to collect it because I was not at the site. Please carry out the inquest investigation in accordance with the law for requital of a life and work off the resentment of my boy's untimely death. Please take this into consideration."

On the same day, the slave coroner's assistant Pong-nok, thirty-five years in age, and registered. [He took an oath saying:] "Now, upon the examination of the body of Mun Chong-ji, if I do not record the correct measurements and subsequently such wrongful deed is disclosed, I shall submit myself for punishment."

On the same day, I examined the body of the deceased boy Mun Chong-ji. The body lay in the accused Ms. Kim's thatched-roof house oriented toward the south, which was 2 *kan* in size. There was one door to the room and another door to the kitchen. Seeing inside after opening the door, there was a side door between the rooms. The body was in the first room. The measurements of the four corners of the room were: 5 *ch'ŏk* 1 *ch'on* to the eastern wall, 3 *ch'ŏk* 1 *ch'on* to the threshold on the southern wall, 3 *ch'ŏk* 6 *ch'on* to the western wall, and 2 *ch'ŏk* 9 *ch'on* to the northern wall. The body was covered with a torn padded-cotton baby blanket. When it was removed, a boy possibly one or two years in age was laid on his back, with his head to the south and his feet to the north.

His dead body was on a woman's underskirt and he was wearing a cotton summer jacket.

I could not conduct the examination of the body because the room was too small. Thus, the body was moved outside the room to a windless area and put on a wooden board. I had the slave coroner's assistant turn the body to wash and measure it. He had bushy hair and was 2 *ch'ŏk* 2 *ch'on* tall. Both hands were open and the legs were straight.

The ventral side of the body [was as follows]: The face color was yellow or white. The crown of the head, fontanel, and left side of the head looked normal. There was a pockmark from smallpox a little behind the right side of the head and the scar looked like a bean.[7] Cranium, forehead, temples, both eyebrows, the spot between the eyebrows, both eyes and the eyelids looked all normal. Both eyes were a little bit open and the pupils looked fine. Cheeks, ears, ear flaps, ear lobes, ear holes, the bridge and tip of the nose, and nostrils were all normal. There was blood trailing from the nostrils. The philtrum, upper and lower lips, and the area around the lips all looked normal. The mouth was a little open but the tongue did not protrude from the mouth. Ten upper and lower teeth began to show and all looked normal. There were scars on the area under the jaw and above the throat that were bright red or blue. They were horizontal and crossing toward below the ears and under the hairline. They were not caused by a binding coil knot. They looked somewhat sparse, like insect bites or nail marks. When pressed, they were a little bit hard. When measured, the circumference was 6 *ch'on* 3 *p'un*. The depressed area above the shoulder blades, the shoulders, and the right armpit looked normal. There was a scar a little below the left armpit and it looked like an insect bite. The upper arms, inside elbows, wrists, palms, fingers, fingertips, underneath fingernails, chest, and left breast all looked fine. There was a pockmark from smallpox a little below the right breast and it had a bean shape. There was a pockmark from smallpox a little left of the area between the chest and belly and it looked like a leaf of a wild jujube tree. Ribs and sides under the arms were good. [However,] the upper belly was bulged. The lower belly, groins, penis and scrotum, thighs, knees, shins, ankles, tops of the feet, toes, and toenails were all normal.

The dorsal side of the body [was as follows]: The occipital and the roots of the ears were all normal. The backs of the shoulders, elbows, palms, backs of the hands, fingers, and fingernails all looked normal. The spine and area along the spine, back ribs and back sides under the arms, waist, buttocks, anus, thighs, crooks of the knees, calves, ankle bones, heels, soles, toes, toe tips, and underneath the toenails all looked normal.

The silver hairpin inserted inside the mouth and anus did not change color.[8] At the same time, when examining the head of the body, the mouth and eyes were open, and both hands were open. All these conditions fit into the category of "strangled to death" in the *Coroner's Guide for the Elimination of Grievances*. Therefore, I record that the true cause of death was strangled to death.

On the same day, Ms. Kim, the principal offender, twenty-one years in age, and registered.

[Magistrate:] "According to the testimony of Mun Yu-mok, the close relative of the deceased, during the inquiry into the criminal case of the deceased boy, he hired you as his two-year-old baby's wet nurse and paid for your service. When he went to see his baby on 1866.4.29 (6/11/1866), he found that the baby was unable to swallow milk and also had some bloody marks on his neck. Therefore, he asked you what had happened and you answered that they were insect bites. Later he heard from Sŭng-mun, a public slave, that you hated the baby's whining and had strangled the baby's neck with the sash of a skirt. At the time, your husband's older brother Ko Kyŏng-sam scolded and hit you, and your niece-in-law Ms. Cho loosened [the sash from around] the baby's neck so that the baby did not die. Having heard that, Mun Yu-mok was shocked and immediately reported it to the authorities to arrest you. You were already paid to breastfeed and raise the baby and must have had the heart to love and protect the baby. Instead, you hated the baby's crying and ended up killing the baby by choking him. It is extremely cruel of you. Now do not dare conceal or hide anything in this court, and state your vicious acts truthfully." In such a way, I interrogated Ms. Kim.

[Ms. Kim:] "I have been poor all the time and living in someone's extra room by their favor. The second month of this year, I unexpectedly lost my baby girl. My neighbor Mun Yu-mok was a poor single [parent] and could not raise his two-year-old boy. He asked me by saying, 'I will pay 2 *yang* per month if you breastfeed and raise my son.' I agreed [to his proposal]. I took 10 *yang* in cash in advance, bought a house to move into, and raised the baby without any trouble. Around the full moon of the fourth month, I became seriously ill and Yu-mok took the baby away. As I came to feel better around 4.20 (6/2/1866), Yu-mok sent back his baby. Therefore, I fed him and raised him like before. Toward the end of last month, I was going to draw water from a well. I worried that flies might bother the sleeping baby, so I covered the baby's face with a tattered skirt. When I returned from the well, the baby cried hard. Therefore,

I rushed in to check on him and found that his neck was bound with the sash of the skirt and his legs and arms were twitching violently. I removed the skirt right away and breastfed him. After that incident, Yu-mok falsely charged me of strangling his baby and reported such to the authorities to arrest me. Stories such as my husband's older brother beating me and Ms. Cho's freeing the baby's neck from choking are all lies. Please take this into consideration."

On the same day, Ko Kyŏng-sam, an eyewitness, no military obligation, forty-two years in age, and registered.

After repeating Mun Yu-mok's testimony, the magistrate continues: "Your sister-in-law should have been kind and nurturing since she nursed the baby for money. Instead, she hated baby's crying and ended up killing him. Her viciousness is extreme. Now, under this investigation, you should state everything straightforwardly without hiding anything. . . ."

[Ko Kyŏng-sam:] "Because of a stroke, my four limbs have been paralyzed and thus I have been bedridden for a long time. [One day] toward the end of the fourth month, the baby my younger brother's wife was nursing [began] crying a lot. So, I investigated and found that the sash of a skirt had been tied around the baby's neck. I scolded my sister-in-law and the sash was removed from the baby's neck [by Ms. Cho] and that was it. . . ."

On the same day, Ms. Cho, an eyewitness, a commoner woman, twenty-four years in age, and registered.

After repeating Mun Yu-mok's testimony, the magistrate continues: "At the time, you were in the room and freed the baby's neck from the sash. You were there and saw what happened at the time. So, you must have seen how Ms. Kim acted and must know the root cause of the baby's death by strangling. Under this deposition, testify everything you know truthfully. . . ."

[Ms. Cho:] "My father Cho Kyŏng-sin and Ko Kyŏng-o are brothers by different fathers. My house and Ko Kyŏng-sam's house are next to one another, sharing the same fence. On the twenty-ninth day of last month, [I] heard some disturbances from Ko Kyŏng-o's house. I peeked through the fence to see what was going on, and it seemed that several men and women were huddled together, having an argument. I rushed over to see what was going on. Ko Kyŏng-o, his wife, and Kyŏng-o's older brother Kyŏng-sam were there: some were sitting inside the room while others were standing and walking around the courtyard. There was a baby lying inside the room and his neck was tightly tied with the sash of a skirt. I felt such pity for him and untied the sash. At the time, Kyŏng-sam was scolding his sister-in-law, saying, 'You have been nursing Yu-mok's son for two months by now and you must have cared for him. How could you choke the baby?' His sister-in-law then replied, 'When I went to fetch water from the well, I covered baby's face with a skirt because I was worried that flies might sting him. When I returned, I found that he had kicked his legs and moved his arms, and [as a result] his neck had become entangled in the sash. How come you scold me like this?' They were arguing like that, and so I returned home. . . ."

On the same day, Sŭng-mun, a related witness, a public slave, thirty-four years in age, and registered.

After repeating Mun Yu-mok's testimony, the magistrate continues: "Now, you were the one who uttered the words about strangulation. As for the most essential component of this criminal case, who could it be but you? Under this investigation, do not dare to hide anything but testify truthfully how that woman Kim carried out her malicious acts and the root cause of the death of Mr. Mun's boy. . . ."

[Sŭng-mun:] "Mun Yu-mok, the father of the dead baby, is my hired laborer. Toward the end of the fourth month, I went back home for lunch from my duties. I then heard that Yu-mok's two-year-old son had been strangled by his wet nurse and that Yu-mok had gone to her house. I thought it was unbelievable and so went there to see what was going on. There, Yu-mok and Ms. Cho were arguing. Ms. Cho said to Yu-mok, 'What on earth did I do wrong by untying the [sash from the] baby's neck?' They came into conflict with one another like that. Although I did not witness the wet nurse strangling the baby, it seems obvious to me that she did it, considering her intention and also all the circumstances. . . ."

On the same day, close neighbors: Cho Tae-rim, no military obligation, and thirty-six years in age; Yun Mi-ryŏk, no military obligation, and nineteen years in age; Ms. Chŏng, a commoner woman, and sixty-seven years in age; and all registered.

[Magistrate:] "The criminal case of the deceased boy Mun Chong-ji took place right in your neighborhood, thus you must know everything in detail from the beginning to the end. In this court, each of you shall truthfully state everything you have heard and seen."

Cho Tae-rim: "I am a craftsman making leather shoes and do not go into the village. Some five or six days ago, I heard that Ko Kyŏng-o's wife Ms. Kim accidentally choked Mun Yu-mok's boy, whom she was nursing. That was what I heard; I know nothing more."

Yun Mi-ryŏk: "I work for someone and go out to the fields every day. I do not know anything about what is happening inside the village. I heard a rumor that Yu-mok's two-year-old baby was strangled by his wet nurse."

Ms. Chŏng: "There is some distance between my home and Ko Kyŏng-o's. Several days ago on my way to the well, I heard a rumor that Ko Kyŏng-o's wife strangled Mun Yu-mok's son. . . ."

On the same day, Yi Hyang-hŏn, district administrator (*p'unghŏn*), forty-four years in age, and registered.

[Magistrate:] "The criminal case of the deceased boy broke out in your district. You are the administrator of this district and there is nothing that you have not observed. Therefore, you must have intimate knowledge about this particular case. In this court, you shall truthfully report everything you heard and saw."

[Yi Hyang-hŏn:] "There is some distance between my residence and the place of the incident. Therefore, I would not have been able to know what had happened. On the seventh day of this month (6/19/1866), I received a report from the subdistrict administrator of Sao Village, Il Subdistrict of this district, in which it was written: 'Mun Yu-mok, a resident of this subdistrict, hired Ko Kyŏng-o's wife Ms. Kim as his two-year-old boy's wet nurse. Around the end of last month, Ms. Kim strangled that baby, who ended up dead today.' That was how I heard, and there is nothing more I can testify."

On the same day, Kim Myŏng-sin, subdistrict administrator (*ihŏn*), fifty-seven years in age, and registered.

After the magistrate asks the same questions he asked the previous witness, Kim Myŏng-sin replies: "There is some distance between my residence and the place where the incident took place. Therefore, I had no idea about what had happened. On the seventh day, I heard that Mun Yu-mok's baby, whom Ms. Kim, Ko Kyŏng-o's wife, was nursing, was for unknown reasons strangled and dead. So, I immediately reported this incident to the authorities, and that was it. . . ."

On the same day, Hong Myŏng-ha, a village headman (*tumin*), forty-eight years in age, and registered.

After the magistrate asks the same questions he asked the previous witness,

Hong Myŏng-ha replies: "I live a little bit away from where the incident took place, although it is in the same village. Around noon on the seventh day, I heard that Mun Yu-mok's baby, whom Ms. Kim, Ko Kyŏng-o's wife, was nursing, was for some reason strangled and killed. That was how I got to know about it. I do not know the exact cause of death. . . ."

On the same day, Mun Yu-mok, the close relative [i.e., father] of the deceased, second deposition.

[Magistrate:] "In your previous testimony, you said you learned from Sŭng-mun, a public slave, that Ms. Kim, your son's wet nurse, strangled the boy with a skirt's sash because she hated your son's crying. And [Sŭng-mun also told you that] Ko Kyŏng-sam, the wet nurse's brother-in-law, hit and scolded her while Ms. Cho, her niece, untied the [sash from the] baby's neck. You hired her as a wet nurse and paid her, and she agreed and nursed the baby. She must have developed a grateful and caring feeling. After several months [like that], how could she suddenly harbor such terrible thoughts and strangle the baby? Under this deposition, tell the truth rather than prevaricating like before."

[Mun Yu-mok:] "I have already told you everything I know. On the twenty-ninth of last month, I went to Ms. Kim's house to see my son after returning from Yop'o. My son was lying inside the room but had some bloody marks on his neck. I asked Ms. Kim the reason why. She replied that some scars were from insect bites and some from his own scratching. The next day, on the thirtieth, Sŭng-mun, a public slave, told me, 'Your wet nurse Ms. Kim strangled your baby for some reason, and her brother-in-law Ko Kyŏng-sam beat her and scolded her while her niece Ms. Cho saved the baby from choking.' Several days passed while I was hoping that my son would recover. Yet he could not suckle and appeared to be dying, so I filed a report with the authorities on the second day of this month (6/14/1866) to arrest that woman. Considering the circumstances, there could be no likely cause for anyone to strangle an infant. Although my son was two years old, he suffered from smallpox and was frail. After being strangled, he was not able to cry or suckle, and finally became a ghost of untimely death. How can there be no bitterness in a father's heart? I only wish to avenge the death quickly."

On the same day, Ms. Kim, the principal offender, second deposition.

[Magistrate:] "According to your previous testimony. . . . Toward the end of last month, when you came back from fetching water from the well, [you discovered that] a sash of the skirt that covered the baby was wrapped around the baby's neck like a binding coil knot, so you removed it immediately and nursed the baby. . . . According to the testimony of Ms. Cho, . . . the baby's neck was tied tightly by a skirt's sash. Ms. Cho felt so badly that she removed it right away. Kyŏng-sam scolded you by saying, 'You have been nursing this baby for two and a half months now and must care about him. Why on earth did you tie [a sash around] the baby's neck?' . . . You said that the skirt's sash was wrapped around baby's neck, whereas Ms. Cho stated that the neck was tied with a skirt's sash. When you said 'wrapped around,' does it mean that the sash wrapped around the baby's neck on its own, [and] that you did not strangle the baby? Ms. Cho clearly testified that the neck was tied intentionally and so she untied it. How dare you speak glibly and invent [such a lie]?! A human life is extremely important and a criminal investigation is very serious. In this second deposition, testify truthfully without telling a lie like before."

[Ms. Kim:] "I have already told you everything I know. On the twenty-ninth day of the past month, when I was about to go to the well to fetch water, I covered the baby's face with a skirt. When I came back soon after, the baby was crying so much. So, I checked on him and [found that] the skirt's sash was wrapped around his neck like a binding coil knot. I removed it right away. Mun Yu-mok is blaming me and I do not know why."

On the same day, Ko Kyŏng-sam, an eyewitness, second deposition.[9]

After repeating the previous testimonies by Ko Kyŏng-sam and Ms. Cho, the magistrate asks: "Now, Ms. Cho has said [she] loosened the baby from strangulation while you are saying that the sash was wrapped around the baby's neck. How come these two testimonies are so different? You have been sick and have long been staying home. Therefore, you must know your sister-in-law's intentions and heart. If you scolded her for strangling the baby, you must know the root cause of this incident in detail. In this deposition, do not hide anything like before, but tell the truth."

[Ko Kyŏng-sam:] "I have already told you everything I know. On the twenty-ninth day of last month, my younger brother Kyŏng-o left the village and my sister-in-law and I were at home. Around noon that day, I went to my neighbor to borrow embers and returned home. My niece Ms. Cho, living next door, also came [to my place], and we all went inside the room. Right then, suddenly, the baby whom my sister-in-law was nursing cried. I checked on him and found that his neck was tied with a skirt's sash. My niece immediately removed it. I could not bear to watch that scene, so I sat facing the wall. I do not know my sister-in-law's mental state well—whether good or bad. When the baby cried, sometimes she spanked him and almost took him back to his father. I have nothing more to tell."

On the same day, Ms. Cho, an eyewitness, second deposition.

After repeating her first deposition to her, the magistrate asks: "You witnessed the baby's strangulation and you saved him; therefore, you must have had some conversation about it with your uncle and his wife. In this second deposition, testify truthfully what conversations you had with them and what kind of sash it was."

[Ms. Cho:] "I have already told you everything I know. That day, I went to see what happened. Yu-mok's son was lying inside the room. The skirt's sash was wrapped around the baby's neck and one end was tucked in. I felt so bad and untied it right away. I then scolded my aunt, saying, 'Although this is someone else's son, you have been nursing him and so he is no different than your own. If you did not want to raise him with love, you should have taken him back [to his father]. Why on earth did you choke the baby?' My aunt Ms. Kim replied, saying, 'I went to fetch water for a while and came back to find that the skirt's sash wrapped around the baby's neck like a binding coil knot. I did not do it myself.' Therefore, I wanted to ask Ko Kyŏng-sam about what had happened. However, Kyŏng-sam is a person who, because of his long illness, is barely able to speak coherently and think clearly. There was no need to talk to him. I therefore returned home."

On the same day, Sŭng-mun, a related witness, a public slave, second deposition.

[Magistrate:] ". . . Although you did not witness the wet nurse strangling the baby, it seems obvious to you that she did it when considering her intentions and also all the circumstances. Now, as for a baby, people do not generally differentiate between mine and yours. Furthermore, the care and affection toward the baby would not likely be so different [whether the baby is your own or another's], when you nurse the baby. What resentment and hatred could have made her strangle this poor child? In terms of rational discussion, as well as imagining what happened, there must have been some other reasons. Therefore, in this second deposition, tell truthfully what you heard and saw without daring to hide anything."

[Sŭng-mun:] "I have already told you everything I know. I live right next to Ko Kyŏng-o. Mun Yu-mok hired Ko Kyŏng-o's wife as his baby's wet nurse and had her raise him. On the twenty-ninth day of last month, I heard a rumor that the baby at the home of Kyŏng-o had been strangled. When I went there, Kyŏng-sam, Kyŏng-o's older brother, was scolding his sister-in-law, saying, 'If you do not want to nurse the baby, you should have sent him back to his father. How come you choked the baby like this?' That woman then replied, 'I must have been possessed by a ghost. How can a person intentionally commit such an act?' When I went to see what had happened, the thing that choked the baby's neck had already been removed. I do not have anything more to add."

On the same day, Mun Yu-mok, the close relative [i.e., father] of the deceased, third deposition.

[Magistrate:] "According to your previous testimonies, your two-year-old baby could not take the breast after being choked and eventually became a ghost of untimely death. When I ponder all that has happened, you hired and paid her and she on her part agreed to it and nursed the baby. Therefore, she should not have had any reason to murder the baby. Suppose that she choked the baby like that only because she hated the baby's crying. That supposition is implausible, and that story does not fit with the reason. After your son suffered from a disease, he did not completely recover from it. On top of that, he suffered from another affliction. It is apparent that he could not take the breast and cried on and on for a long time. But you single-handedly take strangling as the cause of death, out of your desire to accuse Ms. Kim of the crime. Why in the world do you do this? You must have called an herbalist and used medicine while you were taking care of the baby for a number of days. Under this repeated deposition, do not be ambiguous like before but tell the truth."

[Mun Yu-mok:] "I have already told you everything I know. My baby son had the smallpox around the twelfth month of last year, and again had the measles the third month of this year. But his body recovered fast and he had no particular health problems. Only after he was harmed by that woman Kim did he sometimes shut his eyes and drop his head and lose the ability to suckle. Therefore, I did not think of calling on an herbalist and using medicine from the beginning. I have nothing more to say."

On the same day, Ms. Kim, the principal offender, third deposition.

After repeating Ms. Kim and Ms. Cho's previous testimonies in summary, the magistrate continues: "In general, murder always originates from accumulated hatred. This two-year-old baby was unable to speak but only knew how to suckle. How did you come to have this murderous mind, tying the neck with a sash of a skirt, and having him come to die? I cannot understand what is going on with you. Under this repeated deposition, tell the truth about your wicked crime without concealing anything."

[Ms. Kim:] "I have already told you everything that I know. Yet, under these repeated depositions, how can I tell a lie even if I tried? What I did at the time was not my true mind. I was tired of the baby's crying and hated it. I drove out my brother-in-law and had him go to the kitchen to tend the fire. After I snuck inside the room and secured the door [to the kitchen], I choked the baby's neck with a skirt's sash. I lost my mind and my hands and legs trembled. Consequently, I could not tie it tight enough, and only one end was tucked in. It must have been a ghost's deed. There is nothing more to say."

On the same day, Ko Kyŏng-sam, an eyewitness, third deposition.

After repeating selected testimonies from Ko Kyŏng-sam and Ms. Cho's second depositions, the magistrate continues: "You had a stroke. But if the baby cried hard after your sister-in-law went out, would your concerned and rushed mind have let a skirt's sash choke the baby? In this repeated deposition, tell the truth without prevaricating like before."

[Ko Kyŏng-sam:] "I have already told you everything I know. Even if I were a person struck by illness, why on earth would I let the two-year-old baby choke and want him to die? The baby's death was entirely the act of my sister-in-law."

On the same day, Ms. Cho, an eyewitness, third deposition.

After repeating conflicting testimonies by Ms. Cho and Ms. Kim in terms of how the baby was choked, the magistrate asks: "When considering this case with reason, there is no way that a skirt's sash can wrap around a baby's neck all by itself. Those who were present at home were the wet nurse and her brother-in-law. Who else could it be if not one of them? You went to untie the [sash from the] neck and so you must know who strangled the baby. As for the one end of the skirt's sash getting tucked in, was there just one knot or two? Under this repeated deposition, tell the truth without prevaricating like before."

[Ms. Cho:] "I have already told you everything I know. That day, I went to see what was going on. The baby's neck was wrapped around twice and one end of the skirt's sash was tucked in. The baby's death must have been caused by Ms. Kim's doing."

On the same day, Sŭng-mun, a related witness, a public slave, third deposition.

After repeating Sŭng-mun's earlier testimonies to him, the magistrate continues: "This case of the strangulation of Mun Yu-mok's son is beyond ordinary [human] sentiment and reason. Regardless [of whether a baby is] yours or mine, the loving sentiment of a baby is all the same [to every human]. The caring sentiment must be deeper when one nurses a baby for money and there must be no way of killing that baby. How much less could one strangle him—nothing close to such could take place! You went to witness what happened, so you must know everything in detail from the beginning to the end. Under this repeated deposition, tell the truth."

[Sŭng-mun:] "I have already told you everything I know. I heard some commotion, so I went to Ms. Kim's home. Kyŏng-sam, Ms. Kim's brother-in-law, was severely scolding her because of the strangulation of the baby. Thus, I heard and got to know [what had happened]. Indeed, I do not know the root cause of this criminal case in detail."

On the same day, Ms. Kim, the principal offender, fourth deposition.

After repeating Ms. Kim's testimony from the third deposition, when she confessed her crime, the magistrate continues: "Now, if you take care of other people's sons for money, you must have some loving feeling. If you had not been incited by someone else, how could you, out of whatever vengeful thought, have strangled such a pitiful baby? There must have been a person who provoked you. Under this repeated deposition, tell the truth."

[Ms. Kim:] "I have already stated that I strangled the baby. How can I now hide a single thing? When I was first hired as a wet nurse of Mun Yu-mok's son, I got some 11 *yang* in cash advance and bought a thatched-roof house and settled there. Im Ch'ang-nin, a village neighbor, called me and told me that he would have given me more food and clothing than Mun Yu-mok has if I had nursed his baby [instead]. Thus, I asked Yu-mok to take the baby back. Yu-mok in response begged and said, 'That baby of Ch'ang-nin's has her mother, but my son's mother has already run away. If [you] do not breastfeed him, he will die and that is it.' He persuaded me in all manners like this, so I could not ignore personal sentiment and continued to nurse him. The same Yu-mok, however, on account of his advance payment of 11 *yang*, seemed to have some attitude. When he came to see his baby, he showed some disrespect on many occasions. I felt very unhappy and told Yu-mok about my intention of selling the house. Then, in reply, he stated many times that I should pay the exact amount back to him in case I sold the house. I am a small-minded person and

I came to hate this baby. Indeed, on that day, I strangled the baby with a skirt's sash. Now my crime has been disclosed; how can I make an excuse? I have nothing more to testify."

On the same day, Im Ch'ang-nin, a related witness, forty-four years in age, and registered.

[Magistrate:] "According to the accused Ms. Kim's testimony in this criminal case of the death of a two-year-old boy, she was already nursing Mun Yu-mok's son when you begged her, saying that you would provide more clothes and food than Yu-mok did if she nursed your baby. So she talked to Yu-mok to take his baby back, but then Yu-mok in response said that his [Ch'ang-nin's] baby has a mother while his does not, and that it would be impossible to raise the baby if she did not breastfeed him. Yu-mok then often came to see his baby, but showed some attitude on account of his advance payment of 11 *yang*. She was thus very unhappy and came to hate the baby. Indeed, on that day she ended up strangling the baby. If you wanted to hire a wet nurse, there must be others around. How come you tried to steal the one who had been already hired by another? The way that you think is disgusting. Under this interrogation, testify truthfully what had happened."

[Im Ch'ang-nin:] "I am [one of those] poor folks. I just have a daughter two years in age. But my wife and I have been concerned because [her] breast milk was not enough. At the time, Ms. Kim, Ko's wife in the village, lost her baby and thus had breast milk. She sometimes came to my house to eat leftover food, and thus I asked her to nurse my daughter. She replied that she had already been nursing Mun Yu-mok's son. Therefore, I did not mention it again. After she committed this crime, she has now dragged me in. This is really unexpected. If I were in fact capable of hiring a wet nurse, there are others. How would I necessarily steal another person's wet nurse? I have nothing more to tell."

On the same day, Song Chi-hyŏp, head clerk, thirty-nine years in age; Im Si-jŏng, court recorder, fifty-nine years in age; Kim Ing-no, clerk at the Bureau of Penal Affairs, thirty years in age; Hong Hae-bung, herbalist, thirty-five years in age; Hong Chae-u, legal clerk, thirty-five years in age; Kim Ch'i-muk, head officer (*changgyo*), fifty-eight years in age; Yi Hun, assistant director of the Bureau of Local Yangban, fifty-one years in age; Pong-nok, slave coroner's assistant; Mun Yu-mok, the deceased's close relative; Ko Kyŏng-sam and Ms. Cho, eyewitnesses; Sŭng-mun, a public slave, a related witness; Cho Tae-rim, Yun Mi-ryŏk, and Ms.

Chŏng, close neighbors; Yi Hyang-hŏn, district administrator; Kim Myŏng-sin, subdistrict administrator; Hong Myŏng-ha, village headman; all registered.

When the first inquest investigation of the body of the deceased boy Mun Chong-ji was conducted, all of us attended as persons relevant to the investigation. We did not add or delete anything to the record of the proceedings in uncovering this evil crime. There is nothing more to testify. Please take this into consideration.

On the same day, the watchmen [were]: Kim Myŏng-sin, subdistrict administrator (*ihŏn*), fifty-seven years in age; Cho Chong-gap, subdistrict administrator (*chipkang*), sixty-three years in age; Yun Il-yong, subdistrict administrator (*chipkang*), forty-four years in age; all registered.

After a first inquest investigation of the body of the deceased baby Mun Chong-ji, we had the order of guarding [the body]. If there were any unforeseen problems, we will be responsible for them.

. . . .

CONCLUDING STATEMENT OF THE FIRST INQUEST INVESTIGATION

Each person's testimonies are as stated.[10] In general, the most difficult thing to comprehend under Heaven is one's mind, and the most difficult thing to be careful about is the facts of the case (*okchŏng*). As for this particular criminal case, the victim is only two years in age and cannot yet talk. Naturally, he has neither resentment against nor favor toward others. He cries for breast milk three [meal] times a day. The very person whom he relies upon is his mother. If the mother is not good, he would be harmed—would that be what a human being [with] compassion wishes to happen?

According to the examination of the body, there was no single injury on the entire body from top to bottom, except the neck, some parts of which were slightly blue and red. The scars did not form a contiguous line but were sparse. They looked somewhat like insect bites or nail marks. It was difficult to measure their sizes. Whether he was strangled by someone else or he choked himself, he would have died on the spot if his neck was tied tightly. Instead, he died nine days after the incident, and that leaves some room for suspicion. It is common sense that, when a person raises a baby, she would sometimes try to comfort the crying baby and at other times spank him. It is not that she does not know that the baby's behavior is spontaneous, but it is out of her stress and frustration. As for that woman Kim, the reason she choked the baby was because of her stress and frustration, not out of criminal intention. This worry-free baby from yesterday could hardly take the breast after being choked and eventually lost his life. If not caused by the strangulation, what else could [have resulted in his death]?

According to the testimony by the close relative of the deceased, however, there are other things to consider. After suffering from smallpox, he then again had the measles. He was still suffering from aftereffects and lacking in vigor. On top of that, he was strangled and eventually lost his life like this. His death could be compared to disease-ridden leaves that fall in the wind or growing grass damaged by frost. The baby was unable to talk about symptoms of illness. He was freed from strangulation; however, if many days of nursing did not work (*changyang pulhyo*) after strangulation, how can we limit ourselves to the discussion of physical evidence [of strangulation]?

I file with the [Chunghwa] county office that the true cause of death was strangulation and fill out all entries in three preprinted inquest forms with the *un* serial mark: one copy is to be sent to the county office; one given to the close relative of the deceased; and the other attached [to the rest of the inquest report] and sent to the PROVINCIAL GOVERNOR'S OFFICE. Ms. Kim should not have accumulated hatred against the baby since she nursed him for payment. Yet she had her brother-in-law tend the fire, pretending that she was going to the well to fetch water, and then committed the horrible crime with a skirt's sash. Her crime is no different from those punishable by beheading. Not only did the testimonies by neighbors attest to it, but also she herself confessed it. How could she avoid being recorded as the principal offender? Ms. Kim is recorded as the principal offender. However, this case is somewhat different from other criminal cases that fall under the category of "death on the spot" (*sal*).

Mun Yu-mok is the father of the dead baby; therefore, he is recorded as the close relative of the deceased. As for Ko Kyŏng-sam and Ms. Cho, one scolded Ms. Kim while the other untied the [sash from the] neck; therefore, both are recorded as eyewitnesses. Yet, because one is a brother-in-law of the accused and the other is a niece of the accused, there must be procedural avoidance (*kuae chi hyŏm*).[11] However, I was not able to produce any other eyewitnesses because the incident took place in a room and there was no other witness. Thus, I could not but list them in that category. Sŭng-mun, a public slave, transmitted the rumor that the baby had been strangled to the baby's father. Im Ch'ang-nin wished to steal the wet nurse for the sake of his own child. Therefore both Sŭng-mun and Im Ch'ang-nin are recorded as related witnesses. Because Ch'ang-nin came to be mentioned only in the fourth deposition of the accused, his testimony is placed at the end. I interrogated only once because there was not much to ask him further. Cho Tae-rim, Yun Mi-ryŏk, and Ms. Chŏng are all residing nearby; thus, they are recorded as close neighbors. Ko Kyŏng-o is the husband of the accused and appears in the testimonies. We should have questioned him but we did not because of procedural avoidance (hyŏmae). There is no need to discuss the sash of the skirt that was used for strangulation, and thus it has not been collected [as evidence]. The body has been returned to its original location. As for preserving the corpse with ashes and securing it with seals, I commissioned the village administrator (tongim) to take charge [of this]. I also had him guard the corpse. All the people who were interrogated are in the custody of the county office and are standing by for the second inquest investigation. I request that the magistrate of Sangwŏn Lesser County be called in to take charge of the second inquest investigation. I sincerely submit this report and request to [the provincial governor].

. . . .

CONCLUDING STATEMENT OF THE SECOND INQUEST INVESTIGATION

The testimonies are not copied here because they are stored in Sangwŏn, where the second inquest was held.

Each person's testimonies are as stated. The essence of attending a criminal case is in these two words: facts and logic (chŏngni). In cases where facts do not match each other, nothing cannot be settled arbitrarily even if numerous testimonies fit together. In cases where logic does not work naturally, nothing cannot be forcefully decided even if neighbors from all four directions make the same claim. Now, in this criminal case of Mun Chong-ji, the entire investigation, from the examination of the deceased's body to the testimonies of witnesses, raises a suspicion of setting nets [to catch the criminal] and falls into the way of trapping [the criminal]. Therefore, where can [the cause of] the death be found? In terms of the illness [that the baby suffered], while the accuser (koju) testified that the baby's belly was swollen, the body did not show so much [symptoms of] malnutrition. In terms of a vicious act, although the accused woman had nonsensical talk of being possessed by a ghost, the fingernails do not reveal a blue color.[12] Furthermore, in terms of the examination of the corpse, the blue and red colors and sparse scars right above the throat could naturally constitute the cause of the death. If the scars resulted from choking, whether he was strangled by someone else or he choked himself, a person who survives choking may not necessarily die because of that choking. That baby had suffered from smallpox and measles and was weak. Once he was choked, he did not take the breast. He barely managed to breathe nine days. Therefore, would it be appropriate to say that the strangulation led to his death? Alas, what a perilous life this dead baby had! He already lost his mother at the age of seven months. He was nursed here and there. As for his pitiful circumstances, would they not have been [caused by] a certain family's accumulated grudge or someone's bad karma? Alas! That Ms. Kim is poor and stupid. She took the payment of 11 *yang* and bought a house of a few *kan*. At the beginning of nursing, the baby looked more like a miraculous good. After nursing him for a while, she took it as a difficult job. In her small mind, she felt that she was fed up with his father's acts. That day in the morning, she asked her brother-in-law to go down to the kitchen, and that in itself was outside of a proper manner. She suddenly attacked the sleeping baby in the room—why did she do that? Ms. Cho's untying the baby's neck seems to be a praiseworthy act. Who is going to find fault with Kyŏng-sam's scolding Ms. Kim? Yet Ms. Cho's testimony—that there was no need to pay attention to Kyŏng-sam because he was out of his mind and consequently she did not bother asking him [about who was responsible for choking the baby]—is simply an excuse to avoid being held responsible.

Therefore, the true cause of death is recorded as "strangled to death" in the Sangwŏn Lesser County, and three preprinted inquest forms with the *chin* serial mark are filled out. One is to be kept in this office, one [given] to the close relative of the deceased, and one attached and sent to the PROVINCIAL GOVERNOR'S OFFICE. Ms. Kim is recorded as the principal offender. By law, it is difficult to pardon [her]. By the facts, there is room for clemency for the sake of saving a life, because there is a possibility that a pear falls off a tree as soon as a crow flies away.[13] As for [applying] the legal clause of "requital for a life," it is outside the purview of my shallow view and not something in which I should intervene. Mun Yu-mok is the father of the deceased baby and thus recorded as the close relative of the deceased. Ko Kyŏng-sam and Ms. Cho witnessed the scene of strangulation, and thus both are recorded as eyewitnesses. Yet they are either a brother-in-law or a niece of the accused, and the law disqualifies their testimonies as witnesses. Nonetheless, there was no other person who could be closely questioned in this criminal case, and thus there was no choice but to record them as eyewitnesses. Sŭng-mun, a public slave, is the person who went to see [the crime scene] after the baby was freed from strangulation. Im Ch'ang-nin is the person who asked [Ms. Kim] to return the baby to his father when the baby was alive. Therefore, both are recorded as related witnesses. The fact that Im Ch'ang-nin asked [Ms. Kim] to return another person's son in order to nurse his own daughter might likely create room for doubt [regarding Ms. Kim's motive of murder] when considering the story without much thinking. But if one thoughtfully examines another side of it, it is indeed only a futile story, and there is no need to pursue any further. Cho Tae-rim, Yun Mi-ryŏk, and Ms. Chŏng live very close to where the body is, so they are all recorded as close neighbors. I did not interrogate the wife of Tok-san whose surname is unknown, who appeared in a testimony, because there was nothing important to ask her. Ko Kyŏng-o is the husband of the principal offender.[14] In accordance with precedent, I did not interrogate him. As for Ms. Chang, the wife of the public slave Sŭng-mun, I carried out only one interrogation without torture (p'yŏngmun), which also is not included here because interrogating both husband and wife goes against the rule; in addition, she is not an important witness. The body has been returned to its original location. As for preserving the corpse with ashes and securing it with seals, I commissioned the subdistrict administrator (ihŏn) to take charge [of this]. I also had him guard it. The skirt's sash used for the crime has never been presented, so I cannot include its illustration here. All the people who were interrogated are in the custody of the Chunghwa county office and standing by for the order. This magistrate of Sangwŏn is returning to his own post. And as such I submit this report [to the provincial governor].

. . . .

CONCLUDING STATEMENT TO THE SPECIAL INVESTIGATION REPORT (SAAN)

The special investigator is magistrate of Sunan Prefecture.
Yi Sŭng-gyŏng, special investigator, is presently in charge of Sunan.[15]

Each person's testimonies are as stated. Because the body has already been buried, there was no way to conduct the examination of the corpse and it is difficult to seek the facts behind this crime. Testimonies are the only materials to resort to. There are two eyewitnesses. However, one is a thoughtless woman and the other is a patient who lost his mind. Their utterances are out of order and confusing. They bluntly utter what happened, then suddenly swallow their words. If I pressed them, they were verbose. If I relaxed [my questioning of] them, they were prevaricating. Ms. Kim, the principal offender, is also not much different. The reason she changed her testimony was because the evidence of her crime was eventually detected. Now, when I weighed suspicious as well as credible testimonies from both the first and second inquest records and led the witnesses in accordance with select questions, the facts of the crime spontaneously came to the fore and the sequence of incidents was exposed more clearly. The essence was not disclosed in either the first or second inquest records.

If one desires to understand the truth and the lie behind the strangulation, he must first examine the plausible cause that made Ms. Kim choke the baby. Only after that will any doubt disappear and the crime be proved. There is no way to strangle the baby without any hatred and grudge. It does not make sense if she strangled the baby because she found nursing hard work. The stories that Mun Yu-mok [asked her to sell] the house [to pay back his advance payment] or that Im Ch'ang-nin begged for breast milk do not make up a cause for strangulation. These are neither plausible nor credible causes. When reasoning with the testimony by that woman Kim, Mun Yu-mok's personality is not necessarily gentle or affectionate. Worse, he went back and forth to Kim's home several times a day and scolded Kim's mistakes. If the baby suddenly cried, he would blame [her] that the baby was not full. When the baby fell, he would reproach her that she did not hold the baby. From the baby's being hungry or full to his being cold and warm, moving or not moving, and sleeping or awake, there was nothing he did not find fault with. Sometimes he stared at her; sometimes he gave her a dirty look. Sometimes he blurted out lamentations; sometimes he sighed. That woman Kim on her own is small-minded and consequently built up resentment and anger in her heart. Although she did not yell at him and fight, she certainly harbored such sentiment but did not mention it. She wanted to return the baby, but then he did not take him back. She wanted to vacate the house and move, but then he did not allow that. Day after day, things accumulated. She was not at peace at all, and her thinking had become more restless. She feared Yu-mok like a tiger's roar and detested the baby like a thorn in her eye. The baby whined much and she did not have good sleep at all. Love and benevolence did not grow; instead, hatred and irritation got deeper. Every day she wished to get rid of the baby, but she couldn't in the middle of all this. Although there were no particular signs of malicious acts, the truth was that something was waiting to happen.

To talk about the situation of that day, she was going out to fetch water. She managed to breastfeed the baby, who then fell asleep. Yet before she set out to the courtyard, the baby cried hard again. She could not go out but returned, but the baby did not stop crying. Because of existing hatred, vicious and perverse thoughts spontaneously sparked. Consequently, she carried out such an extremely horrifying and cruel act. Alas! How malicious! How merciless! Furthermore, using a single sash to tie fits with Ms. Cho's testimony. Why did she strangle the baby? Ms. Cho's testimony is reliable. [The story that] she was possessed by a ghost to do it is only to cover up her crime and cannot withstand [scrutiny]. Her feeling of trembling and shaking hands can be regarded as a real condition [at the time]. The criminal confessed and there is nothing suspicious in the inquest reports.

The baby died of illness. Illness derived from strangulation. The strangulation was done by Ms. Kim. Therefore, the cause of the crime in both inquest reports has nothing unacceptable. In my humble opinion, however, there is one thing that is difficult to believe. In death caused by strangulation, [the victim] in general loses his life immediately because his inner energy and pulse (*kimaek*) are obstructed and cut off and he cannot breathe. Even if the victim is freed from choking before dying, his obstructed inner energy may not be circulating and his cut-off pulse may not be normalized. Therefore, even though he may extend his life for a while, he cannot avoid his death in the end. If he is still alive after several days, it is because his inner energy has begun circulating [again] and his pulse has normalized. And [it is also because] food and water go through his esophagus and his breath flows freely through the airway. His death [after that], then, could not have been derived from strangulation [in such a case]. In the article concerning "striking others with hands or feet" (*kuch'ŏk*) in the *Great Ming Code*, it does mention "the period of responsibility for crimes" (*kohan*).[16] In contrast, in the entries concerning death by strangulation, there is no such discussion, and this is exactly the reason why. Now, the deceased in this case was strangled, but his cry was heard from outside the room. After his neck was loosened [from the sash], that woman Kim held him and breastfed him immediately. Thus, strangulation was not so critical and he was breathing. From this, we know that his inner energy was not obstructed and his pulse was not cut off. After passing nine days, he then lost his life. Therefore, to say that the death was caused by strangulation may, I fear, not be a very revealing judgment. Speaking of smallpox and measles, these are previous illnesses [that the baby] had already gone through. They are only plausible causes of the death and it is not necessary to discuss them.

Alas! Mun Yu-mok is simply a thoughtless yokel. If he had known a bit the ways to cure the damage after the baby had been choked, his son's esophagus could have been treated with medicine even if it was injured a little. The baby's inner energy and pulse, even if damaged a little, could have been vitalized with proper care. Yet Yu-Mok was indecisive and left the baby unattended, thereby worsening the condition. The baby ended up having a swollen belly; he could not urinate or move the bowels. These symptoms do not match with death by strangulation, but the sick baby [died because he] did not receive proper care. This case fits perfectly with the legal statute, "nursing [of the injury] did not work" (changyang pulhyo). Therefore, the true cause must be stated, "[the baby] died because nursing did not work after having been strangled." In addition, if the true cause is "nursing did not work," Ms. Kim cannot be the accused. Yet, speaking of that woman Kim's crime, it is horrible; thinking of her crime, it is merciless. Considering that a human being does not choke a baby, she did have a murderous mind and the incident was a homicide. If she carried out a homicidal act with a murderous mind, this is also a murder. The murderer shall die, and how can there be clemency? The tying was incidentally not tight enough, and it was the neighbor who fortunately came and saved the baby. The baby did not die on the spot, but died because nursing did not work after being strangulated. Therefore, although it is not possible to simply name Ms. Kim the principal offender, she must be punished appropriately in accordance with the law.

Both Ko Kyŏng-sam and Ms. Cho are close relatives of the woman Kim. The law prohibits interrogation [of close relatives], but both inquest investigations have already taken their testimonies. Therefore, I had to question those, following precedent. There are some inconsistencies in testimonies by the prisoners. But I did not carry out cross-examination in their presence because the inconsistencies are trivial, and also because that woman Kim has already confessed her crime. All people including the accused have been returned to the prison of Chunghwa County, and I will be returning to my post from here. In such a way, I submit this report.

• •

In the adjudication from the Provincial Governor's Office, it is written:[17] The special investigation report has been filed. Ms. Kim committed a homicide but the victim did not die on the spot; this is Ms. Kim's luck. The investigator searches for a way for clemency under the law but there is none; this is the investigator's sadness. The reason there is no clemency under the law for this case is because she committed a homicide. Yet, because the victim did not die on the spot, there is room for saving her life. There are many cases where the victims do not die immediately after a murderous act takes place. Sometimes, it is because the injuries to the affected area are not critical enough; sometimes because the strength [of the victim] and weakness [of the murderer] do not lead to the death. Now, this baby was two years in age. What he faced was strangulation. In terms of affected area and strength and weakness, all is very apparent and there is nothing more to argue. Then why did the baby not die on the spot? The first person who saw the baby's neck tied was Ko Kyŏng-sam, but it was not the moment when the act of choking was taking place. He investigated after hearing the baby's crying. How can a choked baby, whose voice would have become very weak, make a spontaneous sound loud enough for a person to hear? It is understandable that the strangulation was not forceful enough. Strangulation has ultimately been regarded as the cause of the death; how could that be? When reading the concluding statements of both inquest reports, they did cast some doubt [on strangulation as the true cause of the death]. Yet they cannot avoid the charge of handling lightly their decisions on the cause of death and the principal offender. The mistakes by the clerks at the Bureau of Penal Affairs for the first and second inquest shall be officially recorded for now.

Although it is fair to say that human criminality under Heaven is infinite, all falls under ordinary circumstances and logic. As for the reason why that woman Kim's hatred toward the baby had become increasingly intense, and why her crude hatred suddenly exploded, it is all because of [Mun Yu-mok's] censure. Though choking was in the end not forceful enough, she ultimately choked the baby. That was also driven by [Mun Yu-mok's] censure. One word, "strangulation," makes people shudder. Striking a person is out of [the offender's] wish to cause pain, although some do die [because of such injuries]. Strangulation is out of [the offender's] wish to kill [the person]. How can I leisurely discuss illness as the cause of death and loosely say the "nursing did not work and the victim ended up dead"? How can such a cruel crime be completely forgiven? The accused Ms. Kim shall receive another punishment of one round of beating. All other prisoners shall be released since there are no other particular questions. Deliver such an order and have both inquest officials carry it out.

A WIDOWER SEEKS
PRIVATE SETTLEMENT

Ms. Chŏng (Yŏngch'ŏn, Kyŏngsang Province, 1889)

D URING THE CHOSŎN DYNASTY, A DEATH INCIDENT WAS SUP-
posed to be immediately reported to the local authorities, so that they
could carry out a thorough investigation to meet a timely postmortem
procedure.[1] However, it is not uncommon to find a death case that was not
reported to the office but instead settled between the families of the victim
and the offender. While the government discouraged excessive legal suits for
trivial matters that could be resolved by the conflicting parties,[2] it criticized
the private settlement (*sahwa*) of death incidents as an immoral practice and
also strictly controlled *sahwa* for any serious incidents, especially homicide.
Nevertheless, as cases 4 and 8 illustrate, toward the end of the dynasty local
people frequently chose to settle death cases through private negotiations
rather than going to court. So why did people choose an illegal option when
lawful means were available?

Although people understood their legal rights and used the judicial process to address their problems, going through official channels required enormous mental, physical, and material efforts. For example, various expenses
related to an autopsy could be quite a burden for families of the dead, who also
had to be involved in a series of testimonies that were sometimes elicited by
the use of torture.[3] In addition, as we see from all the cases introduced in this
book, nearly everyone in the village was called for public testimonies when a
death case occurred. The village head and administrators were held particularly responsible, since they observed and supervised village matters. When a
death case was filed, it thus involved not just the families concerned, but the
entire community.

On the one hand, the Confucian government viewed abandoning the investigation of a family member's death (especially that of a parent) as immoral and unfilial. There were many occasions when the Chosŏn government forgave and even praised a person who had taken the life of the killer of his or her parent, sibling, or spouse, even deeming such revenge a virtuous act. On the other hand, it is not surprising that private settlement was an obvious choice for ordinary people, as long as the incident was successfully covered up and no further problems ensued. Yet even though families negotiating a wrongful death hoped to hide it completely, quite a number of legal cases reveal that such efforts often failed to bear fruit. This particular case, the death of Ms. Chŏng in 1889, is an example of what could happen when a private settlement between the family of a victim, an offender, and the villagers was later discovered and reported to the local magistrate.[4]

Pak Kyŏng-ju, witnessing his wife Ms. Chŏng's death and knowing of her last wish that he avenge her, carried her body to the offender Yang Su-gŭn's house, a practice quite prevalent among local people at that time.[5] In cases when someone was beaten and hurt, Chosŏn law prescribed that an offender was responsible for all medical expenses. If the victim died within a certain period set by the court, the offender was punishable for homicide; if the victim died after the set time, the offender was prosecuted on the charge of assault instead.[6] The actual cause of Ms. Chŏng's death was determined to have been kicking that led to a miscarriage. "Causing a miscarriage" means, according to the law, "that the child dies within the period of responsibility and that the fetus is more than ninety days old and that the child is formed. [Only under such circumstances shall the offenders] be punished."[7] The offender was subject to "eighty strokes of beating with a heavy stick and penal servitude for two years."[8]

Rather than going to court, a victim's family often attempted to seize monetary compensation for the death by threatening the offender. In this case Pak Kyŏng-ju, a poor peddler who was always in need of money, forgot his wife's last wish and agreed on a settlement that would grant him a deed to some fields. The mediators of the negotiation between Pak and Yang were village elders and administrators who seem to have been quite familiar with such a practice and somehow tried to take advantage of it.

Despite the parties' wish to conceal the event, Ms. Chŏng's death was reported to the magistrate's office by the head of the pack-peddlers' organization in the Kyŏngju region where Pak moved after cashing in the land deed. Although the head peddler, Kim Ch'i-su, stated that Pak had circulated the news of his wife's miserable death to the group, it is not clear whether Pak really wanted the peddlers to file a complaint on his behalf. Despite the fact that Pak told the rueful story to his fellow peddlers, he must also have been aware that he could be punished for the private agreement once the event became known to the court. Why, then, did the peddlers decide to report the incident and make it into a legal case?

Peddlers were merchants during the Chosŏn dynasty, wandering widely in local areas with various materials and selling them at local markets. Though broadly called "peddlers" (*pobusang*), these traveling merchants were a combination of two groups: pack-peddlers (*pusang*) and wrapping merchants (*posang*). The former usually carried and sold large, inexpensive items such as pottery and salt by bearing them on their backs; the latter sold small, expensive items, including fabrics and jewelry, which were wrapped in a cloth to carry around. Therefore, it is assumed that peddlers with wrapped items were more financially secure than those carrying heavy materials on their backs. Pak Kyŏng-ju was a pack-peddler who managed to eke out a living making and selling pottery. As illustrated by his life, many pack-peddlers came from extremely deprived peasant families and engaged in both commerce and other labor.[9]

Peddlers were an indispensable source of various supplies needed by people living in rural areas, where permanent shops were not established and public transportation was underdeveloped. From the beginning of the Chosŏn dynasty, the state promoted three- or five-day-interval village markets based on a peddler's standard travel period—30 to 40 *li* per day.[10] With the growing numbers of local markets during the late Chosŏn, peddlers formed their own organizations (*posangdan*) and began requesting official acknowledgment of their activities.[11] Because peddlers were often exposed to various dangers on the road, the primary goals of the organizations were to establish their identity and reputation and to help fellow peddlers in need. Strict regulations were required of members, both for effective function of the associations and for social recognition of them. These included the proper codes of conduct for merchants and for basic human relations according to Confucian norms. In particular, one of the articles drafted in 1870 states that in the event a member is treated unfairly by yangban or rich people in local areas, the peddlers should hold a grand meeting and wash away the humiliation.[12]

This idea of active response to a member's plight may explain why the pack-peddlers' association in Kyŏngju decided to divulge Ms. Chŏng's death and ask for an investigation, even by locating and digging up her corpse, which had been buried more than a month before. The spouse of one of its members had died from brutal injuries inflicted by a local yangban, and this mattered both to the association's future interests and to the status of peddlers in the local community. Although association members knew that Peddler Pak would be subject to punishment for accepting the private settlement, they may have undertaken this collective act to alert or warn local elites and other people about the very existence of their organization. By 1889 it had already been more than a decade since the Kanghwa Treaty was signed with Japan in 1876, and Chosŏn society was witnessing an influx of Chinese and Japanese commercial goods with the opening of three ports in Pusan (1876), Wŏnsan (1880), and Inch'ŏn (1883).[13] As numerous inquest records do, this case thus brings to light a marginalized yet highly important economic group in Chosŏn society—namely, peddlers—and reveals their active networks in nineteenth-century Korea, which grew even more powerful once they had infiltrated the ranks of foreign merchants and begun to compete with them toward the end of the dynasty.

YŎNGCH'ŎN

Principal Offender: Yang Su-gŭn
Deceased: Ms. Chŏng
True cause of death: Kicking (p'ich'ŏk)

In the official report submitted by Sim Chŏng-t'aek, magistrate of Hayang Lesser Prefecture: On 1889.4.23 (5/22/1889), a secret report came in.[14] On account of that, on 4.24, I, the magistrate, arrived on horseback in Kasu Subdistrict, Koch'ŏn District of Yŏngch'ŏn Lesser County, the location where the dead woman Ms. Chŏng lay, and carried out an examination of the deceased body. It was a woman, about thirty-six or thirty-seven years old.[15] On the ventral part of the body, there was a kicking mark below the left breast with a circumference of 4 ch'ŏn 5 p'un, reddish-purple in color. Upon pressing with a finger, the area was firm and hard.[16] A little above the right breast, there was a slightly depressed part that resembled a huge tree leaf. Expanded and swollen, the upper belly was rigid to touch with a hand. On the dorsal part of the body, the anus and large intestine were a little bit out of place. Because the silver hairpin did not change [color when it was inserted inside] the mouth, no further test [by inserting it inside] her anus was conducted.[17] Therefore, the true cause of death was [first] due to being kicked and later the injury to the baby [in the womb] causing death.

In the testimony of a pack-peddler, Kim Ch'i-su, who filed the complaint: "The fellow pack-peddler Pak Kyŏng-ju and his wife Ms. Chŏng were living temporarily in the servants' quarters of a house owned by Kasu Village in Koch'on District. As a way to make a living, they worked for a neighbor, Yang Su-gŭn. Su-gŭn said that a hired girl in his house stole his rice and gave it to Ms. Chŏng. On 3.18 (4/17/1889), he made a big fuss about it and hit Ms. Chŏng's chest with an oak club. Ms. Chŏng, who was eight months pregnant, died the next day. Although Pak Kyŏng-ju intended to report the death to the magistrate office, Su-gŭn ordered the villagers [to cooperate], tied up Kyŏng-ju, and forced him to settle the matter in private by giving some land to Kyŏng-ju. As the villagers buried Madam Chŏng's body at the edge of the courtyard, there was no recourse to vindicate the death. With such a story, the Kyŏngju peddlers' association sent a circular to us. Based on the circular, we held a meeting and [decided to] file this complaint under our collective names. The Kyŏngju peddlers then returned [home,] and I, as the leader, submit this complaint."

In the testimony of a Confucian scholar, Kim Tŭg-ŭm, district administrator: "On 3.19 (4/18/1889), around supper time, I heard from the villagers that the hired maid in Yang Su-gŭn's house had stolen 1 *toe*[18] of rice and given it to Ms. Chŏng. Yang Su-gŭn made a big fuss about it and grabbed Ms. Chŏng's hair by the tresses and kicked her off. Because of this, the pregnant woman died in two days. Pak Kyŏng-ju and the villagers caught Su-gŭn in the vicinity of O Mountain. Because I heard that Su-gŭn reached a private settlement (*sahwa*) by giving a field of 15 *turak*[19] to Kyŏng-ju, I indeed did not report the incident to the magistrate's office."

In the testimony of a peddler, Pak Kyŏng-ju, close relative [i.e., husband] of the deceased: "I am originally from the Kyŏngju area, but came to live in the servants' quarters of a house owned by Kasu Village of this district. I sometimes sell pottery or rice cakes. Previously, I had sold three pottery jars at a discounted price of 7 *chŏn* to Yang Su-gŭn's household. When I went to Yang's house to collect payment, he did not give me the money but 1 *toe* of polished rice instead. Then the hired girl in Yang's house secretly told my wife: 'This rice is for rice cakes. I will certainly steal the rice and give it to you. Make rice cakes with the rice and secretly give them to me.' Thereby she covertly gave [my wife] a bowl of rice and rice bran, and indeed, my wife took [them], made rice cakes, and gave them to that maid. Yang Su-gŭn and his wife got to know of this, and on 3.18 (4/17/1889), they stormed into our house. They badly beat me and my wife with a club, kicked us with their feet, then left. A little later, Yang Su-gŭn sent his hired slave to fetch my wife. [When my wife went there] he kicked her numerous times and my wife narrowly came back home. She lay down, yet could not get back up. The next day, hardly breathing, she grabbed me and said: 'After I die, please avenge my death.' Watching this situation, I heaved my wife and left her at Yang's house.[20] That afternoon, without even being able to do anything, she died. That same afternoon, I seized and bound Yang Su-gŭn in the vicinity of O Mountain, then confined him in the room with my wife's corpse. The village elders and village administrator advised me to privately settle the matter with the deed to 15 *turak* of rice paddies. After reaching an agreement, I went to the place where the corpse lay, but both the corpse and Su-gŭn had disappeared. I wanted to report it to the authorities, but the villagers said: 'Since the body has already been buried, there is no further need to make a fuss.' When thinking of conjugal sentiment, I had to [seek] revenge for my wife. Yet, concerned about making a living and being driven by cold and hunger, I ended up taking the deed [from the Yang family] and sold it for the price of 110 *yang*. I then went to Kyŏngju, living in my older brother's house. When my fellow peddlers in Kyŏngju learned about the incident, all of them gathered and went to Kasu Village to wash away the mortification. After arresting Yang Su-gŭn, they found and dug up the buried corpse, then filed a complaint. Since I had already privately settled, I fear that my crime deserves death. Now that this has become a criminal matter, I only wish for revenge."

In the testimony of a "youthful student" (*yuhak*),[21] Yang Su-gŭn, the principal offender: "When I called and reprimanded Ms. Chŏng for stealing the rice, she replied: 'Although the rice was stolen, it was done by a thief raised in your own household [the aforementioned hired girl]. How can you lay blame on someone else?' She did not stop her abusive words. Therefore, not being able to suppress my anger, I grabbed her tresses once and kicked her in the middle of the chest once. People nearby stopped me, so I returned home. I called in Ms. Chŏng again, to inquire about the stolen rice matter in front of my hired girl. However, because she made a fuss, I was enraged, grabbing her hair and kicking her in the chest once. She then went back home. Early the next morning, I went to the O Mountain area. That afternoon, Pak Kyŏng-ju and villagers came to O Mountain and tied me, saying, 'Ms. Chŏng died yesterday after fighting with you.' After binding me, they took me to the village. While I was out of my mind and spirit, the district administrator and villagers told me: 'Since Pak Kyŏng-ju does not have stable means of making a living, he himself is asking to settle this privately. If you submit some of your possessions to the village, there will be no problem.' Indeed, I submitted some of my property to the village, and [the village authorities] in turn awarded 15 *turak* of field and 30 *yang* in cash to Pak Kyŏng-ju to conclude the settlement. To avoid later problems in discussing this incident, we put the settlement in writing, buried Ms. Chŏng's corpse, and returned home. As these peddlers have dug up the grave and filed the complaint now, I have no idea what intention they have. How could I have an intention to kill from the beginning? But she unfortunately died. There is no way to cover up [my crime], and I lie humbly waiting your prosecution."

In the concluding statement: [Ms. Chŏng] secretly accepted the stolen rice, but it was not something that she asked for. [Yang] repeatedly pulled Ms. Chŏng's hair and kicked her. How vicious he was! Considering her death, it was not more than two days [after the incident]. In addition, speaking of his abusive acts, all testimonies proved them in unison. Once assaulted, two lives were lost. If there had been no kicking, the baby in the womb certainly would not have been hurt. If the baby had not been hurt, there would not have been [Ms. Chŏng's] death. The true cause of death is recorded as kicking, causing the death of the baby and leading to the death [of the pregnant woman]. It is duly recorded that this Yang Su-gŭn is the principal offender.

In the adjudication of the provincial governor: An autopsy form has been filed. Select a second inquest officer and send out the appointment order.

In the report submitted by the second inquest officer, Yi Sŏk-chin,[22] magistrate of Ŭihŭng Lesser Prefecture: The autopsy and the testimony from each person are the same as before. The concluding statement records that the true cause of death was being kicked.

In the adjudication of the provincial governor: An autopsy form has been filed. Indeed, the injury led to death within two days. As though struck by the legs of a flying pheasant, both the mother and the baby in her womb reached death at the same time. Alas, this is like an egg in an overturned nest.[23] The heartless husband forgot the last words of his wife to [seek] revenge on her behalf and ended up settling [the matter] privately. His fellow peddlers, who became enraged over the incident, dug up the buried corpse and finally filed this complaint. Yet the autopsy was carried out very late [many days after the death occurred], only making the affair more chaotic. The areas between the breast and side (*yuhyŏp*) and between the chest and belly (*simgam*) are all critical parts of the body. The fact that these areas were very stiff and blackened purplish reflects a severe injury. As the mark of the injury did not disappear even after a month but became even more pronounced, it may mean that that part was severely kicked. These injuries would not have allowed even a nonpregnant woman to survive the three-day period of responsibility for crimes. How much worse would it have been for a woman who was eight months pregnant!

It is not that I did not [carefully] consider the two additional characters "injury to the fetus" (*t'aesang*) from the true cause of death [recorded] in the first inquest record. However, the critical injuries [that led to Ms. Chŏng's death] already appeared on the outside of her body. Even if the baby [inside the womb] did not suffer any injuries, the mother would have certainly arrived at death. When looking into the general cause of the death, whether or not the fetus was injured along with the mother, it was due to being kicked and that was all. Therefore, the true cause of death in the first inquest form shall be corrected as simply "kicked to death." As the heinous criminal has already confessed the crime, this fits the true fact of the criminal case and there is nothing more to discuss. The corpse [which has been dug up] is now to be returned immediately for a burial.

Alas, as for Yang Su-gŭn, he could have scolded the young girl working in the kitchen for stealing the rice and reprimanded the neighbor woman for making the rice cakes. Wouldn't that have been enough? Why on earth did his twisted rage explode uncontrollably and he act so viciously, kicking and pushing her without considering that the woman was carrying a baby, and causing both lives to die quickly in two days? The law is very strict, and there should not be even the slightest tolerance shown in the punishment. Those who dare to raise the issue of unintentional killing by pouting their lips and curling their tongues are extremely deceptive. The [two] investigators should set a date to meet and discuss each party in every detail. Punish them accordingly, but not more than one round of beating,[24] and submit a report without delay.

Pak Kyŏng-ju did not consider the plea for vengeance of the deceased, and even privately settled the matter by receiving a bribe. While the situation is understandable, such an attitude is not befitting the close relative [i.e., husband] of the deceased. He shall be sentenced to one round of severe beating and be released after admonition. Kim Tŭg-ŭm failed to report this incident and covered it up. [If unpunished,] this could encourage more problems later [such as not reporting death incidents and encouraging private settlements].

He shall be sentenced to thirty strokes of beating with a heavy stick and will be released after being reprimanded with the others. Send this adjudication to both the first inquest official and the jailer (*okchaegwan*) and have them carry out these orders accordingly.

ADULTERY LEADS TO MURDER

Ms. Paek (Anak, Hwanghae Province, 1897)

TANNERS (*P'IJANG* OR *KATPACH'I*) BELONGED TO THE SOCIAL stratum known as *ch'ŏnmin* (the lowborn), the lowest group in the Chosŏn hierarchy. Although the majority of tanners were engaged in crafting leather goods, particularly shoes, which were worn mostly by the upper class as a symbol of privilege and wealth, they formed a separate status group from the typical commoner craftsmen because they treated dead animals and their hides.[1] However, it is unclear whether the law restricted tanners to residing within a designated administrative area, as it did butchers (known as *paekchŏng*) and entertainers.[2] The *Great Code of Administration* (Kyŏngguk taejŏn) lists a certain number of tanners as being involved in producing a variety of items (such as long, short, and embroidered shoes and bearskin products), and indicates that they were registered and hired by the government (both central and local) along with other craftsmen, whose social status might either be commoners or public slaves (*kong nobi*).[3]

Whereas it is not too difficult to find traces of slaves (*nobi*) in various official and unofficial documents—despite the fact that slaves were illiterate—the lives of tanners are rarely visible.[4] This 1897 legal case, then, not only introduces conflict, conspiracy, and homicide among tanners, but reveals people's perspectives toward this most marginalized group. Throughout the original document, these tanners are referred to as "brutes" (*han*). In 1894, the historic Kabo Reform introduced a number of radical changes, which included officially abolishing the entire social hierarchy system in Korean society (including private slavery).[5] One of the reform articles outlines that "post station attendants, vaudeville performers, and tanners shall no longer be treated as lowborn (*ch'ŏnmin*)."[6] However, the deep-rooted awareness of social status did not disappear overnight. Compiled three years after the Kabo Reform of

1894, the case file translated here shows that tanners were still quite isolated from the rest of the society and that their daily networks and social relations were limited to their own circles. Ms. Paek, the wife of the tanner and victim Cho P'al-bok, is also identified as "female tanner (*p'ijang nyŏ*) Ms. Paek" in the original text in her deposition. It is no surprise that lower-status women engaged in physical work and that status-group endogamy was still in force.

Although most inquest records are titled with the victim's name, this case is headed by the name of the female prisoner Ms. Paek, who was charged with committing adultery and being complicit in the murder of her husband. The case initially seems to be that of a typical murder sparked by fighting among drunken men. Yet the death here proves to be a more complicated one, connected to an illicit affair, a frequent cause of the homicides recorded in many legal archives of nineteenth-century Korea. Though not every adultery leads to homicide—the most extreme manifestation of emotional conflict—adultery can, of course, generate motivation for revenge because it involves the betrayal of trust in that most intimate of relations, marital loyalty.

Homicide can occur when a spouse (usually a wife) is caught (by a husband) in an adulterous relationship, as in case 1, in which the husband killed the adulterous widower Yang Hang-nyŏn and was exempted from capital punishment.[7] Though it might be taken for granted that an outraged husband is more likely to kill than to be killed himself, a number of cases in the inquest records show that a husband was often susceptible to being killed by his wife, her lover, or both.[8] In other words, an adulteress may kill her husband to continue her affair, and an adulterer, too, can be inclined to murder his lover's husband in order to keep her. Although there are not many cases of adulteresses actually killing their husbands, testimonies show that the adulteress was usually complicit. The tanner Cho P'al-bok's death exemplifies this: the adulterer Kim Kyŏng-un's desire to continue his affair with Cho's wife led to his plot to murder Cho and thus achieve his goal.

In this case, the discovery of a suspicious grave outside of the village opens the investigation, even though none of the local people have any idea whose body is buried there. A village elder informs the magistrate in writing, through the proper administrative channels, of this unprecedented state of affairs. As the *Coroner's Manual for the Elimination of Grievances* (Muwŏllok) outlines, the initial investigation goes through repeated testimonies by eyewitnesses of the unidentified grave, as well as by subcounty administrators, until it reaches a unified statement—namely, that a fight among strangers near the village entrance a day before the discovery of the new, unmarked grave must be related.

The exceptional length of the various oral depositions and redundant interrogations in the first round of the investigation highlights the efforts of the judicial official to ascertain the background of this elusive death incident for which there was almost no tangible evidence. The roles played by local people in reporting and detailing the fight largely contribute to the further development of the case, leading to the second round of investigation with the capture of the runaway suspect, Yi Haeng-mun. Although the first inquest official, while expressing the difficulty of investigating this vague case, concludes with full confidence that Yi is the principal offender, the provincial governor assumes that it was either Yi or another man in the fight who was wearing a bamboo hat. As a suspect, Yi was soon taken into custody, thanks to a proactive and private investigation carried out by the victim's family members, and his confession became crucial both in untangling the mystery of this case and to the entire judicial process.[9]

Yi's confession reveals a cold-blooded conspiracy to murder the tanner Cho, the husband of the adulterous Ms. Paek. According to the article on plotting to kill others in the *Great Ming Code*, "In all cases of plotting to kill others, those who formulate the plan shall be punished by decapitation. The accessories who aid in the crime shall be punished by strangulation. . . . Only if the killing takes place shall they be punished."[10] Therefore, although the plot itself was formulated by Ms. Paek's lover, Kim Kyŏng-un, Yi remained guilty of joining the plan and carrying out the actual murder. Unfortunately, the case ends with Kim's absence—it is unclear whether or not Kim was ultimately captured,[11] and how the magistrate's investigatory performance for this case was evaluated for not being able to capture Kim in time.[12]

Ms. Paek, the adulterous lover and the victim's wife, was also caught and brought to court. In her testimony, Ms. Paek tries to escape the heavy guilt of adultery by claiming that, as a weak woman, she could not resist Kim's threatening her with a knife. Since the Chosŏn state valued a woman's reaction to the threat of coercive sexual intercourse—the most crucial factor in determining whether the act was adultery or rape—many women accused of adultery claimed that they had been coerced in an attempt to avoid punishment. As long as a woman's intention to rebuff a coercive sexual attempt was proved (even orally), the intensity of her resistance mattered little in prosecuting the case.[13] But because the law clearly outlined that "if the adulterous lover himself kills the husband, the adulterous wife shall be punished by strangulation even if she *does not know* the circumstances" (emphasis added),[14] it was critical for Ms. Paek to assert that she had not committed adultery. Although Ms. Paek understood and utilized this common strategy of denying her adulterous relations, the court did not believe her. The court reasoned that she had gone away with Kim despite the fact that she may have known that her husband had been murdered. In the end, she could not avoid being charged both with committing adultery and with being complicit in the plot to kill her own husband.

This report begins with the first autopsy of the victim Cho P'al-bok in the tenth month of 1895, though the identity of the victim was unknown at the time of this first inquest investigation. Exactly a month later, the principal offender, Yi Haeng-mun, was arrested, and a special investigation was carried out about fifty days later, in the first month of the next year, 1896. Chosŏn law stipulated that legal decisions on penal affairs be concluded within a certain number of days, depending on the degree of severity of the crimes after all evidence and witnesses were presented.[15] Yet, the second cover page of the original report notes that it was drafted sometime in the ninth month of 1897, more than a year and a half after the special investigation was conducted.[16] The reason for this delay is not clear: perhaps the case was left open in order to keep searching for the other principal offender, Kim Kyŏng-un, or perhaps the local administration dropped the ball, as there were frequent changes of magistrates and governors during this period. This region—particularly Anak and Sinch'ŏn in Hwanghae Province—experienced considerable unrest after 1895, when a number of participants in the Tonghak uprisings in the southern provinces fled to northern Korea and began to lead tax resistance movements there.[17] Most likely because of such unstable social conditions at the time, all three local officials in charge of the investigation of this case either resigned from their posts or were punished for their inability to deal with tax collection. This administrative instability and social insecurity may well have prolonged the processing of the case.

The entire document consists of two sets of reports: the first inquest investigation report and the special investigation report. The first inquest report begins with the initial report of the incident made by the villagers and maps out the development of the death incident. It ends with the concluding statement made by the first inquest official, a provincial governor's directive, a short report on the arrest of Yi Haeng-mun, and another provincial governor's directive to carry out another investigation. The special investigation report includes the investigator's concluding statement and the provincial governor's directive in addition to the usual testimonies.

[title page]

The principal offender: Yi Haeng-mun
The deceased: Cho P'al-bok

THE INQUEST REPORT OF THE FIRST INQUEST AND THE SPECIAL
[REPORT] CONCERNING A PRISONER, MS. PAEK FROM ANAK LESSER
COUNTY, [UNKNOWN] DAY OF THE NINTH MONTH IN THE SECOND YEAR
OF KŎNYANG REIGN (1897)

Review completed (kyŏl)[18]

. . . .

On 1895.11.14 (12/29/1895), the accused Yi Haeng-mun from Anak Lesser County was imprisoned for beating Cho P'al-bok to death and received two rounds of beating with a light stick.[19]

In the report made by Yu Myŏng-han, the village elder (hyangjang) of Samso, An'gok District of this county, and Chŏng Kwŏn, the subdistrict administrator (chipkang): A tanner, Cho P'al-bok, was beaten to death by Yi Haeng-mun, who secretly buried Cho's body and fled.

In the first inquest: Cho P'al-bok is a male about forty-one or forty-two years old. His hair is not in disarray, eyes closed, mouth a little open, and the teeth shown.[20] Both hands are slightly folded and legs are straight. The injury was dislocation of the neck bone. Therefore, the actual cause of the death is recorded as breaking of the neck bone. The autopsy was conducted on 1895.10.14 (11/30/1895).

In the testimonies of Yu Myŏng-han, village elder, and Chŏng Kwŏn, the subdistrict administrator, during the first inquest investigation.[21]

Yu Myŏng-han, village elder, [said]: "On the thirteenth day of last month, I went . . . and returned home. Around . . . in the evening,[22] an elder from Pear Blossom Hamlet (Yihwa-ch'on), Yi Hŭng-guk, dispatched a messenger to me saying, 'Around sunset yesterday, the tanner Yi Haeng-mun and two other people were fighting at the entrance to the village. Therefore, I sent some people to chase them off. This morning, a villager, Yi Ik-ch'ŏl, went to Old Temple Valley on Namwŏl Pass in front of the village entrance to fetch firewood, and happened to find an unfamiliar grave at the landslide site on the way, which was covered by soil with traces of hand- and footprints. Thinking it to be suspicious, I could not keep silent and am now submitting a report.' Therefore, I do not know well how the circumstance developed."

Chŏng Kwŏn, subdistrict administrator, [said]: "Having been ill since several months ago, I was unable to keep my eyes on public funds and also visit the county seat to oversee accounting matters for several months. On the twenty-sixth day of last month, I was carried in a palanquin to the county seat and did my best to take care of various business. On the third of this month, An Yŏng-dŭk, a district servant, brought a report made by the village elder and asked me to submit it to the authorities. The report was about those brutish tanners burying a corpse after fighting each other. I learned about the incident through the report and subsequently submitted it to the county office. Therefore, how could I know the context of the incident? Please take this into consideration."

In the first investigation of Yi Hŭng-guk, a village headman (*tumin*) with no military obligation (*muyŏk*); Yi Hang-nok, no military obligation; and Yu Chin-ch'ŏl, a village administrator (*tongim*) and no military obligation.

In the testimony of Yi Hŭng-guk, [he said]: "The twenty-ninth of last month was the funeral for the villager Yi Sŭng-o. After the funeral, around dusk, the villager Chang Mun-wŏn and my son Yi In-myŏng went to the village entrance in order to return the funeral bier to storage, and saw three unfamiliar people fighting loudly close to the village entrance. After witnessing the fight, both men [my son and Chang] came to tell me about it. Because I cannot let such fighting happen like that near the village entrance, I had [them] report the incident [to Yu Myŏng-han]. Then, Chang Mun-wŏn and my son In-myŏng went and drove them away. When these two men came back, they told me that one of the three who had been fighting was lying on the road, while another man was standing right by him, and the third was fleeing the scene away from the village. Therefore, they chased and caught him. The runaway was the brute, the tanner Yi Haeng-mun; the two brutes lying and standing were not familiar to them. They had the two—who stood and fled—assist the one lying, and kicked them out [of the area], over the mountain pass in front [of the village]. This was all I knew.

"Then on the next day, the thirtieth, our village man Yi Ik-ch'ŏl went to the firewood farm at Old Temple Valley over Namwŏl Pass in front of the village entrance to fetch firewood, and happened to see a new grave at the landslide site along the mountain trail. He immediately noticed that it was not made with hoes and shovels but was covered with [traces of] hands and feet. After I heard this [from Yi Ik-ch'ŏl], we pondered and became suspicious since there had been no funeral held in neighboring villages recently, and also because the shape of the tomb was different from [any other ordinary mounds]. If it had to do with those brutes, including the tanner who fought yesterday, we could not overlook it. So, we had those village men, Yi Ik-ch'ŏl, Yi Nak-to, Yi Ch'un-gŭn, and Yu Myŏng-hak, tell this to the village elder who had to subsequently write and submit a report to the authorities. Now, I did not know who the dead [person] was, by whom he was beaten, when he died, or where his family was from the very beginning."

Yi Hang-nok and Yu Chin-ch'ŏl [said]: "What we heard and saw was the same as what Yi Hŭng-guk stated. We hope you take this into consideration."

In the first testimony of Yi Ik-ch'ŏl, a related witness (saryŏn) with no military obligation: "I did not go out and stayed up for three nights in my relative Yi Sŭng-o's house for checking food preparation for [his] funeral on the twenty-ninth of last month. Thus, I did not know anything about the tanners' fight at the village entrance. On the next day, the thirtieth, I heard from village people that those tanners had been expelled [from the village] while fighting each other the day before. Because I had been totally occupied by the funeral and did not have enough firewood at home, I went to the firewood farm in Old Temple Valley near Namwŏl Pass to gather firewood. To get there, I had to follow a narrow mountain path, and I noticed a new tomb mound that had not been there before under the landslide site of the mountain trail. There were no traces of hoes and shovels, but only those of hands and feet. So, I became very suspicious. Just then I recalled the story of the tanners' fight; thus I went and informed the villagers of it. The village people agreed that this was a suspicious thing that should not be ignored but be reported to the village elder, who should in turn report it to the authorities. Therefore, I went with the other three men to the village elder's house, told everything, and had him write and submit a report on this. There is nothing else to testify; please take it into consideration."

In the first testimony of Chang Mun-wŏn, an eyewitness (kanjŭng) with no military obligation: "On the twenty-ninth of last month, I went to the funeral of Yi Sŭng-o. When I was returning the funeral bier to storage with another village man, Yi In-myŏng, I saw three brutes fighting each other loudly a little [distance] away on the road. I informed the village head of this, and he asked us to chase them away. Upon going back to the place with Yi In-myŏng, we noticed that among those three fighting, one was lying on the street, another was standing by him, and the other wearing a coarse bamboo hat (p'yŏngnip) was running away.[23] When we pursued and caught him, it was the brute, the tanner Yi Haeng-mun. We reproached them, saying: 'Why are you guys fighting here, for what reason? One guy is lying on the road and one is trying to flee. Why is this so? Go and carry the person lying on the road and leave.' Those brutes did not answer right away. Then the guy who was standing there and wearing a bamboo hat helped the person lying on the road to get up from the ground, and put him on Yi Haeng-mun's back, and left toward the hill. I was not able to ask the name of the fallen man, but saw his appearance very briefly. He seemed to have injuries on his face and his hair was in disarray. His upper jacket was soiled with bloodstains here and there. There were no particular weapons nearby. After watching this scene, we came back. Except for me and Yi In-myŏng, there was no one else who returned to the [fighting] place and saw them. Please take this into consideration."

In the first testimony of Yi In-myŏng, an eyewitness: *After repeating Chang Mun-wŏn's testimony as a witness to the fight, reporting the incident to the village headman, and chasing the three men away, he continues:* ". . . At that time, I saw bloodstains on the fallen man's face and he was groaning from pain. We neither knew how this incident began and which part [of the body of the fallen man] was hit, nor saw what weapons [they used to beat him]. It was chaotic and [we] did not think of asking their names. No one else went to the place except for me and Chang Mun-wŏn. Please take this into consideration."

In the first testimony of An Yŏng-dŭk, a subdistrict administrator (*ijŏng*): "As a servant of this subdistrict, I take care of all matters, whatever those are. Since the village elder prepared a written report on the tanners' fight in front of Pear Blossom Hamlet on the second day of this month and sent it over to me, I delivered it to the subdistrict administrator's place inside the county seat. There is nothing I saw or heard [about the incident]; please take this into consideration."

In the second testimonies of village headman Yi Hŭng-guk, Yi Hang-nok, and Yu Chin-ch'ŏl: *After repeating the reports about the fighting and an unfamiliar grave, they continue to say:* ". . . According to Yi Ik-ch'ŏl, the grave was not covered by grass. There were only the traces of hands gathering soil to cover it, and it was indeed located under a crumbled hill alongside a mountain trail. It was as clear as daylight that [someone] had hidden and buried a corpse there. Because the tanners fought on the previous day and now there was a secret grave, everything was suspicious. Therefore, we told this to the village elder, who then submitted a written report. There is nothing we did not state. . . ."

In the second testimony of Yi Ik-ch'ŏl, a related witness: "I told everything in the previous testimony. On that day, I went to the Old Temple Valley to gather firewood and happened to find a new grave that looked to have been covered with soil by [using] hands and feet. Thinking it to be suspicious, I immediately recalled the tanners' fight. When I told this to the village people, they all agreed, 'This is indeed a strange incident. If we cover this up, it will definitely cause us trouble later. By reporting this to the magistrate's office, it should come out into the open.' All discussion fell into one agreement, which was delivered to the village elder, who then submitted a report to the office. . . ."

In the second testimony of Chang Mun-wŏn, an eyewitness: *After repeating his first testimony, he continues to say:* ". . . We were stupid and did not have the chance to ask who beat whom and for what reasons. It was around sunset when we had the injured man be carried and [made them] leave, so we saw them [only] in passing. The fallen man's face had open wounds that were bleeding and soiling his clothes. Upon being carried on the back, we heard a slight groan of pain that did not sound quite urgent. Yi Haeng-mun was a lowly tanner originally from Ŭnyul County, temporarily residing in Chŏng Hwan-sŏp's house in the Eastern Village and working as a tanner. Because I had happened to meet him around 8.20, I immediately knew it was Haeng-mun upon meeting him on that day. . . ."

In the second testimony of Yi In-myŏng, an eyewitness: "I told everything in the previous testimony. On that day, upon putting a funeral bier back into storage, I witnessed two brutes grabbing one another by the collar and fighting, while another man wearing a bamboo hat seemed to hold them back. As advised by village headman, I returned to the [fighting place] and saw one man lying on the road, his face bleeding onto his jacket. . . . The injured man groaned a few times. . . . As for the names of the beater, [the man] being beaten, and the reasons for the fight, I did not even get a chance to ask. . . ."

In the third testimony of Chang Mun-wŏn, an eyewitness: "I have already told everything in the first and second testimonies. When I first witnessed the fight in front of the [village] storage, I was unable to see things in detail because it was getting dark. There were three brutish men fighting: two of them were holding and fighting each other, and one wearing a bamboo hat was standing a little behind them. Being foolish and scared, I did not mention a minute thing in my first and second testimonies. I have some acquaintance with Yi Haeng-mun, who is in his thirties and has a small figure. He has neither whiskers nor scars on his face. As for the one wearing a bamboo hat, though it was difficult to see his face carefully because of darkness, he looked quite tall. Except for this, I have nothing more to say, though I die under punishment."

In the third testimony of Yi In-myŏng, an eyewitness: "I have already told everything in the first and second testimonies. When I saw them in front of the storage building, two men were holding and fighting each other, and the one stopping them from fighting was a man with a bamboo hat. When [we were] approaching to expel [them], the man wearing a bamboo hat was standing on the road, and it was Yi Haeng-mun who tried to run off down the road. Then we caught him to [make him] carry the fallen man on his back and leave. As we were ignorant, we only had the idea of kicking them out quickly and never really thought of asking the names of the two other men besides Haeng-mun. Haeng-mun is about twenty-six or twenty-seven years old and has a small frame. I did not carefully examine whether he had whiskers and scars or not. Also, I did not observe in detail the appearance of the man wearing a bamboo hat. Except for this, I have nothing to add, though I die under punishment."

. . . .

In the concluding statement (kyŏlsa) of the first inquest investigation by Yu Ki-dae,[24] the inquest official and the magistrate of Anak Lesser County: This criminal case took place [in an area] surrounded by high peaks, which is not unlike the territory of the Jiuyi (K: Kuǔi) Mountains.[25] A handful of sand is [the result of] ten thousand years of weathering. That Pear Blossom Hamlet cannot avoid unexpected wind. A fallen leaf from another mountain has caused unbearable resentment [to the villagers].

What happened at the time was as if a heavy frost fell. What is not traceable is as if the sun was blocked by clouds. Was it because of drinking? Or were they crazy? We just do not have any clue why they began to fight. Mountains like to know; roads like to know. But it is impossible to locate any clue. When facts of the case come to this point, investigation has to be done with extreme care.

I had the corpse placed in a bright place and washed it all over. Then I used my own hands to examine the body meticulously. The skin on the right shoulder blade was open, creating a hole there. The left eyelid has a light abrasion, but it is not a critical injury and there is no need to discuss this. The neck bone on the dorsal side of the body is broken and dislocated, so [the head] goes right or left as my hand touches it, as if it were a hanging cucumber. Therefore, I record the true cause of death as death by broken neck.

Oh, this poor dead man. He might have put his arms around other men's shoulders and formed a close friendship. As they traveled through unknown villages, how could he have expected to meet such rage? On their return home as the sun set, he was attacked by the other. The incident took place so suddenly, and the lonely spirit [wandering around] the green mountains had no one to call for. His bitterness [was great enough to] reach Heaven. How horrible his death was! How sad the entire circumstance was.

Now, these three men were on the road together; one was dead and two were alive. Both of them are culprits. However, between the two, there must be a difference between the primary offender and the accomplice. When considering testimonies, the one who was fighting was Yi Haeng-mun and the one who tried to flee was Yi Haeng-mun. It was also Yi Haeng-mun who carried away the fallen man after being caught. Considering the circumstances and evidence, there is no need to doubt that Yi Haeng-mun was the principal offender. I could not interrogate him because he had already run way; this is an extremely regrettable situation. As for the man standing by and wearing a bamboo hat—who is that person? It might have been difficult to stop the fight when it was a bloody one. However, from the fight to death, from death to burial, from burial to fleeing, this man must have also committed some crimes. He is at large; therefore I do not put him in any category [in this inquest report].

I compile and submit this report after having excavated and examined, in accordance with law, the body of this anonymous dead male who was buried in Old Temple Valley over Namwŏl Pass in Pear Blossom Hamlet, Samso, An'gok District of this county.

. . . .

In the directive issued by former provincial governor Yi Myŏng-sŏn:[26] The autopsy report has been filed. This death case is about [the grave of] the unknown man in front of Pear Blossom Hamlet. Who is this dead person? [The grave] was constructed only with hands and feet along the stream by the landslide site, and the grave never existed there before. As for who beat and who was beaten, we simply do not have any clue, just as the traces of a snow-white goose are imperceptible. Frustratingly, we simply do not know anything, just as one cannot distinguish the shadows of cranes from the reeds. The words in the village people's report are like [trying to] scratch [an itchy] foot with the shoe one is wearing [that caused the itch in the first place,] and the circumstances of the tanners' fight are like the [dim] light thrown off by burning a screen. With insufficient evidence, it is like hearing sparrows chirping; and without a critical clue, it is like seeing the same indistinguishable colors of pine and cedar trees.

In examining the autopsy form, the cause of the death was a broken neck that resulted from beating. The bloodstains were small, but [the injury] was very deep and long. The neck bones were broken and out of joint, and the head swung from side to side. Although there is some vagueness in conducting this investigation, the real cause of death is not in doubt at all. Indeed, three men went together, yet one died and two survived. I am confident about the suspect: if not Yi Haeng-mun, it is the man wearing a bamboo hat; if not the man with the bamboo hat, then Yi Haeng-mun. However, Yi Haeng-mun has been named as a principal offender [by the first inquest official]. Widely search for both Yi and the one wearing a bamboo hat and arrest them as soon as possible to resolve the case. Yi Hŭng-guk and Yi Hang-nok are village headmen who heard about [the fight] from Chang and Yi and had them chase away those who were fighting. If they had handled the matter well, they would have gotten the names [of these men] as well as the reasons for the fight. [Because they did not,] they gave the vicious criminals a chance to escape. After witnessing those men fighting from afar, Chang Mun-wŏn and Yi In-myŏng chased down and caught the man who was fleeing the scene. But they were clumsy and did not care about getting their names and the reasons for the fight, thereby ruining and delaying this important murder case. As for these four men, I order them to be put in jail. After serving the set time in jail, punish them with thirty strokes of beating with a heavy stick, and report this back to me. The second inquest investigation shall be suspended, and the corpse should be reburied. All other people shall be released.

. . . .

[I] report that on 1895.11.14 (12/29/1895), the five-hundred-and-fourth year of the dynasty's foundation, the accused, Yi Haeng-mun, was arrested and interrogated.[27]

In the directive of former provincial governor Yi Myŏng-sŏn: The interrogation report has been filed. With the shining light of Heaven's will, the heinous criminal was caught. Finally, the victimized soul can be comforted and the legal procedure can be carried out properly. Now, a one-time investigation is not sufficient. Thus, I appoint the magistrate of Sinch'ŏn Lesser County as a special investigator (*myŏngsagwan*)[28] for this case. The arrested Yi Haeng-mun should be imprisoned, Kim Kyŏng-un arrested as soon as possible, and Yi Hŭng-guk and the other people confined in jail.

[no title page]
Special Investigation: As for the wounded area, based on Yi Haeng-mun's testimony, Yi Haeng-mun first picked up a stone and hit Cho P'al-bok's face. When P'al-bok fell down, Yi Haeng-mun and Kim Kyŏng-un alternately trampled all over Cho's head, neck, and spine. Therefore, I record that the direct cause of the death is a broken neck by being trampled on. The special investigation was carried out on 1896.1.6 (1896/2/18), the five-hundred-and-fifth year of the dynasty's foundation.

In the first testimony of Cho Kuk-po, the close relative of the deceased, a tanner: "The deceased Cho P'al-bok is my younger cousin. P'al-bok used to live in Harŭng Village in the Munhwa area, but moved into Kodu Subdistrict in the Songhwa area. Early in the last ninth month, he went out for leather-making and did not come back home. His wife had already run away for no reason. I heard from people that an unknown tanner had died near a tavern at Wa Hill of Anak Lesser County. Since my cousin had never come back, I was worried. I hurriedly went to the office for investigation in Anak and requested to see the deceased. However, the clerk at the bureau replied, 'An autopsy was already conducted the other day, and the corpse has already been marked and sealed. You cannot see him until we receive adjudication (*chesa*) from the provincial governor's office.'[29] Therefore, I waited for the day when the adjudication arrived, then went to see the deceased with the head officer. Indeed, it was my cousin P'al-bok. Not being able to control my surprise and bewilderment, I asked the villagers about what had happened. Two men said, 'On 9.29 around supper time, three unfamiliar men were fighting on the road in front of the village. Among the three, one of them was injured and collapsed in the street;

another stood by him; and the other was a tanner, Yi Haeng-mun, who resided in the neighboring Ch'ŏnggye Village. Upon seeing that we were approaching, Haeng-mun was scared and fled, yet we pursued and caught him. We had him carry the wounded man on his back and expelled them [from the village]. Haeng-mun and the two other men, including the one on his back, left and went over the hill.' After listening to this, I told my nephew living in the Hwangju area about it. [He] then searched all over for Haeng-mun's whereabouts, and finally went to Kan Village in Chunghwa and caught him there. My sister-in-law [Cho P'al-bok's wife] had already been arrested in New Hamlet, in the West District of Anak. Both Yi Haeng-mun and my sister-in-law stated that they had no relations at all. My cousin, P'al-bok, was a healthy man without any illness, but was injured and met a violent death. What on earth is there that is a [more] bitter thing than this? Please conduct a meticulous investigation and clear the resentment of this untimely death."

In the first testimony of Cho Kwang-p'il, the close relative of the deceased, a tanner: "Cho P'al-bok is my father's cousin.[30] I moved to the Hwangju area, where I live now. On 10.26, I heard from my father's cousin [Cho Kuk-po] that P'al-bok had gone to Anak for leather work and was beaten to death by Yi Haeng-mun, another tanner. While searching for him everywhere, I caught him in Kan Village in the Chunghwa area. I asked him why he killed [my uncle, P'al-bok]. Haeng-mun answered, 'My relative Kim Kyŏng-un from the Munhwa area came to my house, saying, "I had a secret affair with Cho P'al-bok's wife. Although having an affair is confidential, it is difficult to develop a deeper relation with her because her husband is alive. I will entice P'al-bok [to come here] sometime soon. Please kill him for me; then I will be able to marry her." Since he requested, I accepted it. Indeed, a few days later, [Kyŏng-un] came with P'al-bok and I killed him.' Upon hearing this, my eyes were glittering with such fury that I only thought of seeking revenge right there [on my uncle's behalf]. Yet, considering that this would violate the law, I suppressed my anger and decided to deliver him to the authorities. I wandered around the New Hamlet area in Anak to look for Kyŏng-un's traces, but only caught my aunt [my uncle's wife, Ms. Paek]. I asked her about Kyŏng-un's whereabouts and she replied, 'He is a criminal. Last night, he saw torches held by people in the next village. He became alarmed and ran away. I do not know where he went.' On listening to this, I felt my blood boiling in my body and wanted to beat her to death. But there is a law and I did not dare kill her like that. So, I arrested [her] and presented [her] to the authorities. Now both are caught. Please punish them with death and clear the resentment of the deceased. As for close relatives, there are none but us; do take this into consideration."

In the first testimony of Chang Mun-wŏn, an eyewitness (kanjŭng) with no military obligation: "On 9.29 last year, it was our neighbor's funeral. When I was returning home from the funeral work around sunset, a village headman said, 'Three brutes were fighting in front of our village. When a fight becomes excessive, one could die. You and Yi In-myŏng should go and stop them from fighting and drive them out of the village.' Therefore, we hurriedly went there. Of the three men, two were strangers and one was Yi Haeng-mun, a tanner. One guy was lying on the road; one wearing a bamboo hat was standing right there; and Haeng-mun ran away. We chased and caught Yi Haeng-mun, scolded him, and asked them to leave. Haeng-mun carried the fallen man on his back and left with the guy wearing a bamboo hat. It was already getting dark, and I do not remember whether the fallen man was injured or not. I went back home, slept, and left for day labor early the next morning. I do not know any other affairs but this. Yi In-myŏng, who was with me at that time, is here [waiting for a chance to testify], and if you ask him, things will be clearer. Please take this into consideration."

In the first testimony of Yi In-myŏng, an eyewitness with no military obligation: "9.29 last year was the funeral of a villager. The village headman then was my father. On my way back home from the funeral work with Chang Mun-wŏn, my father said, 'You and Chang Mun-wŏn both go, keep those [men] from fighting in front of our village and kick them out.' Therefore, we went there immediately and it was getting dark. Seeing us approach, one of the three men fled. When we caught him, it was a tanner, Yi Haeng-mun, [who was] living in a neighboring village. After we scolded them several times and asked them to carry the fallen person and leave, Haeng-mun together with the man wearing a bamboo hat carried the fallen man and rapidly left. It was around sunset and it was hard to see a short distance, so we just came back home. There is nothing else we saw, and please take this into consideration."

In the first investigation of Yi Hŭng-guk, a village headman with no military obligation; Yi Hang-nok with no military obligation; and Yu Chin-ch'ŏl, a village administrator with no military obligation:

Yi Hŭng-guk [said]: "Since I am the oldest in this village and called a village headman. . . ." *After repeating what Chang Mun-wŏn and his son Yi In-myŏng had testified, he continues to say:* ". . . Yet next day, Yi Ik-ch'ŏl, who went over the mountain pass[31] to gather firewood, came back and told me, 'On my way back from fetching firewood, I saw a strange grave alongside the crumbled mountain slope, which looked suspicious. I wonder if it was made by those fighting last night in front of the village. They might have killed one of them and buried him there to cover up the traces.' Since I was a village headman, I sent my son and other village people there to examine the grave. The shape of the grave was suspicious, as Ik-ch'ŏl said. Therefore, I passed this story on to the village elder and subdistrict administrators. There is nothing else to report."

Yi Hang-nok and Yu Chin-ch'ŏl said: "Except for what our village headman Yi Hŭng-guk said, we have nothing to report. Please take this into consideration."

In the first testimony of Yu Myŏng-han, a "youthful student" (*yuhak*)[32] and the village elder, and Chŏng Kwŏn, a youthful student and subdistrict administrator:

Yu Myŏng-han, the village elder, said: "I resided in Nak Village, and it is about 7 *li* away from Pear Blossom Hamlet. On 9.30, in the afternoon, Yi Ik-ch'ŏl and others from Pear Blossom Hamlet came and said to me: 'There were three strangers fighting in front of our village last night and the villagers expelled them. Two men carried the wounded one on their backs and left [going] south, over the mountain pass. There was a new, unfamiliar grave near a crumbled valley under the hill, and it must be that one of the men fighting last night beat another to death and buried him secretly there.' Because I, as a village elder, was shocked to hear this, I had a district servant, An Yŏng-dŭk, report this in writing to the authorities. I do not know anything else; please take this into consideration."

Chŏng Kwŏn, a subdistrict administrator, said: "I have nothing that differs from what the village elder just stated. Please take this into consideration."

The first testimony of An Yŏng-dŭk, a subdistrict administrator: "I am a subdistrict servant. I take care of all the matters of the subdistrict, following the village elder and subdistrict administrator's orders. I was told to report about a strange murder on 9.30 in front of Pear Blossom Hamlet, and so I only submitted it to the county office. I do not know anything else; please take this into consideration."

In the first testimony of Yi Ik-ch'ŏl, a related witness (saryŏn): "On 9.29 last year, when there was a funeral in the village, I only stayed inside the house to check funeral preparations and did not hear what was happening outside. I returned home and slept that night. Next day, when I went to the house of mourning and was eating leftover funeral ritual food, I heard about the fight involving Yi Haeng-mun and the two other men. I then went to Old Temple Valley over Nam Pass[33] to fetch firewood and saw a new, unfamiliar grave at the entrance of the valley near a crumbled hill. It looked suspicious, and there were only the traces of hands gathering soil without using hoes. Pondering for a while, I thought that those three men fighting the previous night must have killed one of them and buried the dead here to eliminate any traces. I told what I suspected to the villagers and they replied, 'If that is true, it must be a disaster. You go to the village elder and subdistrict administrators and report [this incident].' I only delivered the message and there is nothing else to state. Please take this into consideration."

In the first testimony of Ms. Paek, a female tanner: "My husband, Cho P'al-bok, and Kim Kyŏng-un lived in neighboring villages. Kyŏng-un was a drunk-ard with a violent temperament. While my husband was away from home, he came to [my house] and threatened me with a knife in order to rape me. As a powerless woman, I could not withstand his threats and allowed him once. After that, [we] moved to the Songhwa area. At the beginning of the ninth month, my husband went to the Anak area to do leather work but did not come back after a month or so. Early in the tenth month, when I and my six-year-old daughter were about to sleep late at night, that evil Kyŏng-un entered my room harboring a knife and saying: 'You run away with me tonight. If you do not follow me, I will kill you with this knife.' I wanted to yell, but he stuffed my mouth with the blanket and I was not able to cry out [for fear]. That night, he put my sleeping daughter on my back and dragged me away from home. In my ignorant and delicate heart, I did not even think of scolding and stopping him, yet was only afraid I would be stabbed to death. Since I obeyed him reluctantly, how could I feel comfortable? It was natural that my pace was tardy and slow. Alas, that Kyŏng-un said, 'I plotted to kill your husband. If you reveal this, I will kill you, too.' I delayed on the way by making all kinds of excuses and also hurting my own calf and thigh, which was very painful. We eventually arrived in New Hamlet in An'gok, and rented a small room in a mountain home. That criminal brute [Kyŏng-un] saw torches held by people in a neighboring village the day before yesterday, and he panicked and has already fled. The following morning, I heard that a constable (*saryŏng*), my husband's brother, and my husband's nephew were looking for me. I went out to the road first and met them. Now I am here, after being caught. The truth is that Kim Kyŏng-un is like a bitter enemy whom I hate most in my mind. If I knew his whereabouts, why would I not tell you? I do know nothing else, and please take this into consideration."

In the first testimony of Yi Haeng-mun, the principal offender, tanner: "I originally resided in Ŭnyul. About a year ago, I happened to move to Anak. In the early ninth month, I did leather work for the Kim family at Suun Bridge in An'gok District. Around the twentieth of the ninth month, my relative uncle, the tanner Kim Kyŏng-un, who was living in Harŭng Village in Munhwa, visited the house where I was working and said, 'I have had an affair with a woman who wants to move in with me. Please buy a house for me. . . .'" Then he left. On 9.28, Kim Kyŏng-un came to my work place with his fellow Cho P'al-bok and stayed overnight. Kyŏng-un slipped out and asked me to come outside the door. When I followed him, he told me, 'What I am saying now is something that I can only tell you. Cho P'al-bok's wife and I already had a secret affair. Although we want to build deeper relations, her husband is a problem. I enticed him to come here now. If you understand my intention and handle him, I can live with her in the same house.' In the beginning, I did not assent to [his suggestion], sternly reproaching him that it was out of reason. Yet, I finally agreed to help him when he came and asked for it again. After having breakfast next morning, together with P'al-bok we went to a tavern near Tongp'yŏng Mountain under the excuse of trading leather. We all drank heavily until it was around sunset time. I held P'al-bok by his sleeve and tried to take him to an isolated place, but he was very drunk and rambling, not following me obediently. Before we reached an isolated place, we came near Wa Hill. Without realization, I picked up a big stone and hit P'al-bok's forehead hard, and P'al-bok's arms and feet dropped to the ground. With Kyŏng-un, I kicked and trampled on P'al-bok, who was near death. At that moment, people from Pear Blossom Hamlet witnessed our beating from afar and a few of them approached us. Out of fear, I ran away, yet was soon tracked and caught by those people. I then put P'al-bok on my back and went over Nam Pass with Kyŏng-un. It was around twilight and no one was around. Being afraid P'al-bok would revive, we beat and stepped on him more, buried his body by the crumbling hill, and fled to the Chunghwa area. Thanks to Heaven's will, I am now here under arrest. It is all a disaster I made by myself, and how can I wish for life after killing someone? Even if I die under the flogging, how can I alter my statement? I only wait for a punishment."

In the second testimony of Cho Kuk-po, the close relative of the deceased, a tanner: "I told everything in the previous testimony. When I went to see my cousin's corpse, his left eyebrow had cuts with dry bloodstains, and his head and neck swayed, not being fixed. In pressing with my hands, bones were broken and torn apart, yet there was no bloodstain on his back, shoulder, or chest. If that evil Haeng-mun had half a human heart, he could not have dared to kill [my cousin] even though he himself was a relative of Kyŏng-un's. While the killing plot was made by Kyŏng-un, it was Haeng-mun who did the [actual] murder. Please arrest Kyŏng-un immediately, who is at large. And punish him together with Haeng-mun, so that even a fraction of P'al-bok's deep grudge can be satisfied. Alas, that woman tanner Ms. Paek had had a secret affair with Kyŏng-un and then went away with him. If she had not really joined in the plotting earlier, would she have maintained the adulterous relation and followed him? In this way, I believe that Ms. Paek, Yi [Haeng-mun], and Kim [Kyŏng-un] were all in this together. Please punish this cunning evil woman and clear my dead cousin's grave resentment."

In the second testimony of Ms. Paek, a female tanner: "I already stated everything in my mind in the previous testimony. In fact, I do not deny the crimes I committed—having a secret affair and following Kim Kyŏng-un—even if I die under punishment. Truly, however, I did what I did not want to do, yet how can I show that this is so? Even if I am severely interrogated a hundred times, I do not have anything to say. I only wait for a punishment."

In the second testimony of Yi Haeng-mun, the principal offender: "I told everything in the previous testimony. Indeed, we were as drunk as a broom walking on a twisting path. Our conversation under the circumstance became sour. I picked up a stone and smashed his face with it. After getting to a dark place, Kyŏng-un and I alternately beat and trampled on P'al-bok's neck. It was during this time that his [P'al-bok's] neck was broken. It was a severe bout of fighting. As for how many times we did [it], and which one was strong or weak, how can I remember [in the midst of such commotion]? I am the one who hit P'al-bok's face with my hands first and stepped on his head and neck. Since Kyŏng-un is on the run, I have no reason to make any excuse about who did what. I have confessed everything and am only waiting for a punishment. There is nothing more I have to say; please take this into consideration."

. . . .

In the concluding statement of Nam Hyo-wŏn,[34] a special investigator (*myŏngsagwan*) and the magistrate of Sinch'ŏn Lesser County: This criminal case consists of three men who traveled and drank together. Yet one lost his life as if [he] were a bird hit by an arrow. After fighting each other, [P'al-bok] fell on the road. This fits with the witnesses' testimonies. When reburying the corpse, the close relative of the deceased saw that the corpse's head was dangling. In addition, as Yi Haeng-mun stated in his testimony, he first picked up the stone and badly hit the face of Cho P'al-bok, who then collapsed on the road. Then Haeng-mun and Kim Kyŏng-un even trampled on his neck and backbone. Considering this, there is no doubt that the real cause of the death is breaking his neck after being stepped on. Alas, that Cho P'al-bok was born into the unavoidable lowest status and that the traces of his death were also concealed by those evil brutes. The resentful bones [covered with] yellow sand were spotted by the cow [driver] who collected firewood. It seems as though the lonely soul [of P'al-bok] on a blue mountain relied on a sole bird to cry out [for help]. What an extremely miserable incident it is! Ah, that Yi Haeng-mun is only one of ten thousand creatures in the world. Yet, by accepting Kyŏng-un's heinous instigation, he harbored the intention of murdering P'al-bok and brought up a loud commotion on their way back at dusk. He violently hit P'al-bok's face with a stone and stepped on P'al-bok's neck with his feet, beating and trampling to his satisfaction. Carrying the dying P'al-bok on his back, he covered up the traces of the dead man with sand. In the middle of running away and hiding in Kan Village like a deer in the woods, he was caught by the accuser like a turtle in a jar. Therefore, it is not avoidable to record Haeng-mun as the principal offender.

. . . .

In the directive of Yi Myŏng-sŏn, a former provincial governor: An investigation report has been filed. From ancient times, there has never been a time when people did not murder each other, yet nothing was crueler than this case. Although the principal offender was indicated in the first inquest investigation, how could the traces of the murder plot by those two evil people have been disclosed and the truth about P'al-bok's sudden death have become known if the accusers had not scouted around for the criminals? Haeng-mun was caught in Kan Village, while P'al-bok's wife was arrested in New Hamlet. With one investigation, the criminals confessed their crimes and the judgment can now be made based on the law.

Alas, that Yi Haeng-mun made a pretext for the horrendous crime by heavily drinking at the Chŏng family's tavern, after being secretly incited [to commit the murder] by the adulterer Kim, who had an affair with Cho's wife. He pulled P'al-bok's sleeve and grabbed his topknot, then smashed P'al-bok's face with a stone. While stepping on P'al-bok, he was afraid that P'al-bok would not die. He carried P'al-bok on his back to the mountain pass and finally killed him there. After hurriedly burying the corpse, he hid away here and there. Now he is here arrested, thanks to Heaven's mirror lighting up [the world]. He has confessed the heinous crime in every detail. How could he avoid capital punishment? A meeting shall be scheduled with the first inquest official to review the case. Punish him with something comparable to thirty strokes of beating with a heavy stick and imprison him in a cangue in accordance with the regulations.[35]

As for Ms. Paek, she relied on a brute [Kim Kyŏng-un] who was from the same place as her husband, and finally drove the affair to the point of her husband's violent death. Without thinking of rectifying and clearing her husband's resentment, she followed evil instead. When considering her role as an accomplice, her crime is almost the same as Kim Kyŏng-un and Yi Haeng-mun's. Imprison her after rendering a special punishment of thirty strokes of beating.

Kim Kyŏng-un had an affair with P'al-bok's wife in secret and murdered P'al-bok. As for the crime of murdering P'al-bok, there is no way that it is forgiven in Heaven and Earth. Yet, because apprehending him has been delayed, the king's law has not been properly conducted. How deplorable! He should be immediately arrested and punished. As for Yi Hŭng-guk, Chang Mun-wŏn, and Yi In-myŏng, they were disciplined enough for their guilt. Release them with the other people. Send this order to the first inquest official so that he can implement it one by one, accordingly.

AN ILLEGAL BURIAL BEGETS A SON BUT KILLS A RELATIVE

Kim Kap-san (Hoeyang, Kangwŏn Province, 1899)

As briefly examined in case 2, gravesite litigation had become an increasingly widespread social problem in late Chosŏn Korea and often developed into physical confrontations between the families involved, sometimes resulting in homicide. The death of Kim Kap-san was one such incident, although he only assisted his clansman Kim Mun-ho of the Kyŏngju Kim lineage in carrying out an illegal burial at another gravesite (that of the apical ancestor of the Kwangsan Kim lineage). Kim Mun-ho's intention when carrying out the illegal burial was clearly articulated during the investigation: he became the father of a son at a rather late age (in his forties) and he clearly attributed such blessing to the illegal burial. He did not seek direct economic gain by claiming ownership of the forestland surrounding the illegal burial because the burial was meant to remain a secret forever.

The secret burial itself constituted a crime, but the way Kim Mun-ho dug into the side of the existing tomb—creating a hole right by the coffin and placing his father's bones there as though it were the resting place of a man and wife (in comparison to case 2, in which the violator placed an illegal burial near the tomb of the violated)—was regarded as an unthinkable violation of the apical ancestor of the Kyŏngju Kim lineage. And whereas Mun-ho thought that the birth of his son had to do with the blessing emanating from his father's illegal tomb, members of the Kwangsan Kim lineage believed that the many unusual deaths among their members in the preceding years had been caused by this desecration of their ancestral grave. Both parties evidently believed in a geomantic prescription, namely, that the ancestral gravesite brought either fortune or misfortune. It was natural even to the investigators that the Kwangsan Kims would be extraordinarily furious, both because of how the illegal burial had been carried out and because they believed the violation of the ancestral grave had resulted in many abnormal deaths in the lineage.

One subtle aspect of the conflicts between the two Kim lineages seems to be derived from the native place of the members of the Kyŏngju Kim lineage who were involved in this case. The victim, Kim Kap-san, was originally from Hamgyŏng Province but had migrated to Hoeyang, Kangwŏn Province, a county bordering Hamgyŏng to the north, where his relatives were residing. Social, political, and cultural prejudice against people of the northern provinces was pervasive in the late Chosŏn, and the Kwangsan Kims did not hide their ill feelings toward the northerners, for they called Kap-san and Mun-ho "wicked people from Hamgyŏng" (*Pukkwan han'ak*).[1] The Kwangsan Kims' disdain for northerners made them suspect that Kap-san had placed additional illegal burials somewhere in their ancestral cemetery. Despite Kap-san's denial, they subjected him to further torture to elicit the facts, and such extra punishment must have caused his death, whereas Mun-ho, who was the primary culprit in the illegal burial, survived.

The outrage of the affected lineage members was understandable, especially since they believed that the disturbance of their ancestor's peace inside the grave had brought inconceivable disasters to their lineage. However, their private way of handling the matter, as well as the end result—the death of Kim Kap-san—were crimes that called for official investigations. Private punishment or torture (*sahyŏng*) by inserting wooden sticks between bound legs and twisting the lower limbs (*churoe* or *churi*)[2] was illegal even in official settings, though not all forms of private corporal punishment were prohibited (see fig. 1). For example, according to the *Great Ming Code*, "If [slaves or hired laborers] disobey orders and [their household heads, or household heads' relatives of the second degree of mourning, or maternal grandparents], according to the law, punish them and unexpectedly cause death, or accidentally kill them, in each case they shall not be punished."[3] Various local community organizations, such as village compacts, often had regulations allowing corporal punishment of those who violated the prescribed rules of conduct.[4] However, yangban overlords in the late Chosŏn often went beyond the law and arbitrarily punished and tortured their underlings or even their fellow yangban, which in rare cases resulted in death. According to the regulations prohibiting arbitrary punishments issued in 1740, yangban used such cruel tortures as setting fire to a fuse placed between the toes, hanging a person upside down and pouring water into

그을이줄

FIG. 1 "Twisting the Legs by Inserting Wooden Sticks" (*Chyuli [churi] t'ŭlgo*). A genre painting by Kim Chun-gŭn. Watercolor painting on paper; 26.5 x 18 cm. Late nineteenth century. Courtesy of the Korean Christian Museum at Soongsil University.

his nose, or hanging a person by his or her big toes, which often caused the toes to tear off.[5]

The Chosŏn state modified its penal laws and gradually removed punishments and torture methods that were considered overly cruel and inhumane, such as prohibiting the previously mentioned *churi* in 1732, putting a hot iron on the soles of a criminal's feet (*nakhyŏng*) in 1733, tattooing a character on a criminal's face or arm (*chajahyŏng*) in 1740, and the indiscriminate beating of the soles of a criminal's feet (*nanjanghyŏng*) in 1770.[6] Yet despite such efforts to control the yangban's abusive exercise of power in the countryside, which eroded the authority of the state, local yangban apparently continued to rely on private punishments to resolve their problems, and it does not seem that the state was able to proactively enforce the new laws. The Kwangsan Kims' choice of *churi* without much hesitation also indicates that this particular form of private punishment had often been employed despite legal prohibition. The fact that artists like Kim Chun-gŭn (see fig. 1) and Kim Yun-bo in the late nineteenth century produced a painting of *churi* also testifies to the practice of this punishment at the time.[7]

One dire difficulty for the courts that investigated and tried this case was that they had to find the principal offender for the "requital for a life," yet the torture, which was found to be the true cause of death, had been carried out not by one person but collectively. Ms. Ch'oe, the widow of the deceased Kim Kap-san, named one of the Kwangsan Kims, Kim P'yŏng-il, as her husband's antagonist, stating that her husband had accused P'yŏng-il on his deathbed. One matter that the courts were not able to resolve seems to have been whether the purported last words of the deceased were true or not. Even if they were true, the court had to have corroborating evidence to name Kim P'yŏng-il as the principal offender. Yet no one from among either the complainants or the defendants came forward to corroborate that Kim P'yŏng-il was the leader of the entire incident, despite the courts' repeated grilling of the witnesses.

Instead, Kim Pyŏng-nyŏl, the lineage chief, was designated as the principal offender because he had issued a circular to the lineage members calling for a meeting to investigate the matter of the illegal burial, authorizing the use of torture if necessary to obtain the facts. The problem, however, was that Kim Pyŏng-nyŏl was quite old and ill, and thus had not been present at the mountain cemetery where the torture took place. Another complication was that although Pyŏng-nyŏl told his lineage members that they should torture Kap-san and Mun-ho if needed, he also said that they would have to rely on the law to resolve the matter. Pyŏng-nyŏl did not intend to kill anyone. The concluding statements by the inquest officials reveal their quandary: there could not be two principal offenders for one crime who would presumably receive capital punishment to avenge the murder. Despite such inconclusive and conflicting evidence and testimonies, the initial inquest as well as the subsequent special investigation found Kim Pyŏng-nyŏl to be the principal offender.

Thanks to a rich paper trail, we were able to reconstruct the legal processes and judgments made for this case, though not completely, as there were some missing pieces. Besides three full inquest reports (initial, first special, and second special investigations), we identified six pieces of correspondence written by judges (p'ansa) of the Kangwŏn Provincial Court (Chaep'anso) and addressed to the minister (taesin) of the Ministry of Justice (Pŏppu).[8] One such report, dated 1900.9.9 (10/31/1900), informs the minister that judgments and sentencing of the case have been made in accordance with the recommendation from the ministry—namely, that Kim Pyŏng-nyŏl has been downgraded to an accused (p'igo) and is to be sentenced to ten years in prison, though the sentence would not be enforced because of his old age and illness; and that Kim P'yŏng-il has been downgraded to an involved witness (kallyŏn) and subsequently released. The author of this particular report disagrees with these judgments and argues that Kim P'yŏng-il is the principal offender in the case, referring to relevant codes in the Great Ming Code.

Apparently, this challenge prompted the Ministry of Justice to revisit the case and issue an order to conduct another special investigation, which was carried out a few months later. The second special investigation, however, did not find any evidence to support Kim P'yŏng-il as the primary offender, and concluded that Kim Pyŏng-nyŏl should be named as the accused, though he had already been released on 1900.9.29 (11/20/1900), not because he was innocent but because he was not subject to corporal punishment because of his old age, as regulated in the legal code. The judge recommended that Kim P'yŏng-il, as an accomplice (ch'abŏm), receive one hundred strokes of beating with a light stick, and Kim Mun-ho eighty strokes with a light stick and two years in prison.

One more—and most likely the last—face-to-face interrogation of Kim P'yŏng-il and Kim Mun-ho was conducted on or before 1901.5.5 (6/30/1901), upon the order of the ministry. Kim P'yŏng-il was finally found innocent and released while Kim Mun-ho was sentenced two years in prison, though he probably didn't serve the term because he had already been in and out of jail for many months since the inception of the case. It seems that the Kwangsan Kims subscribed to the strategy of naming Kim Pyŏng-nyŏl, the lineage chief, as the person entirely responsible for the death incident, knowing that by law Pyŏng-nyŏl would not receive corporal punishment because of his advanced age. According to the law concerning the original conspirator in the article "Killing Others in Affrays or by Intention" (K: T'ugu kŭp kosal in; C: Dou'ou ji gusha ren), in section 2, "Homicide" (K: Inmyŏng; C: Renming), in the *Great Ming Code*: "In all cases where those who are 70 years of age . . . commit crimes punishable by life exile or lighter, they may redeem their punishment." In addition: "If those who are 80 years of age or older . . . commit crimes involving homicide or other actions punishable by the death penalty, deliberate on the matter and propose a provisional sentence, petitioning for a decision by the throne."[9] In this case, the state's repeated efforts to uncover the truth did not bear fruit, both because of the lack of evidence and because Kim Mun-ho changed his mind at the time of the special investigation and decided not to single out Kim P'yŏng-il as the principal culprit and thereby further antagonize the Kwangsan Kims.

The texts translated here show how written correspondence was carried out between different levels of offices in the very last decade of Chosŏn Korea, as well as the legal reasoning of judges who specifically mention the codes pertaining to different crimes and relevant punishments. By the end of the complex court processes, the inquest officials' initial anxiety over their inability to determine one principal offender in the homicide seems to have melted away, and more lenient rulings are made, as occurred in many other death cases in the late Chosŏn.

While following the investigators' process of discerning the principal offender, we meet Ms. Yu, a woman who turns out to be at the center of the entire investigation, if not the incident. She was an itinerant yeast merchant but also a shaman and healer (and perhaps a geomancer), and thus is called an "enlightened woman" (*yŏ myŏngin*). Ms. Yu was involved in a number of monetary transactions that may have caused her to have some personal animosity toward the village headman (*tumin*) Kim Chung-ok and his relative Kim Mun-ho. Although she changed her story or told a new one every time she testified, it is clear that she got to know about Mun-ho's illegal burial and leaked that secret to others who eventually told it to the Kwangsan Kims. Did she commit any punishable crime in this? Perhaps not. However, the first inquest official concludes by saying, "This criminal incident originated from *one woman's tongue*, which led to the death of a person under torture" (emphasis added). The same disdain for and accusation of Ms. Yu surface again and again in all three documents, and all three interrogating officials recommend that she be punished. Notwithstanding the trust bestowed on her by Mun-ho, who made her his son's godmother and shared his deepest secret with her—not to mention her reputation as a shaman and healer—local officials did not hesitate for a moment to accuse her of a crime she did not commit, viewing her as though she were a poison in society.[10] Yet, at the central level, the law does not find her guilty of any of the crimes in this murder case, and her name does not frequently appear in the correspondence between the provincial and central courts.

Some notes about the original documents are in order. Unusually, three separate sets of inquest reports for this particular case—the first inquest report, the first special investigation report, and the second special investigation report—are extant and preserved at the Kyujanggak Archive. Since each document consists of more than twenty double pages and there are many repetitions in content, we translated most of the first inquest report here and then translated only new information from the testimonies of the two special investigation reports, plus their introductory and concluding statements, which reveal the legal reasoning of the investigators. The first inquest report is accompanied by the inquest form (*sijang*) and the illustration of the Kwangsan Kims' cemetery (included here), along with samples of the cover page and main text, thanks to generous permission from the Kyujanggak Archive (see figs. 2 through 7). Readers who know Korean or Chinese may be able to follow along in the translated texts from these reproduced images. Together with these three inquest reports, we are fortunate to have official correspondence between the Provincial Court and the Ministry of Justice, as mentioned earlier. Thinking that these short documents would enrich our understanding of the legal system, we translated them here in the chronological order of all the original texts.

The homicide took place on 1899.10.23 (11/25/1899), after King Kojong (r. 1863–1907) and his cabinet had introduced some sweeping institutional changes, as discussed in the introduction. Thus, the original texts carry evidence of these changes. In terms of the procedural changes, only one inquest was carried out instead of two. A special investigation was conducted because of doubts present in the case, but the examination of the body was not part of the special investigation because the body had already been released to the relatives and buried. Although the first inquest report was addressed to the Ministry of Justice, it seems that it was initially filed with the Provincial Court, which reviewed the report and issued an order of further investigation to the relevant magistrate (the magistrate of Ch'ŏlwŏn in this case). After the spe-

TABLE 2 Timetable of Inquests and Official Correspondence for the Case of Kim Kap-san

Date of incident	1899.10.24 (11/26/1899)
Complaint filed	1899.11.1 (12/3/1899)
First inquest	1899.11.1 (12/3/1899)
Submission of the first inquest report	1899.12.14 (1/14/1900)
Directive issued to the special investigator	1899.12.28 (1/28/1900)
Special investigation	1900.1.9 (2/8/1900)
Submission of the special investigation report	1900.2.13 (3/13/1900)
Report No. 11 to the Ministry of Justice	1900.4.9 (5/7/1900)
Reports filed with the Ministry of Justice	1900.4.12 (5/10/1900)
Report No. 3 to the Ministry of Justice	1900.9.9 (10/31/1900)
Order No. 26 from the Ministry of Justice	1900.9.29 (11/20/1900)
Second special investigation	1901.1.9 (2/27/1901)
Submission of the second special investigation	1901.1.27 (3/17/1901)
Report No. 7 to the Ministry of Justice	1901.2.6 (3/25/1901)
Report No. 19 to the Ministry of Justice	1901.3.18 (5/6/1901)
Inquiry No. 3 to the Ministry of Justice	1901.5.15 (6/30/1901)
Report No. 31 to the Ministry of Justice	1901.5.27 (7/12/1901)

cial investigation, the Provincial Court reviewed those reports and forwarded them to the ministry. Though it was named the Provincial Court, it was either the provincial governor or one of the magistrates in the province who acted as the judge (as we learned from discerning the issuer of the reports), for there were as of yet no trained judges stationed at the provincial level under the new system. Likewise, the ways in which the inquest was conducted were no different from prereform days, and thus local magistrates were in charge of the investigation and trial.

One visible change is observed in the format of the report and its language. Whereas the prereform inquest reports were written in literary Chinese mixed with *idu* (clerk's writing), postreform reports were often written in so-called Sino-Korean, in which some parts previously rendered in *idu* were now in the Korean vernacular script (as seen in fig. 4). In format, too, postreform reports are better organized, and formatted with headings, line breaks, and indents, so that it is easier to distinguish different sections of the report.

[cover page]

The third year of Kwangmu reign (1899)

FIRST INQUEST RECORD OF THE DECEASED MALE KIM KAP-SAN FROM HANCH'I SUBDISTRICT, CHANGYANG DISTRICT, HOEYANG LESSER COUNTY, IN KANGWŎN PROVINCE

• •

[title page]

Kim Pyŏng-nyŏl, principal offender

~~Xxxxx~~ Kim P'yŏng-il, accomplice (kanbŏm)

~~Kim Pyŏng-nyŏl~~ Ms. Yu, a related witness

Report No. 346

Report No. 11

Received on the twelfth day of the fourth month in the fourth year of the Kwangmu reign (5/10/1900)

Review completed (kyŏl)[11]

[seal]

[UNKNOWN] DAY OF THE TWELFTH MONTH IN THE THIRD YEAR OF THE KWANGMU REIGN. FIRST INQUEST RECORD OF THE DECEASED MALE KIM KAP-SAN FROM HANCH'I SUBDISTRICT, CHANGYANG DISTRICT, HOEYANG LESSER COUNTY, IN KANGWŎN PROVINCE

[seal]

• •

REPORT, UNNUMBERED (POGOSŎ HOOE)[12]

I [the magistrate of Hoeyang Lesser County] received a petition (sojang) submitted by Kim Pyŏng-nyŏl and others, people from Changyang District of Hoeyang, which said in summary: "The lŭineage cemetery (sŏnsan) of the plaintiffs (wŏn'go) for the last ten generations has been located on top of Swae Pass (Swae-ryŏng) in this district. Because there was a widespread rumor that Kim Mun-ho, a resident of Hanch'i Subdistrict, carried out an illegal burial (t'ujang) for his father there, we had lineage members investigate the source of the rumor and we also climbed the mountain to examine the condition of the cemetery. After that, we caught Kim Mun-ho and Kim Kap-san and

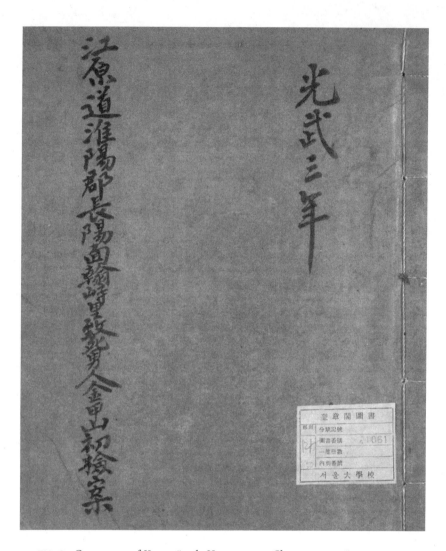

FIG. 2 Cover page of *Kangwŏn-do Hoeyang-gun Changyang-myŏn*
Hanch'i-ri ch'isa namin Kim Kap-san ch'ogŏman (First inquest record of the
deceased male Kim Kap-san from Hanch'i Subdistrict, Changyang District,
Hoeyang Lesser County, in Kangwŏn Province). Kyujanggak Collection,
kyu 21061. Courtesy of Seoul National University, Kyujanggak Institute for
Korean Studies.

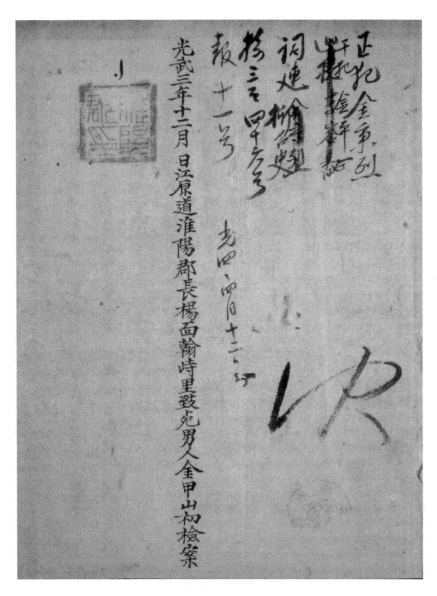

FIG. 3 Title page of *Kangwŏn-do Hoeyang-gun Changyang-myŏn Hanch'i-ri ch'isa namin Kim Kap-san ch'ogŏma* (see fig. 2). Kyujanggak Collection, kyu 21061. Courtesy of Seoul National University, Kyujanggak Institute for Korean Studies.

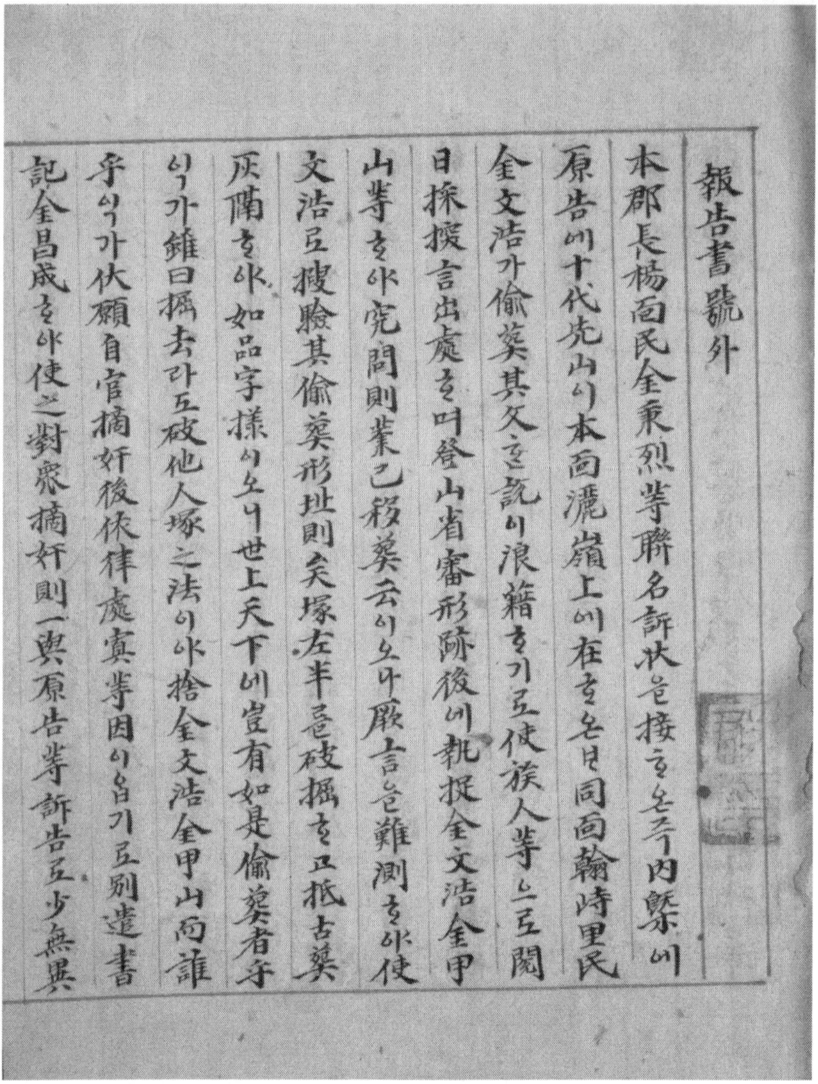

報告書號外

本郡長楊面民全秉烈等聯名訴狀을接호온즉內繇에

原告川十代先山이本面瀧嶺上에在호온바同面翰詩里民

金文浩가偸葬其父호 說이浪籍호기로使族人等노로閱

日採捜言出處호叫登山省審形跡後에執捉金文浩金甲

山等호야宛問則業己穀葬云이오나嚴言을難測호야使

灰備호야如品字樣이오니世上天下에豈有如是偸葬者乎

文浩가捜驗其偸葬形址則矢塚左半을破捉호고抵古葬

식가雖曰捆去라도破他人塚之法이外捨金文浩金甲山而誰

孚식가伏願自官摘奸後依律處真等因이읍기로別遣書

記金昌成호야使之對衆摘奸則一與原告等訴告호少無異

FIG. 4 Report, unnumbered. In *Kangwŏn-do Hoeyang-gun Changyang-myŏn Hanch'i-ri ch'isa namin Kim Kap-san ch'ogŏman*, 1a (see fig. 2). Courtesy of Seoul National University, Kyujanggak Institute for Korean Studies.

questioned them. Although they replied that the burial had already been removed, it was difficult to trust their words. Subsequently, we had Mun-ho demonstrate how he had carried out the illegal burial. [We found that] he had dug into the left half of the tomb and placed [his father's bones] under the plaster encasing the original coffin. This would have resulted in the shape of the character *p'um* 品 [in terms of the location of the original coffin and the illegal burial]. How under Heaven could this sort of illegal burial have happened? Even if they removed the illegal burial, if not Kim Mun-ho and Kim Kap-san, then who else violated the law concerning the violation of other people's graves? We humbly request the authorities to investigate and punish them in accordance with the law."

On account of this petition, I dispatched Kim Ch'ang-sŏng, a court clerk (*sŏgi*), to look into the matter in the presence of all concerned people. [It turned out that] everything was exactly as the plaintiffs claimed and there was nothing different. Therefore, the court clerk subsequently returned to the office with the report, and the case was to be judged when both parties would appear in court.

Meanwhile, on 1899.11.1 in the lunar calendar (12/3/1899), Ms. Ch'oe, a commoner woman residing in Hanch'i Subdistrict of Changyang District, submitted a complaint (*palgwal*). In the complaint, she said: "My husband Kim Kap-san was beaten by Kwangsan Kim clansmen of this district because of the illegal burial by his relative Kim Mun-ho. On 10.23 (11/25), he was carried and taken to the county seat because he was sued by the Kwangsan Kims. On the night of 10.24 (11/26), he eventually died. I sincerely ask you to find the grounds to avenge this resentful death."

After hearing this complaint, I was stunned by the reported death of Kim Kap-san. I, along with various inquest personnel, immediately departed the office around eight in the morning on the same day, arrived at the community funeral home (*sangyŏga*)[13] by the Sŏjin River, 3 *li* from the county office, where Kim Kap-san's corpse was located, and conducted the inquest.

Deposition (*ch'ugo*):
On 1899.11.1 (12/3/1899), Ms. Ch'oe, the wife of the deceased male Kim Kap-san, twenty-eight years in age.

Interrogation: "The examination of the body of your husband Kim Kap-san is about to begin. Truthfully state his age, whether there were any scars, and whether he had any illness when alive, as references for the examination."

Testimony: "My husband was thirty-three years in age. As for scars, there are two scars from previous moxibustion on the waist. He had no illness at all. Please make a note as such."

On the same day, Kim Ch'ŏn-gil, coroner's assistant (*ojak saryŏng*), thirty-three years in age: "Now, upon the examination of the body of the deceased male Kim Kap-san, if I do not record the correct measurements and subsequently such wrongful deed is disclosed later, I shall submit myself for punishment."

On the same day, Kim Ch'ŏl-gyu, head court clerk (*susŏgi*), sixty-three years in age; Song T'aeg-yŏng, court clerk, thirty-three years in age; Yi Tong-sik, herbalist, twenty-eight years in age; Song Hwan-ik, legal clerk, thirty-five years in age; and Pak Nae-ch'un, sheriff (*sun'gyo*), thirty-two years in age: "Now, upon the examination of the body of the deceased male Kim Kap-san, we, as the officers of this examination, shall carry out the examination with [relevant] people in attendance."

The body of the previously mentioned deceased male Kim Kap-san was inside the outer room of the community funeral home by the Sŏjin River. The four corners of the room were: 1 *ch'ŏk* 7 *ch'on* to the eastern wall; 16 *ch'ŏk* to the western wall; 1 *ch'ŏk* 5 *ch'on* to the southern wall; and 1 *ch'ŏk* 3 *ch'on* to the northern wall. The room was 8 *ch'ŏk* and 5 *ch'on* high. The table for the corpse was composed of three baseboards and two supporting logs. The head of the body was to the south; the feet were to the north. We could not conduct the examination of the body because the room was too dark. Thus, we moved the body outside to the yard. The four corners of the yard were: 29 *ch'ŏk* to the gate to the east; 16 *ch'ŏk* 4 *ch'on* to the road toward the Sŏjin River to the west; 31 *ch'ŏk* to the small waterway to the south; and 42 *ch'ŏk* 4 *ch'on* to the horse market to the north. These measurements were by the land-measuring ruler (*chi-ch'ŏk*).[14]

The dress was like this: one black silk hat, one Chinese cotton unlined summer jacket, one Chinese cotton jacket, one cotton jacket, one cotton short jacket, a pair of Chinese cotton arm warmers, a pair of padded arm warmers, two cotton underpants with bloodstains, one pair of Chinese cotton pants with bloodstains, one cotton short underpants soaked with blood, two Chinese cotton belts, a pair of Chinese cotton short ties with bloodstains, one pair of silk socks soaked with running blood.[15] I had the coroner's assistant Kim Ch'ŏn-gil undress the victim one article of clothing at a time and examine the body in its dry condition first. Then the entire body was further examined by turning it over and applying inquest instruments (*pŏmmul*) to it. The deceased person was a male in his thirty-second or thirty-third year of age. He lay on his back with his head to the south and feet to the north. His height was 4 *ch'ŏk* 8 *ch'on*, and the length of his hair was 2 *ch'ŏk* 5 *ch'on*. These measurements were by the official ruler (*kwan-ch'ŏk*).

The ventral side of the body [was as follows]: The crown of the head and left side of the head were yellowish white. The right side of the head was a little red. The fontanel, cranium, and forehead, temple on both sides, both eyebrows, [and] both corners of the eyebrows looked normal in color. Both eyelids were closed and the pupils looked normal. As for both cheeks, the right side was a little red while the left was yellowish white. Both the ears, ear flaps, ear lobes, ear holes, and the bridge and tip of the nose were yellowish white. Stench secretion was [issuing] out of the nostrils. The philtrum looked normal. The upper and lower lips were slightly open. The silver hairpin inserted [inside the mouth] did not change color.[16] The mouth was slightly open. One upper and bottom molar were missing. The tongue was by the lower teeth. Below the jaw was blue. The throat and esophagus looked normal. Both the depressed areas above the shoulder blades, shoulder blades, armpits, and upper arms were normal. Inside the elbows on both sides had traces from tying and they were consistently purple in color. Both wrists and palms were normal. The hands were clenched loosely in fists. The fingers and fingertips looked normal. Underneath the right fingernails was yellowish white, while the other side was blue. The chest, both breasts, between the chest and belly, the upper belly, both ribs, both sides under the arms, and the lower belly were all blue. The right side of the groin was yellowish white and its skin was scraped, while the left side was slightly red and swollen. The penis and scrotum looked normal. The lower inner part of the right thigh had one purple-black spot, which was also slightly swollen. Inside was shallow while the outer part was deeper. Its circumference was 9 *ch'on*, with 3 *ch'on* in length and 1 *ch'on* 7 *p'un* in width. The left thigh was normal. The right knee was slightly swollen and purple-black in color, while the left knee looked fine. The upper part of the right shin had an open wound with torn flesh. When pressed, blood came out. Its circumference was 3 *ch'on*. The lower part of the right shin was a spot with sunken bone and dry skin. Its circumference was 3 *ch'on* 5 *p'un* and purple-black in color. A little below that, there was one scar with broken skin and bruises. It was in a willow-leaf shape with a surrounding bloodstain. There was one wound with a sunken bone and purple-black in color on the left shin. The flesh was curled and contracted, and its circumference was 9 *ch'on* 5 *p'un*. On both ankles, there were bloody traces caused by tying, with widespread extravasation. Both tops of the feet, toes, and toenails were yellowish white.

The dorsal side of the body [was as follows]: The occipital and neck hairline were normal. The roots of the ears and back of the neck were slightly red. The backs of both shoulders and upper arms were slightly red. Both elbows had traces from tying, with widespread extravasation. The palms, backs of the hands, fingers, fingernails, and spine and area along the spine were all slightly red. Both back ribs and back sides under the arms were blue. The waist was blue and had two old moxibustion scars in the shape of a jujube leaf. The color of the buttocks was yellowish white. The silver hairpin inserted inside the anus did not change color. Both thighs were yellowish white. The crook of the right knee was purple but the left side was normal. The left calf was bruised all around. The right calf from the crook of the knee down to right above the ankle was bruised in purple color. There were bruises all over both ankles. The heels, soles, toes, toe tips, and underneath the toenails looked yellowish white. And both legs were straight.

After examining the body of the previously mentioned deceased male Kim Kap-san in accordance with legal procedure, we dressed him again and moved him back to the room. Then guards were placed to watch the site.

On the same day, the watchmen were: An Yu-jong, forty-six years in age; Kang Chae-yŏl, twenty-nine years in age; Han Ho-ban, fifty-four years in age; Song Sŏn-yŏl, forty-seven years in age; Yi Pyŏng-ch'ŏl, forty-two years in age: "Now, after examining the body of the previously mentioned deceased male Kim Kap-san, we moved the corpse back to the room. The corpse was preserved with ashes and secured with seals. We watchmen shall take charge of this site. If anything unusual takes place, we shall submit ourselves for punishment."

On the same day, Ms. Ch'oe, a close relative [i.e., wife] of the deceased and the complainant, a commoner woman and twenty-eight years in age.

Interrogation: "You have already reported the cause of your husband Kim Kap-san's death. For what reasons in origin and with whom and where did he have trouble? With what sort of tools and on which parts of his body was he beaten to death? And which month and day did he end up dying? Present the murder weapons if you collected them. Also, who is closely related to the deceased besides yourself? Answer truthfully."

Testimony: "My husband is originally a person from Hamgyŏng Province and has been temporarily living in Hanch'i Subdistrict of Changyang District for the last four or five years. Kim Mun-ho in the same subdistrict is his remote relative. I do not remember the exact year, but some time ago Mun-ho illegally buried his father at the apical ancestor's gravesite (*sisan*) of the Kwangsan Kim lineage. Subsequently, several hundred members of the same Kwangsan Kim lineage gathered to catch my husband and all the lineage members of my husband as soon as they encountered them on 10.13 (11/15). Although all lineage members near and far fled, Kim Mun-ho was caught first. My husband would naturally have fled, but he thought he could not run away because he was serving as the subdistrict administrator (*chonwi*). Thus, he was caught and taken to the house of Kim Chung-ok, a senior in his lineage. On the next day after the night [he was caught], I heard that the Kwangsan Kims had taken him to their apical ancestor's tomb and repeatedly applied a torture of twisting his legs (*roehyŏng*) by inserting something like wooden sticks between bound legs. Only after deep nightfall did they return and take him to the village study hall (*sŏjae*). For two days, staying there, they again twisted his legs. I did not witness all the things that happened with my own eyes, but my grudge cut right to the bone when I learned that. I would have risked my life to run there and save him. But all the Kwangsan Kim people stayed at my home and forced me to feed them, and so I could not go see him. Meanwhile, the Kwangsan Kims submitted a petition about this conflict over the gravesite (*sansong*) to the authorities, and the court clerk showed up in order to investigate the event and make a drawing of the disputed site on 10.19 (11/21). The Kwangsan Kims again bound my husband and took him to the graveyard and applied the torture of twisting legs again. After that, they took him to a roadside tavern on Swae Pass. My husband could not move his body because of the cruel torture. After spending a night there, his relatives carried him to the county administrative seat in order to attend the hearing (*songbyŏn*). The day before his travel to the county seat, when I met him quietly, he left his dying wish, saying, 'If I do not die, that is it. But if I die, please seek vengeance upon Kim P'yŏng-il for my death.' After having gone through cruel torture multiple times, he finally died on 10.24 (11/26). His relative Kim Mun-ho, who was at the county seat, sent the message of his death. Regardless of Heaven and Earth, I hurried and ran all night to get there, and filed a complaint. In his last words, he indicated Kim P'yŏng-il as the culprit for his death, [and] I beg [the court] to avenge his unfair death. As for the murder weapons, I could not collect them because I was not there [when he was tortured]. As for other close relatives of the deceased, there are older and younger brothers of his father and his father's cousin."

On the same day, Kim Kyŏng-hŭi, a close relative of the deceased, thirty years in age.

Interrogation: "You, together with Ms. Ch'oe, filed a complaint concerning the death of your older cousin Kap-san. State with whom and for what reasons he had trouble from the beginning, by whom and with what he was beaten, from what injuries he died, and the date of the first beating and the date of his death."

Testimony: "I reside in Changdong Subdistrict of Hŭpkok Lesser County. I learned of the death of my older cousin Kap-san from my adopted younger brother (*suyangje*) Pak Yun-sŏk on 10.29 (12/1).[17] I immediately ran to the county seat and found that my older cousin Kap-san was indeed dead. I asked Ms. Ch'oe, my older cousin's wife, what had happened to him, and she replied that Kap-san's relative Mun-ho had carried out an illegal burial at the apical ancestor's gravesite of the Kwangsan Kims located at Swae Pass. From wherever the Kwangsan Kims learned that, they [then] arrested and bound her husband and Mun-ho to dig up and remove the illegal burial. Then they applied torture by twisting their legs numerous times, and Kap-san consequently died of it. When her husband was still alive, he spoke his last words to her, saying: 'If I do not die, that is it. But if I die, how can I list so many members of the Kwangsan Kims? Avenge my death by [killing] Kim P'yŏng-il.' I, in my conscience as the younger cousin of Kap-san, could not overcome my resentment and filed a complaint together with his wife. Please punish Kim P'yŏng-il in accordance with the law to avenge his death. Because I live separately away from him, I do not know the details about where he was beaten, whereabouts of murder weapons, or the date of his death."

On the same day, Yi Kyŏng-ch'an, district administrator, fifty-one years in age.

Interrogation: "This criminal case involving the deceased Kim Kap-san took place in your village. Your job is to collect and report all matters under your jurisdiction, regardless of whether they are big or small. In the complaint submitted by Ms. Ch'oe, the close relative of the deceased, the Kwangsan Kims' causing of trouble lasted for four or five days, and their torturing of Kap-san and so forth was done five or six times. Why did you not go right away to stop it, and how come did you not make a report about it? Considering the entire circumstances in which you [did not] carry out your responsibilities, it must be that you have either received favor from or harbor resentment against one of these [two lineages of the] Kims. What sort of hidden sentiment do you have [toward either lineage of Kims]? Truthfully testify what you heard in terms of what sort of terrible things happened, without hiding anything."

Testimony: "I am an administrator of this mountainous district, and my primary responsibilities are to collect and submit taxes and report on various matters. The previous taxes had been taken care of while the new taxes do not need to be distributed yet. Taking advantage of this lax season, I went to Kosŏng to trade salt on 10.20 (11/22) and returned home on 10.23 (11/25). Then I heard that both Kims were in the county seat for the hearing of the dispute over the gravesite. Because I was not there at the site of the incident as it took place, how could I hear or see what had happened at all? It is difficult to avoid the charge that I was away from my duty, but I have no idea about the cause of the incident."

On the same day, Kim Chung-ok, village headman, sixty-seven years in age.

Interrogation: "This criminal case involving the deceased Kim Kap-san took place in your village. As the village headman, you should have immediately run to report this. In addition, you are Kap-san's relative at some remove, and [so] have [that] much more reason to come forward to report the incident to the authorities. How come you were leisurely watching the event and began to show up only after your name was mentioned in the testimony as a result of the incident? There must be reasons. You must know in detail the origins and the hidden causes of the incident and who caused the troubles. The criminal court is extremely solemn. Testify truthfully."

Testimony: "I am a ten *ch'on* relative of Kim Kap-san.[18] The reason I did not report this murder to the authorities was that there were relatives closer to the victim in their blood relations, and thus I just followed the precedents. Because my relative Kim Mun-ho had placed an illegal burial of his father at the apical ancestor's gravesite of the Kwangsan Kim lineage located at the Swae Pass, several hundred members of the Kwangsan Kims gathered at Hanch'i Subdistrict on 10.13 (11/15). They first caught Kim Mun-ho and Kap-san, followed by myself and Yŏ-su, who is a junior successor of our lineage. They tied us up and applied torture. On 10.14 (11/16), after a night, they bound us all and took us to the top of their lineage graveyard and again arbitrarily tortured us. While we were going through such trouble, the Kwangsan Kims filed a litigation about this dispute over the gravesite with the county authorities. On 10.18 (11/20), a court clerk arrived to investigate the incident and also to make a drawing of the site. On 10.19 (11/21), after he climbed to the graveyard and finished drawing the site, the Kwangsan Kims again tortured Mun-ho and

Kap-san by twisting their legs. After dusk, they took them to the study hall in my village. Mun-ho and Kap-san were scheduled to go to the county seat together with the Kwangsan Kims to attend the hearing, but they could not move at all because of the terrible torture they had received. On account of the Kwangsan Kims' order, I made arrangements to carry them there and I also followed them. Before the hearing, Kap-san died, on the night of 10.24 (11/26). I sent a message of his death to Kap-san's home, and Kap-san's wife Ms. Ch'oe and his cousin Kyŏng-hŭi came and filed a complaint. In the midst of being tortured, this old man was so fearful and stunned, and thus does not know who the leaders were or who among the Kwangsan Kims applied the torture. When the Kwangsan Kims first came to my house because of Mun-ho's illegal burial, the expenses for food incurred at the time were 37 *yang*. The number of food tables to feed several hundred people of the Kwangsan Kims for eight to nine days was 6,000. The Kwangsan Kims demanded that we cough up some 780 *yang* for other miscellaneous expenses. We could not overcome their threat that we should submit the money right away, and all lineage members close by prepared for it. Subsequently, we are on the verge of losing our homes and having to wander. How resentful it is!"

On the same day, Chŏng Tong-baek, a close neighbor, forty-three years in age.
Interrogation: "As a person living in a nearby village, you are the only one closely involved in this criminal case of Kim Kap-san besides the plaintiff and the accused. Since you directed everything from the beginning to the end, and all matters front and back, who else could be the official witness (*kongjŭng*) in this case if not you? How was Kim Kap-san connected to this incident in the beginning? How did he eventually die? There must be reasons for this. Testify truthfully what you heard and saw during this incident."
Testimony: "The distance of my village from Hanch'i Subdistrict, where Kim Kap-san lived, is about 5 *li*. I stopped over in Hanch'i Subdistrict on my way to T'ongch'ŏn on 10.15 (11/17). Kim Mun-ho of that subdistrict had plotted together with his relative Kap-san and secretly buried his father at the apical ancestor's gravesite of the Kwangsan Kims located on top of Swae Pass. Because of that, several hundred Kwangsan Kims gathered in said subdistrict and arrested Kim Mun-ho in order to force him to dig up and remove his father's bones. At the time, all of Mun-ho's relatives got scared and fled in all directions. Arresting only Mun-ho and Kap-san, the Kwangsan Kims took them to the graveyard and caused the entire trouble, which was extremely severe and depraved. When the Kwangsan Kims asked me to arrange food

tables [for their people], I, as a person living nearby, could not ignore their request. Therefore, I busily took care of this from 10.15 to 10.20 (11/22). As a result, I did not witness how Kim Mun-ho and Kim Kap-san were tortured. I only heard people saying that the Kwangsan Kims conducted illegal torture while I was busily coming and going. Kim Chung-ok, village headman of said subdistrict, was present there and witnessed the whole scene."

On the same day, Kim Tŏg-wŏn, a close neighbor, fifty-six years in age.

Interrogation: "Now, the criminal case involving the deceased Kim Kap-san originated from Kim Mun-ho's illegal burial. And, according to Ms. Yu's testimony, Kim Mun-ho's illegal burial in turn was revealed by that woman Yu, who was furtively instigated to do so by you. As for provoking this terrible incident, you are the one, and who else could it be? As Mun-ho's relative, it would have been appropriate for you to encourage good deeds while hiding evil ones. Yet you invoked and stirred a secretive matter [to be exposed] and caused it to turn into a criminal matter. What sort of hidden resentment do you have [against Mun-ho to cause this]? Do not hide anything under this deposition. You also know in detail all the troubles wrought by the Kwangsan Kims. Say all that truthfully."

Testimony: "Around the seventh month last year, Pak Tŏg-yun from Hamgyŏng Province, but living in Chik Village, invited Ms. Yu to this county to treat his brother's illness. That woman acted as a shaman (munyŏ) and also called herself a geomancer (chigwan). In the same month, she was patronized by my relative Mun-ho living in Hanch'i Subdistrict, and moved there. I heard that Mun-ho forcefully sold off a calf to Ms. Yu, but she cut the calf's bridle and returned that calf to him because it was in nature a needy baby that required its mother's care. On 10.13 (11/15), the Kwangsan Kims arrested Kap-san first, under the excuse that my relative Mun-ho had placed a secret burial at their apical ancestor's gravesite. When they came to me and asked about the matter, I pretended I did not know anything. Then they said that they had already dispatched people to get that woman geomancer from Koho [i.e., Ms. Yu] because they could get to the bottom of the matter only after bringing her over. They also said that I should wait for her arrival to defend myself. In such a way, they forced me to go with them. Subsequently, I followed them and went to the study hall in Hanch'i Subdistrict. On the next day, after spending a night there, the woman geomancer did arrive. The Kwangsan Kims tied Mun-ho, Kap-san, and my son Yŏ-su and drove them up to the graveyard. Then I heard that they illegally tortured them by twisting their legs. I heard that all the relatives of Mun-ho, regardless of whether they were remote or close, would be tortured when caught. Therefore, I just stayed in the study hall, but then fled because I was afraid of being caught. Thus, I do not know details of disturbances wrought by the Kwangsan Kims on the mountaintop. I first learned of the death of Kap-san because a relative who went to the county seat sent a message. In the testimony of Ms. Yu, the story that I furtively instigated her to reveal the matter of illegal burial is not true. Now, I have thought about it and know why she told such a lie and made a false charge. In the past, I loaned her 1 *yang* of cash, but she extended the loan and did not pay it back. So, I dunned her to pay back 1 *yang* 2 *chŏn* 4 *p'un*, including both principal and interest, in the tenth month of last year. She must have harbored her resentment over this. Please firmly interrogate her to differentiate the truth from lies. I have nothing further to say."

On the same day, Kim Mun-ho, an eyewitness (*kanjŭng*) as well as an involved witness (*kallyŏn*), forty-five years in age.

Interrogation: "In the complaint filed by Ms. Ch'oe, Kim Kap-san died after he was beaten by the Kwangsan Kims and also was tortured numerous times because of your illegal burial at the lineage cemetery of the Kwangsan Kims. The direct cause of Kap-san's untimely death is related to the illegal torture of twisting legs applied by the Kwangsan Kims, but the seed of the disaster lies in your illegal burial. Kap-san's unfair death was because of you— if not, then who else? Because you were also gruelingly tortured at the same time, you must know the leading figures and all other assailants among the Kwangsan Kims, the number of tortures applied, and the tools they used for torture. You went to the county seat together with Kap-san and also spent a few days in the same place. Therefore, you must have had some conversations with Kap-san about how he felt. State straightforwardly what had happened from the beginning to the end without hiding a bit."

Testimony: "I am an eleven *ch'on* relative of the deceased Kim Kap-san and I am in the rank of his uncle. In the second month of last year, the so-called enlightened woman (*yŏ myŏngin*) residing in Koho in T'ongch'ŏn came to Pak Tŏg-yong's house in Chik Village to treat illness in that family.[19] Everyone from near and far acknowledged and recommended her because she had three volumes of books by Yuan Tiangang [?–627][20] and had mastered all worldly matters. Therefore, I also invited her over to find an auspicious gravesite. That woman said to me, 'It would be good to place a tomb on the gravesite of the apical ancestor of the Kwangsan Kims located at Swae Pass, because that is an auspicious site.' I was surprised to hear that and asked her, 'How could I place a tomb at another's lineage cemetery?' That woman then replied, 'I would use my divine power to gather and infuse illuminating energy into the tomb after you dig a hole on the side mound of the Kims' tomb and bury [your father's bones there].' As I was a fool who was obsessed with this mystical talk, I indeed buried my father on the left side of the Kims' tomb in the fifth month of last year. That same woman asked me to pay back the money I had borrowed from her. So I gave her a big calf, whose price was set at 100 *yang*. Then, after only a few days, she came to return the calf, but I did not allow it and let the matter go like that. Alas! That woman, with ill intention, spread the word about my illegal burial at the Kwangsan Kims' tomb all over the world, and the rumor came to be all around. Kim Chung-ok, my five *ch'on* relative, came to learn this and begged me, saying, 'Why on earth did you illegally bury your father at another's gravesite?! If this is true, it will cause big trouble. Dig and move it immediately.' Therefore, in the early tenth month of this year I removed the tomb to our lineage cemetery.

"On 10.13 (11/15), the Kwangsan Kims paid 200 *yang* of money to that enlightened woman and led her to the Kwangsan Kims' cemetery. Three to four hundred of the Kwangsan Kims arrested Kap-san and myself and took us to the graveyard to be questioned face to face with that enlightened woman. From 10.14 (11/16) to 10.19 (11/21), they tortured us daily by twisting our legs. At the time of torture, they tied our knees first and then tied our ankles. They inserted two oak sticks between the shins. One or two people took turns and pressed [the sticks], sometimes with their hands and sometimes with their feet. Although I was only half conscious under such cruel torture, Kim P'yŏng-il among all those Kwangsan Kims led all his relatives and said, 'All descendants of this apical ancestor, regardless of how many there are, take turns and punish them. We shall break the legs of people like this who carried out an illegal burial.' I indeed heard this and saw him saying this. The Kwangsan Kims asked me where my father's corpse was and demanded to see it. Being unable to overcome fear, I had to dig up the new grave and show them my father's corpse. They still tortured me like before, not to mention that there is no way to appease my resentment over being forced to dig up my father's grave. Kim Kap-san had to meet such a horrible fate because he had helped me as a hired laborer at the time of my illegal burial. There is nothing further to say about what I had done.

"On 10.22 (11/24), when the court clerk from the county office investigated the matter, the Kwangsan Kims wanted to go face to face at the court and had my relatives carry Kap-san and myself. On 10.23 (11/25) we arrived in the county seat, but before the hearing, on the night of 10.24 (11/26), Kap-san told me, saying, 'As the subdistrict administrator, public funds that I have been dealing with for each individual are not small. I recorded [them] here and give it to you, so that you can collect them on the basis of this list. I do not think I can recuperate. I was tortured because of Kim P'yŏng-il, while it is the enlightened woman who is the root source of all this resentful matter. You shall avenge my death.' Then he passed away. Please punish the designated culprits in accordance with the law to avenge the death of Kap-san and settle my grudge over being tortured."

On the same day, Ms. Yu, a related and involved witness (saryŏn kallyŏn), forty-six years in age.[21]

Interrogation: "This criminal case involving the deceased Kim Kap-san originated from Kim Mun-ho's illegal burial at the Kwangsan Kims' lineage cemetery. All involved witnesses have testified that it was you who disseminated the story of an illegal burial. From somewhere you learned of Mun-ho's illegal burial and Kap-san's assistance in it and caused disturbances among people. You sowed the seeds of the disaster; if not you, then who else? Why did you spread the word? How did the Kwangsan Kims start the incident, and to whom among the Kwangsan Kims did you spread the word? Tell the truth from the beginning to the end without hiding anything, so that you can avoid a heavy punishment."

Testimony: "I am originally from Seoul, but came to live in Koho, T'ongch'ŏn. I am a diviner and I was invited to treat an illness by Pak Tae-gyŏng in Chik Village, Changyang District under this county's jurisdiction, in the eighth month of last year. Maybe because of Tae-gyŏng's recommendation, Kim Mun-ho, living in a nearby village in Hanch'i Subdistrict, also invited me over. He said to me, 'I have a son at this late age. I'd like to find a godmother (suyangmo).' In such a way he wanted me to stay, so I agreed [to be his son's godmother] and was there several days. In the meantime, he wanted to show me his lineage cemetery and said, 'The weather is mild. How about going together to take a look at our cemetery?' In response, I said, 'I am a woman and what sort of capability to discern a gravesite would I have?' Kim Tŏg-wŏn, a neighbor and Mun-ho's relative, happened to come by Mun-ho's house. Because we had met the other day, he called me 'a sister-in-law' and whispered in my ear while poking my waist, saying, 'You will earn double fame if you point out an empty grave when you go take a look at the cemetery.'

Subsequently I was able to learn from him the story about an empty tomb. I am a fool, so I talked about an empty tomb on the basis of Tŏg-wŏn's information when I went to see the cemetery with Kim Mun-ho and Kim Kap-san. Mun-ho only smiled then, but on our way down from the cemetery, Mun-ho said to me, 'You know exactly about the empty tomb in our cemetery. How can I deceive you about this? Indeed that tomb is empty, and the body was buried at the gravesite of the apical ancestor of the Kwangsan Kims.' So I asked, 'How did you do the illegal burial?' He answered, 'I just made a burial.' I asked, 'Where is the Kwangsan Kims' cemetery? And in which spot in the cemetery did you bury your father?' He said, 'The Kwangsan Kims' burial ground is located in the Umyŏn area on top of Swae Pass. I dug a hole on the left side of the Kims' tomb and placed my father [there] like a couple's burial.'

"On my way back to T'ongch'ŏn several days later, I arrived at the tavern on top of Swae Pass, where I happened to meet Mr. Yi, whose given name I do not know. He was an itinerant merchant living in the Blue Dragon Temple in Ch'ungch'ŏng Province. Because of rain, I stopped there a bit and then set off on my journey. Mr. Yi followed me and suddenly came up to me and asked, 'Whose grave is that?' So I answered, 'That is the tomb of the apical ancestor of the Kwangsan Kims.' As we chatted together a bit while traveling together, I leaked the story of an illegal burial by a person from Hanch'i Subdistrict at that apical ancestor's tomb. After that, we parted and I returned home.

"In the early tenth month of this year, two men of the Kwangsan Kims, allegedly from Sŏgu Subdistrict, Sadong District in Hoeyang, visited my home and requested me to come with them to treat an illness. So I followed them without thinking anything [of it]. On the way, they revealed their identity and said that they were men from Changyang District and took me to Pukch'angha Subdistrict in Changyang. There were several hundred Kwangsan Kims. They put me on an open sedan chair and right away went to the gravesite of their apical ancestor on top of Swae Pass. The Kims had already arrested and brought Kim Mun-ho and Kim Kap-san there. They coerced me and said, 'You as a geomancer provoked Mun-ho to place an illegal burial on the side of our ancestor's grave. People like you shall be badly punished on the spot.' I felt so afraid and, facing Mun-ho, asked, 'When did I have you carry out an illegal burial?' Then Mun-ho said, 'This is a face-to-face interrogation involving all three parties of the accused, plaintiff, and witness. It is fine for you to confess what I had told you about the illegal burial last time.' After I told them everything, I wished to go home. Then the Kwangsan Kims offered an ox to me and seven Kwangsan Kim members escorted me home. I do not know what sort of disturbances the Kwangsan Kims stirred up after that. I fully uphold your order and have testified everything that I know; please resolve the matter fairly."

On the same day, involved witnesses are: Kim Ch'ae-wŏn, sixty years in age; Kim Chŏng-hyŏn, sixty-five years in age; and Kim Yun-sŏp, forty-one years in age.

Interrogation: "When you took Kim Kap-san and Kim Mun-ho for a face-to-face interrogation about the gravesite conflict, among the many lineage members [there], how come you were chosen to lead the process? Where did you hear about Kim Mun-ho's illegal burial of his father? If you had reported what you heard to the authorities, it would have been possible to take care of the matter on the basis of the law. How come you privately applied the torture of twisting legs, which led to the death of Kap-san within 'the period of responsibility for crimes' (kohan)?[22] If it were not for your vicious crime, how could this inquest find injuries all over the body? The criminal court is extremely solemn, and a person's life is absolutely important. Who is the leader and who are the followers among you? What tools did you use for torture? Tell truthfully the circumstances of the crime without hiding at all for the sake of this court."

Testimony [of Kim Ch'ae-wŏn]: "The grave of our apical ancestor, the honorable former magistrate of Changyŏn Prefecture, is located on the slope of the Hanch'i Mountain in this district. All lineage members went up to the gravesite on 10.3 (11/5) to offer the anniversary ancestor ritual (sije). Mr. Yi, an itinerant merchant from Ch'ungch'ŏng Province whose given name was unknown, came up the cemetery to beg food and said, 'I earlier heard from the so-called female geomancer from Koho, T'ongch'ŏn, who is the wife of Yu Sŏnjŏn,[23] that someone had placed an illegal burial in this cemetery.' We were very surprised to hear that and had to investigate it. Therefore, after sharing ritual food, we dispatched people to get her [i.e., Ms. Yu] and asked her what she knew. She answered that Kim Mun-ho residing in Hanch'i, together with Kim Kap-san and Kim P'yŏng-san, illegally buried his father on the side of the Kwangsan Kims' apical ancestor's tomb. After we had her put her handprint [on her confession paper] as proof, she went back home to attend to her business. Meanwhile, the chief of the lineage sent out a circular to our lineage members. By 10.13 (11/15), nearly three hundred lineage members came to gather for a meeting. All went to Hanch'i Subdistrict and arrested Kim Mun-ho first, followed by Kim Kap-san. The next morning, we took those two to the cemetery and interrogated them as to where they had placed the illegal burial. Mun-ho testified as though he had not carried out an illegal burial, and took out his jackknife and slashed his own chest. Since blood soaked his jacket, we just tied them, worrying if something serious might happen. To find out the location of the illegal burial, we tied them and applied torture. After Mun-ho indicated the side of our apical ancestor's tomb as the illegal burial site, we had him dig to prove it. Then Mun-ho dug up the site, but there was only an empty cavity because he had already removed the burial. He said that he had already removed his father to another place on 10.5 (11/7). We could not trust him, so the next day on 10.15 (11/17) we had him show us his father's corpse to prove his words. We went to the new gravesite together and had him demolish the mound to see the corpse. Indeed, there was no [need to] worry [about his telling us a lie], and thus we traveled at night and returned to the study hall in Hanch'i. After spending the night there, lineage members discussed the matter of submitting a petition and selected Kim I-hyŏn and Kim Yun-sŏp to go to the county seat. Other members tied and took Kim Mun-ho and Kim Kap-san to the tavern at Swae Pass and waited for the decision from the authorities. On 10.19 (11/21), a court clerk arrived to investigate. He climbed to the gravesite first; we tied Mun-ho and Kap-san and took them there. After the clerk investigated the site, he questioned both parties and drew the site. We could not overcome our bitter anger against them; we again tortured Mun-ho and Kap-san by twisting their legs. The clerk made every effort to prohibit us from torturing them, as [he said] it should be resolved by law. However, at that point all those descendants were so upset as a result of this unresolvable grudge that they strove to be first to torture them. In this situation, who could have prohibited it; who would be pointed out as the leader, and who did it first and last? After dusk, we dragged them to the tavern at Swae Pass and spent the night there. The clerk returned to the county seat the next day, and we, as well as Mun-ho and Kap-san, also needed to go to the county seat to attend the hearing. But because Mun-ho and Kap-san could not move as a result of the punishment they had received, we had their relatives carry them to the county seat. We also went to the county seat on 10.23 (11/25) to attend the hearing. Before the hearing, however, Kap-san died on the night of 10.24 (11/26). From the beginning, we punished them out of the same heart. How could we be the leaders and the first actors? As for the tools we used, they were oak sticks."

[Testimony of] Kim Chŏng-hyŏn and Kim Yun-sŏp: "We came to the county seat because our branch of the lineage dispatched us [as their representatives]. At the same time, we are also here as the original petitioners. There is nothing different from Kim Ch'ae-wŏn's testimony in terms of the entire circumstances."

On the same day, Kim Pyŏng-nyŏl, the principal offender, eighty-two years in age.

Interrogation: "In the complaint submitted by Ms. Ch'oe, the wife of the deceased Kim Kap-san, she reported that her husband Kap-san was beaten to death by the Kwangsan Kims of Changyang District. On what month and day and for what reasons did you cause the disturbance? What did you use to beat him? Who was the leader when the melee took place? Who first hit him and who was assisting? And who was present? You as the lineage chief (*munjang*) must know all of this. Tell truthfully the causes of the incident and how it ended without hiding anything."

Testimony: "How can I say that I do not know the entire incident as the lineage chief? However, I am bent with the weight of the years and quite forgetful, so I cannot remember everything. In the beginning, when [lineage members] mentioned that they wanted to censure the person who had placed an illegal burial at our cemetery in Hanch'i as an entire lineage matter, I held them back and advised that we should solve the problem by law and should not hurt people. Yet things have gotten this way and a person is dead. I have nothing more to say."

On the same day, Ms. Ch'oe, the close relative [i.e., wife] of the deceased, age.[24]

Second Interrogation: *After repeating Ms. Ch'oe's testimony concerning her husband's last words, the interrogator continues*: "Designating an enemy for revenge relates to the life and death [of the accused]. This was not usual talk. [Kap-san's] mind was greatly agitated and he had no need to shut his mouth and stop talking. There were close relatives everywhere, and there must have people who heard and spread his words. Point out who else heard your husband's last words, and who else heard them secondhand. From when to when was your husband retained and tortured by the Kwangsan Kims? And how many times was he tortured on each occasion? . . ." *Here the interrogator repeats Kim Mun-ho's testimony about Kap-san's last words indicating both Kim P'yŏng-il and Ms. Yu antagonists, and asks Ms. Ch'oe*: "Now, how come the designated antagonist is different from [what you said]? Tell the truth and do not cause confusion in this court."

Testimony: "I already said everything in my mind in the last testimony.

Because I learned from others that my husband was tortured, I do not know how many times and how many days he was under torture. There was no one [besides me] who heard my husband's last words in which he pointed out Kim P'yŏng-il as the antagonist. That enlightened woman is that female geomancer. It is not just Kim Mun-ho who knew [that she was my husband's antagonist]. When my husband was alive, he in fact also told me that she became his antagonist. Please avenge my husband's death right away on both Kim P'yŏng-il and the female geomancer to settle the score."

On the same day, Kim Kyŏng-hŭi, a close relative of the deceased, age.

Second Interrogation: *The interrogator questions which one—Kim P'yŏng-il or Ms. Yu—is the victim's antagonist, referring to the differing testimonies by Kim Mun-ho and Ms. Ch'oe.*

Testimony: "There is no doubt that my cousin Kap-san left his last wish to his wife on his deathbed, in which he indicated Kim P'yŏng-il as his antagonist. As for that enlightened woman, she should be also punished."

On the same day, Chŏng Tong-baek, a close neighbor, age.

Second Interrogation: "You have already testified that, out of neighborly compassion, you had made arrangements of food for the Kwangsan Kims. In such a case, you must know all the actions taken by the Kwangsan Kims. Testify again as to what you saw in terms of the root cause of Kim Kap-san's death and the leading culprits among the Kwangsan Kims."

Testimony: "When I stopped over in Hanch'i Subdistrict on my way to T'ongch'ŏn to take care of some business, several hundred of the Kwangsan Kims had gathered there because of Kim Mun-ho's illegal burial at their apical ancestor's tomb and had confined Kim Mun-ho and Kim Kap-san in the study hall. Kim Chung-ok, a relative of Kim Mun-ho, begged me, saying, 'Our lineage will have to provide food for these hundreds of Kwangsan Kims gathered here. But there is no one to be in charge. Please, out of neighborly compassion, make arrangements to supply food.' So I took his request and carried out my job. I was busily running around to suddenly feed several hundred people day and night. Thus, I did not get to know the root cause of Kap-san's death and the leaders and followers among the Kwangsan Kims."

On the same day, Kim Tŏg-wŏn, a close relative, age.

Second Interrogation: "According to the first and second testimonies by Ms. Yu, a related witness, you are the one who poked her waist and whispered into her ear the story of Kim Mun-ho's illegal burial of his father on the side of the Kwangsan Kims' apical ancestor's tomb. Yet you spoke as though there had been no such thing. What an evil practice is your deceitful testimony! Moreover, as a relative of Kap-san and living in the same subdistrict, it was natural that you go to save him when he had difficulty and assist him if he had some problems. Does it make sense that you got terrified and fled rather than going to see them when you heard that your relatives Mun-ho and Kap-san, as well as your son Yŏ-su, had been caught and tortured? Considering what you have done, you are extremely sly and deceitful. In this solemn court, do not make excuses like before, but state truthfully whether you really poked Ms. Yu's waist and whispered in her ear and how you fled in the middle of the incident."

Testimony: "That woman Yu accused me of poking her waist and whispering in her ear about Kim Mun-ho's father's tomb being empty. But she must have said this in order to take revenge [because of] her small grudge against me. Even if I die under penal beating, there was nothing like that at all. I did flee for a while out of fear when the Kwangsan Kims caught Mun-ho, Kap-san, and my son."

On the same day, Kim Mun-ho, an eyewitness and an involved witness, age.

Second Interrogation: *After repeating Kim Mun-ho's previous testimony, the interrogator continues*: "According to that so-called enlightened woman's second testimony, when the Kwangsan Kims arrested and interrogated Mun-ho's wife, she confessed that it was geomancer Pak who had divined the site when Mun-ho placed an illegal burial at the Kwangsan Kims' cemetery. As for that woman's spreading the word, the story of the empty tomb in Mun-ho's cemetery first came from Kim Tŏg-wŏn. Also [she heard about it] from Kim Kap-san's aunt. She learned of Mun-ho's burying his father at the Kwangsan Kims' cemetery when she was taking a look at Kim Mun-ho's cemetery at his request. When your testimony is compared to Ms. Yu's testimonies, how come they do not fit together and are so different? . . . Now, the death of Kap-san originated solely from this illegal burial at the Kwangsan Kims' cemetery. Only after your and Ms. Yu's testimonies become consistent can a judgment be made. How wicked is it that after committing a crime punishable by death, you are confusing the court by telling lies! Both Kap-san and you were tortured at the same time, but you are alive while Kap-san is dead. There must be reasons why the Kwangsan Kims were generous to you. There must be reasons why Kap-san came to die. You should testify everything one by one without hiding anything."

Testimony: "Around the tenth month in the year of *chŏngyu* (1897), Kap-san and I indeed placed an illegal burial on the side of the gravesite of the Kwang-san Kims' apical ancestor. It was geomancer Pak Kun-hae from Kansŏng who divined the spot. The reason I testified initially that Ms. Yu divined the spot for the illegal burial was because I was in confusion and terror because of having been severely tortured and subsequently spoke nonsense. As a host and a guest, I felt close to Ms. Yu, and we have also known [each other] for a while. So I told her about the illegal burial without thinking much. How could I have known this would lead to the disaster?! When I mentioned the matter of illegal burial to Ms. Yu sometime after the fourth month of last year, she mentioned that with her divine power she would gather and infuse illuminating energy into it, but she eventually did not do it. When Kap-san and I were arrested by the Kwangsan Kims, those Kims told Kap-san, 'You also committed a crime because you were of one mind [with Mun-ho and] helped out when Mun-ho buried his father illegally. We also heard that you were planning to move your grandfather's and grandmother's tombs from Hamgyŏng Province here. You must have wanted to secretly bury them in our cemetery in the same way. Tell the truth.' Yet, even to my knowledge, there was no such thing. And how much could Kap-san say about a matter that did not exist? So he said there was no such thing. Then the Kwangsan Kims were convinced that Kap-san was telling a lie and applied harsher torture, leading to eventual death. How could the Kwangsan Kims be more generous to me? I do not know about those stories that Ms. Yu testified, that it was Kim Tŏg-wŏn who first mentioned the illegal burial and an empty tomb and that she also heard that from Kim Kap-san's aunt. I indeed revealed that to Ms. Yu and there is nothing more to say, even if I die at this court."

On the same day, Ms. Yu, a related and involved witness, age.

Second Interrogation: *After repeating Kim Mun-ho's first testimony, the interrogator continues:* "Now, Mun-ho's initial illegal burial [of his father] was because of you. Spreading the story of his illegal burials also originated with you. It is possible to try to harm Mun-ho because of your personal grudge against him. But you mixed up and implicated Kap-san, who only helped Mun-ho, as a culprit of illegal burial. Now your directing of Mun-ho's illegal burial has been disclosed. Even if you have one hundred mouths, how can you avoid the charge? . . . If not for you, would Kap-san have [suffered] an untimely death? When you spread the word of illegal burial, whom among the Kwangsan Kims did it reach first? Who listened to this first? When you had a face-to-face interrogation with Kim Kap-san, you must have seen the scene of torture. Who were the leaders and followers? Now the circumstances of your involvement have been revealed. How can you testify like before? The court is solemn; tell the truth without prevaricating like before, so that there is no confusion in this investigation."

Testimony: "As for the matter of directing Mun-ho to place an illegal burial at the Kwangsan Kims' cemetery, Mun-ho's wife had already revealed to the Kwangsan Kims that it was the making of a certain passing geomancer, Mr. Pak, whose given name was unknown. . . . I heard [about the empty grave] when Kim Tŏg-wŏn poked my waist and told me, and also when I chatted with Kim Kap-san's aunt. Yet I did not know the site of the illegal burial. I later heard [where the site was] when Mun-ho spontaneously revealed that he had dug a hole at the side of the Kwangsan Kims' grave and buried [his father] illegally. Now, in this deposition, I was pointed out as the one who caused the illegal burial. Even if I die from this investigation, I did not do it. Maybe because I spread the word about the illegal burial, [Mun-ho] was resentful and made a false charge. I was rash to disclose the story of illegal burial, but it was not intentional. Around the twelfth month of last year, I went to collect the debt of 25 *yang* from Mun-ho's relative Chung-ok. But Chung-ok showed no intention of paying it back. Because I was small-minded, I could not take patience as a virtue, but was upset that he had lost his loyalty and betrayed me. So I muttered to myself that Kim Chung-ok's entire lineage would be in big trouble if I opened my mouth. Then, I told the woman accompanying me [i.e., Ms. Chang from Kaesŏng, her adopted older sister] everything about Mun-ho's illegal burial. Mr. Yi, an itinerant merchant from Ch'ungch'ŏng Province who happened to be passing by, overheard this conversation and in turn transmitted the story to the Kwangsan Kims. I deeply regret that I did not watch my mouth. I did not witness if Kim Mun-ho and Kim-Kap-san were tortured."

On the same day, Kim Ch'ae-wŏn, an accomplice (*kanbŏm*), age.[25]

Second Interrogation: "On account of the illegal burial at your lineage cemetery, you went to discuss it with the lineage chief, worked on the circular (*t'ongmun*), and directed the lineage gathering. Present the circular now. Kim Kap-san's death was caused by torture by your lineage members. From when to when and how many times did you torture him? You must have hit and kicked him during the torture. Which part of the body did you hit and kick and how many times? State every detail. It was Kim Mun-ho who carried out the illegal burial. But you arbitrarily arrested Kim Kap-san and punished him as though you were the authorities in charge. For what crimes did you punish him? On what matters did he commit a crime? You drove him to his death. Who else is responsible for Kap-san's death, if not you? Although the senior members may have displayed initial leadership, you were actually in charge of the incident. Speak straightforwardly now."

Testimony: "The illegal burial [carried out] by Kim Mun-ho and Kim Kap-san beside our apical ancestor's gravesite should be considered to be 'digging out a tomb' (*kulch'ong*), not just an illegal burial. How can I, as a descendant, not hold a deep grudge? That was why I went to the lineage chief's house and had him issue a circular to gather lineage members. Those gathered numbered several hundred. On 10.13 (11/15), we all went to Hanch'i Subdistrict and arrested Kim Mun-ho and Kap-san. We were quite distressed and tortured them for two rounds in order to make them confess. From the beginning we did not hit or kick them. The death of Kap-san is a misfortune for both families. Initially, lineage leaders (*sujok*) put out the call for a lineage meeting. Eventually, the torture was also directed by the lineage leaders. Every lineage member gathered there participated in the torture, regardless of who was first or last. The circular is now presented here."

On the same day, Kim Chŏng-hyŏn, an involved witness, age.

Second Interrogation: "Your lineage's conduct was originally because of Kim Mun-ho's illegal burial. So arresting Mun-ho is understandable. Yet for what reasons did you arrest and torture Kim Kap-san in the same manner? You mentioned that many descendants of your lineage fought to torture Kap-san first. Even in the middle of such a struggle, there must be leaders and followers and the first and the last. You must have witnessed it all. Do not mix up and hide names but point out each person clearly, so that no one in your lineage is falsely implicated."

Testimony: "On 10.12 (11/14) I received the circular sent out by the lineage chief, [calling for] a lineage-wide meeting to investigate and resolve the matter of the illegal burial by Kim Mun-ho and Kap-san on the side of our apical ancestor's gravesite. I was extremely upset and arrived at the cemetery on the same day. There were already several hundred lineage members who had arrived before me. They bound and tortured Mun-ho and Kap-san. Because everyone fought to torture them, how can I remember who went first and last and who [meted out] a harsher or lighter [punishment]? At the time of the illegal burial, Kap-san led and helped carry it out. So together with Mun-ho, he is one and the same. That was why he was tortured in the same manner."

On the same day, Kim Yun-sŏp, an involved witness, age.

Second Interrogation: "Of the many lineage matters, you are the first one who petitioned, and you also contentedly followed such criminal actions. What were your intentions? You can say that you were one of the many who committed the crime of illegally torturing Kim Kap-san. Now, after the death of Kim Kap-san, with what intention do you volunteer to be punished? If you knew that this sort of serious matter should have been reported to the authorities and resolved by law, then you must have known it was illegal and criminal to privately investigate and torture Kap-san. It is not just you who committed the crime. Point out the leaders and followers one by one so that you do not receive added punishment."

Testimony: "On 10.10 (11/12), the lineage chief learned that someone had carried out an illegal burial in our apical ancestor's tomb. On 10.12 (11/14), there was a circular stating that every household representative should come to the cemetery to search for the site where the illegal burial was placed and find the culprit and uncover the truth, even [if it meant using] private torture. Yet I did not go to participate because that day was the anniversary ancestor ritual for one of our remote ancestors. I arrived there around dusk on 10.14 (11/16) and found that Kim Mun-ho and Kap-san had already been bound and tortured. So I did not witness the incident. When going to the county seat to report the matter, I was selected because I was young and walked fast. I could not decline, so I held the petition and submitted it. With the order to go investigate the matter, draw the site, and report back, I went up to the cemetery with the court clerk. After completing the drawing, because there were concerns that [Kap-san] had carried out illegal burials at some other sites [too], we tortured Mun-ho and Kap-san again. At this time, all members took turns torturing them, and I also participated. Yet I did not see what happened the other day because I was not there. I cannot tell who was first and who was last, [and who carried out] light or heavy [torture] on that day because we all fought to do it. Everything—from the lineage meeting to the torture—was done on the basis of the circular issued by the lineage chief."

On the same day, Kim Pyŏng-nyŏl, principal offender, age.

Second Interrogation: "As the chief of your lineage, you issued a circular to gather lineage members after learning of the Kim Mun-ho matter. Some three hundred members gathered, went to Hanch'i Subdistrict, arrested first Kim Mun-ho [and] then Kim Kap-san, and bound and tortured them. As such, your relative Kim Ch'ae-wŏn and others testified. You led in issuing the circular and directed all your lineage members. You must have sat in the hall and sent down orders. You must have been the one who was in charge when your lineage members tortured them. When reviewing your previous testimony, you arrogantly called yourself 'old' and dared to say 'forgetful.' You speak nonsense and make pathetic excuses in this solemn court in order to save your life. Your sly [ploy] has become your trap; what could be worse than this?! The law is absolutely strict and clemency is difficult to come by. Tell the truth without hiding like before, so as to assist this investigation."

Testimony: "On the first day of this court, I came to arrive here after traveling more than 100 *li*. Because I was old and confused, I was not able to testify to my utmost. The third day of last month was the anniversary ritual day for our tenth-generation ancestor at the gravesite on top of Swae Pass in Hanch'i. I was not able to attend the ritual because I was old and ill. After the ritual, those who had attended came and said to me, 'An itinerant merchant, who came to beg ritual food yesterday when we were making the offering, told us that he [i.e., Mr. Yi] had earlier heard from a female geomancer living in Koho that a person whose surname was Kim, living in Hanch'i Subdistrict, had carried out an illegal burial on the side of this grave. This is such a serious matter and we came to report to you because we could not do anything on the spot.' I was stunned and enraged to hear that. So, while I sent out a circular to lineage members, I called in relatives and sent them out to look for the site of illegal burial. I also ordered them to find the culprit so that we could locate the exact place of the illegal burial. I advised them to use private torture if the culprit would not admit the crime, because we would be able to submit a petition only after we learned the truth. Kim P'yŏng-il and three hundred other lineage members then went to that subdistrict and arrested Kim Mun-ho and Kim Kap-san, the culprits. When they were trying to learn the truth, they tortured the culprits by twisting their legs. But how could we have done that with the intention of killing someone? Those people are in origin wicked people from Hamgyŏng Province (*Pukkwan han'ak*) and did not confess straightforwardly but tried to conceal the criminal traces that had been already disclosed. All three hundred lineage members took turns and tortured them once or twice. The cause of this death originated with me, who stayed home and was in charge of the entire matter. It is wrong that close relatives of the deceased pointed out Kim P'yŏng-il as the antagonist. Please punish me in accordance with the law."

On the same day, Ms. Ch'oe, a close relative of the deceased, age.

Third Interrogation: "Your husband Kim Kap-san was involved in the illegal burial [carried out] by your relative Kim Mun-ho. So it should be the case that you regard Mun-ho as your antagonist. But instead, you pointed your finger at Kim P'yŏng-il and the female geomancer and called those two people antagonists. You are resentful like that, referring to your husband's last wish. You said that there was no one else nearby who heard your husband's wish. This criminal matter is very serious; how could you carelessly name the culprits on the basis of some story [and use the excuse of your husband's last words]? The law dictates that one crime shall not have two offenders (*ongmuyangbŏm*). Furthermore, there must have been one person who was in charge of your husband's torture and who caused [his] subsequent death. Why did you not just identify one person as the antagonist, but instead cause havoc and suspicion in this investigation by submitting confusing testimonies throughout? Can you say that this is the original intention of identifying an antagonist? This court is absolutely solemn. Do not dare submit a confusing testimony; instead, just point to one person on the basis of the facts, so that the investigation is resolved."

Testimony: "My husband's being tortured to death was a result of his assistance with Kim Mun-ho's illegal burial. [Mun-ho] then is also his antagonist, so please punish him in accordance with the law. Yet it is true that when my husband spoke his last words at the county seat, he indicated Kim P'yŏng-il and the enlightened woman as antagonists. He mentioned Kim P'yŏng-il first and the enlightened woman next. This was what I heard, and that is it. Please make judgment in accordance with the law. Indeed, there was no one else at his deathbed who heard [these words]."

On the same day, Kim Mun-ho, an eyewitness and an involved witness, age.

Third Interrogation: In your first and second testimonies, you said that it was true that Ms. Yu talked about gathering and infusing illuminating energy into the illegal burial. Why does Ms. Yu consistently deny this in her testimonies? According to Ms. Yu's testimonies, the talk of the empty tomb of your father came from Kim Tŏg-wŏn first, and then she also heard it from Kim Kap-san's aunt. Thereafter, you revealed your secret to her. From this, one can tell how the disastrous event evolved. With what intention do you try to accuse other people instead of reflecting upon your own wrongdoing? You and Kap-san are distant relatives. When Kap-san willingly worked with you to carry out the illegal burial, he must have been rewarded [in some way]. It was not unreasonable for the Kwangsan Kims to be concerned about whether Kap-san had [helped with] other illegal burials in their cemetery. Anyway, Kap-san's death as a result of torture originated from your illegal burial. Therefore, you are Kap-san's antagonist, are you not? Speak truthfully of what happened so that Kap-san's deep resentment can be resolved."

Testimony: "The story that Ms. Yu was going to infuse the [illegal burial with] illuminating energy is really true, as I said in my previous testimony. The illegal burial and Kim Kap-san's death as a result of torture all originated from my crime. When I ponder my crimes from the beginning to the end, I no longer have anything to say. There were no more illegal burials [of any of Kap-san's relatives] in reward for Kap-san's help."

On the same day, Ms. Yu, a related and involved witness.

Third Interrogation: "You have already said in your first and second testimonies that you spread the word of Kim Mun-ho's illegal burial at the gravesite of the Kwangsan Kims' apical ancestor. Therefore, you are the key person in this criminal matter. If not you, then who else? The story of infusing the [illegal burial with] illuminating energy appeared in Kim Mun-ho's first and second testimonies. Considering that, you were the person who was in charge of finding the auspicious site. If not you, then who else? The Kwangsan Kims gave you a cow; that must have been reason for you to cooperate with them. In this matter concerning a person's life and death, even if you are a woman, you must know how serious the law is. You have already mentioned face-to-face interrogation involving all three parties. Then you must have witnessed how horribly Kim Kap-san had been [injured] while being tortured. Testify one thing at a time without daring to hide [anything], so that there is no suspicion in this investigation."

Testimony: "As for the talk of infusing the illuminating energy, I had a conversation with Mun-ho when I stayed at his house, saying, 'I heard from a master ascetic (*taebangsulgaek*) that the illuminating energy could be gathered and infused after a burial using a mystical technique. But with my own mystic power I do not know how to gather the illuminating energy and infuse it.' We chatted like that. As for the matter of finding the auspicious gravesite, it was the work of geomancer Pak whose given name is unknown. As for the Kwangsan Kims' awarding [me with] a cow, I do not know why, but two or three of them voluntarily brought [it over] and gave it to me. So I temporarily held it and there was no reason for me to render cooperation to them. I did not witness any torturing of Kim Kap-san or the other."

On the same day, Kim Pyŏng-nyŏl, principal offender, age.

Third Interrogation: "According to your second testimony, you issued a circular after learning of Kim Mun-ho's illegal burial and took charge of all matters. So why did the close relatives of the deceased designate Kim P'yŏng-il—among numerous Kwangsan Kims—as their antagonist and not you? Also, according to the testimony of village headman Kim Chung-ok, three or four of your lineage members extorted several thousand *yang* of money from the households of Kim Mun-ho, Kim Kap-san, and others. You must have been in charge of this, too. State straightforwardly your criminal actions involving extortion and other matters."

Testimony: "Because I am so old, I did not go there to take charge. I had P'yŏng-il and Ch'ae-wŏn direct the matter for me. It must be that the accusations of those close relatives of the deceased are based on their witnessing [events where I was not present]. As for the mention of extortion by Kim Chung-ok and others, nothing like that happened. There are seven branch families directly descended from our apical ancestor. Every household sent over one or two family members. All lineage members live around 40 or 50 *li* from the cemetery, and they were unable to carry their own food because things happened so unexpectedly. Altogether, for three to four hundred people for six or seven days, it required five to six thousand food tables to feed them. When converted to cash, it did not cost more than one thousand *yang* or so. I had promised to pay the expenses for food and fuel right away. However, I had to rush to come here and have not been able to make a payment yet. That must be why the village headman said such a thing. How could I extort from others for the matter concerning our ancestor? Such an accusation is unfair.

"Speaking of Kim Mun-ho and Kim Kap-san's crimes, they caused our apical ancestor's tomb to be dug up three times. This is a crime that exceeds carrying out an illegal burial. Speaking of what should have been done, even if all of our thousands of descendants skinned Kap-san's and Mun-ho's flesh and chewed their gall bladders, our deep grudge would not disappear. How much less so for me, the chief of the lineage! I am almost ninety years old and my movement is restricted. So I was not able to interrogate them face-to-face. The death and the related trial emerged while trying to obtain the facts out by torturing them, after sending out a circular and mustering lineage members. From the beginning, I took charge of the matter in order to learn the facts, not necessarily to kill a person. Now, when I think back, I deplore the fact that I did not punish them with my own hands to bring honor to my ancestor, even if I would have had to crawl to get there. I seem to have ignored proper ethics by forgetting my ancestors while only considering my old age. Anyway, I have no regrets, even if I were to be punished by the law. I beg to know, though, how are you going to punish Mun-ho and Kap-san's crime of digging up the tomb of a scholar-official (*sabu*) three times?"

On the same day, Kim Ch'ang-sŏng, the court clerk who investigated the Kwangsan Kims' cemetery, twenty-eight years in age.

Interrogation: "As the court clerk, you went to the Kwangsan Kims' cemetery. You must have witnessed the disturbances there. Tell us about the commotion without hiding anything."

Testimony: "The distance from the county seat to the Kwangsan Kims' cemetery in Hanch'i Subdistrict, Changyang District, is 130 *li*. I could not get there in one day, so I arrived only on 10.19 (11/21). Kim Mun-ho and Kim Kapsan had already been subject to atrocious torture and had their legs twisted. My job was to investigate the illegal digging at the tomb site, thus I only measured and illustrated the scene to submit them. The hearing was to take place after both the defendants and plaintiffs appeared later at court."

. . . .

The petition submitted by Ms. Ch'oe, age, and Kim Kyŏng-hŭi, age, close relatives of the deceased.

We the close relatives submit this petition. Our initial complaint had to do with getting the facts and obtaining justice (*chŏngŭi*). However, our aunt is on her deathbed because of her chronic illness. Therefore, we have changed our minds and would like to withdraw this complaint. With the special benevolence of honoring life, please release the corpse to us for the benefit of restoring harmony.

In the order issued by said county, the deceased has died and that is it. But it is very difficult to straighten out the matters concerning those who are alive. The inquest report is about to be completed, but this office cannot arbitrarily release the corpse.

. . . .

[Concluding statement of the first inquest investigation]
Testimonies by each and every person are as stated. This criminal incident originated from one woman's tongue, which led to the death of a person under torture. The skeletal remains [of the two Kims] in the cemetery are as indis-

tinguishable as a handful of dirt; clamor in the field [over the bones] led to the lamentable death of a person. Everyone involved became very upset and agitated. So how could one argue that [the torture] was just for the sake of their ancestor? When reviewing everyone's testimonies, each has made an excuse to accuse the other. The entire criminal investigation should be absolutely prudent, and the original intention of the inquest is [written] in the legal codes. I had the body of the deceased Kim Kap-san moved to a bright spot. After examining the corpse in its dry condition, I had the body washed and then sprayed with lees and vinegar. Each and every condition of the entire body was subsequently revealed. All itemized injuries have been recorded on the inquest form (*sijang*) and there is no need to repeat them here. But on the ventral side of the body, wounds on the right thigh and knee were purple and black in color. There were broken skin and sunken bones on the right and left shins and the injured area was considerable. Although it looks terrible, these injuries are not in vital areas. So why did the death occur within the period of responsibility for crimes?

Next, when considering the facts of the incidents and tracing what had happened, after [the Kwangsan Kims] first learned of the illegal burial, they arrested the culprits. A descendant, even if he were there all by himself, would have a bloody fight to the death [to revenge the disturbance to the gravesite]. And no one could prevent that. In this case, three to four hundred descendants living near and far, ten or more generations removed from the apical ancestor, circulated the news and gathered swiftly. That was natural. The several people who arrived first arbitrarily tortured [Mun-ho and Kap-san]. Would they have worried about the outcome? Furthermore, Kim Kap-san, who was an evil person from Hamgyŏng Province, did not confess straightforwardly at first. [Seniors of] the Kwangsan Kims had already mentioned [digging up the truth even if they had to] break his legs. Those who arrived later immediately said, "You haven't killed that bastard?" They tortured him as they arrived. In such a way, they continuously took turns and tortured him countless times for five or six days. Even if Kap-san had a big, well-built body, how could he have survived?

Both Kap-san and Mun-ho were in similar trouble, but one is dead while the other is alive. This is suspicious. The Kwangsan Kims said to Kap-san that they heard that Kap-san had planned to move the tombs of his grandfather and father from Hamgyŏng Province. And because Kap-san was plotting together with Mun-ho and helped him, [they said] Kap-san might have also carried out illegal burials. Then they twisted his legs more. This is why Kap-san was tortured more. It was lucky that Kap-san died after five days and not immediately. At any rate, [since] the cause of his death was a result of being tortured, I record the true cause of death as "death as a result of torture" (*p'ijang ch'isa*). I thereby fill out three of the county's inquest forms, including the ventral and dorsal sides of the body, with the *chi* serial mark: one copy is to be given to the close relative of the deceased; one is to be kept in the county office; and the other is to be attached [to the rest of the inquest report] and sent to the MINISTRY.[26]

The deceased Kim Kap-san assisted Kim Mun-ho with the illegal burial [of his father's bones]. No matter how many thousands of Kwangsan Kims there were, Kap-san should have said, "The primary culprit was Mun-ho. I assisted him once, because as a lineage member I felt obliged to. How could my assisting constitute the same crime [as the illegal burial by Mun-ho]?" If he had done so, would things have turned out like this? Alas, this poor, small-minded Kap-san had already helped out with [the illegal burial]. Alas, the power of the Kwangsan Kims must have been far reaching. In his multitude of thoughts, [Kap-san should have realized that] there was no way to survive except to confess everything. The [enraged] cries of the Kwangsan Kims did not stop, and the torture with sticks became increasingly worse. When imagining the scene, it is apparent that his life hung by a thread. He was carried to the hearing site, but he eventually died after five days. His death was gruesome; the facts surrounding the incident are brutal. Why was he not forthcoming, letting his perilous life go so easily? I cannot imagine what was in his reserved mind. At any rate, how could he have avoided [receiving punishment for] the crime of digging up another's tomb, even after his death?

The root cause of the entire matter lies in Kim Mun-ho's illegal burial. In accordance with the law, Mun-ho is liable for the crime. However, this case is not like that. According to the testimony of a close relative of the deceased [i.e., his wife, Ms. Ch'oe], the dead man in his last wish indicated Kim P'yŏng-il as the antagonist, whereas those in the accused party testified that the one who issued the circular and directed the entire incident was the lineage chief [Kim Pyŏng-nyŏl]. By law, there cannot be two criminals for one crime. When many people are involved in torture, the chief commander and conspirator must be identified. And then the leaders and followers, as well as those who participated, whether a little bit or a lot, must be discerned. In such a way, finding the one offender is how the criminal court works properly. It is Ms. Ch'oe's word that Kap-san quietly left such a wish when alive, but there was no one else who heard this and can prove it. Many testified that Kim Pyŏng-nyŏl, the lineage chief of the Kwangsan Kims, issued the circular and took charge of the entire incident. In addition, Kim Pyŏng-nyŏl unreservedly confessed that he did take charge and plan everything from the beginning to the end. As the closest descendant to the apical ancestor, he felt an urge to gather all the lineage members after learning about the terrible incident of an illegal burial in his ancestor's gravesite. It is understandable that he was completely committed to this matter. The true mindset of Kim Pyŏng-nyŏl is [seen] in his words where he regretted not being able to go punish the culprits with his own hands, even if he had to crawl. Pyŏng-nyŏl's testimony that he would have no regret about being punished by death in accordance with the law is evidence of the old man's sincerity. On the one hand, it is pitiful that he knew that he could not run away from the law. On the other hand, the law is extremely strict: how could he avoid punishment? Therefore, I revise and record Kim Pyŏng-nyŏl as the principal offender.

As for Kim P'yŏng-il, his name was mentioned in the testimony of the close relative of the deceased. Thus, there was no need for another discussion to make him the culprit in accordance with the law. However, when Kap-san was tortured, he did not know that there was someone else who was in charge, and as a result indicated Kim P'yŏng-il as the primary offender because that was what he witnessed. [If the court charged Kim P'yŏng-il as the principal offender,] how would it not provoke the resentment of the living? The testimony by the close relative of the deceased is exactly as an ancient classic says, "He saw the ox, but had not seen the sheep."[27] I record P'yŏng-il as an accomplice (ch'abŏm) because he was physically in charge of the torture at the scene [of the crime]. However, it is very regrettable that I could not interrogate him because he has fled. I have deployed officers to arrest him immediately.

As for Ms. Yu, she spread the word because of her personal feeling. Her words provoked a disturbance and eventually caused this death. She is the most critical person in this case. If not her, who else? When considering her crime, even capital punishment may not be satisfactory. Her object of hatred was Kim Mun-ho. But this lamentable incident arose in relation to Kap-san, and, when discussing the origin [of the entire matter], there are things that refer to and involve her. Therefore, I record her in the categories of both related and involved witness.

As for Kim Mun-ho, this criminal case single-handedly originated from him. He is the source of this calamity. If not him, who else? He dug up the tomb to bury his father. He dug up the tomb [again] to remove his father's bones. When facing the Kwangsan Kims, he dug [up the tomb a third time] to show the spot for illegal burial. After that, he dug [once again, unearthing] his own father's [relocated] tomb to prove his father's burial. When discussing his crimes, we cannot stop with one or two of them. He dug up one tomb three times—this crime itself is already a very serious one. He argues that he was forced to do that, but I humbly refer the HIGHER COURT to make a judgment in accordance with the law. Because he witnessed the entire incident with his own eyes, I record him as an eyewitness and an involved witness.

Kim Ch'ae-wŏn, Kim Chŏng-hyŏn, Kim Yun-sŏp are all involved witnesses. They followed the issue on the table and carried out their leader's command. It is difficult to avoid the punishment for participating in the incident. It is true that Kim Kyŏng-hŭi, a close relative of the deceased, simply listened to what Ms. Ch'oe said and filed a complaint together with Ms. Ch'oe. So, I only interrogated him twice and stopped. As for close neighbors Chŏng Tong-baek and Kim Tŏg-wŏn, one provided services to prepare for food and the other became afraid and fled. There is no need to investigate them further. The village headman Kim Chung-ok, also a very close relative of Kim Mun-ho, personally took care of all the expenses incurred by [having to] host the Kwangsan Kims and [their] various extortions. There is no need to talk about him because he did as he was ordered under such precarious circumstances. The Kwangsan Kims' arbitrary exaction is illegal and extremely depraved. All those expenses must be calculated as stated in the testimony, and [the Kwangsan Kims] shall be urged to pay them back. District administrator Yi Kyŏng-ch'an was out of town before the incident took place and thus did not know anything about it. There is no need to examine him any further. Because the legal clerk Kim Ch'ang-sŏng was carrying out official business [regarding the illegal burial], I interrogated him only once. The following people shall be imprisoned in accordance with the law and await a further decision: Kim Pyŏng-nyŏl, principal offender; Ms. Yu, a related and involved witness; Kim Ch'ae-wŏn, Kim Chŏng-hyŏn, and Kim Yun-sŏp, all involved witnesses; and Kim Mun-ho, an eyewitness and an involved witness. All other concerned people shall be temporarily released because it is regrettable to keep them in custody in this harsh, cold weather. The corpse has been placed back inside the room, marked with ash seals, and guards have been assigned to watch it. I revise and submit to you the list of all criminals and imprisoned people as well as the measurements of the affected Kwangsan Kims' tomb. The murder weapons have not yet been obtained, so I cannot produce their illustration.

This criminal matter originated from an illegal burial. However, [Mun-ho and Kap-san] dug up the tomb. Therefore, their crime of illegally digging up a tomb cannot be deliberated on the basis of the law concerning the perimeter of the tomb (kungnae). The judgment for this case cannot be made in accordance with ordinary legal prescriptions. The discussion of applying the law must concern Mun-ho. Mun-ho and Kap-san, members of the same lineage, carried out this unlawful action. Therefore, they would have nothing to say even if [they were sentenced to] death.

Because Kap-san's death was caused by torture, the consideration of requital for a life must involve the Kwangsan Kims with absolutely no clemency. After the inquest, the close relatives, out of whatever thinking, dared to request the withdrawal of their accusation because they had changed their minds and wished for the release of the corpse to restore harmony. I am not thoughtful enough and cannot make a decision on my own regarding this request. Thus, I have attached the petition submitted by the close relatives of the deceased to the end of this report. There is not much to discuss in making a judgment for this case. However, I wonder what you think of making a judgment on the basis of one inquest. Thereby, I humbly submit my report and sincerely request your review.

On 1899.12.14 (1/14/1900), around six in the evening (yu-si).[28]

Pak Yong-dŏk, the first inquest official and
the magistrate of Hoeyang, Kangwŏn Province [seal]

To the minister, Ministry of Justice
[seal][29]

. . . .

[Inquest form (sijang)]

Around ten in the morning (sasi) on 1899.11.1 (12/3/1899), [I] arrived in the community funeral home by the Sŏjin River, 3 li north of the county office, where Kim Kap-san's corpse was located, and conducted an inquest to determine the root causes of death. I document the true cause of death in [the drawings of] the ventral and dorsal sides of the body on the county's inquest form with the chi serial mark.[30] Everything is collated and filed here.

The Ventral Side of the Body (angmyŏn)

[Illustration of the ventral side of the body, with the following entry of the true cause of death written in between the two legs.]
The true cause of death is recorded as torture.

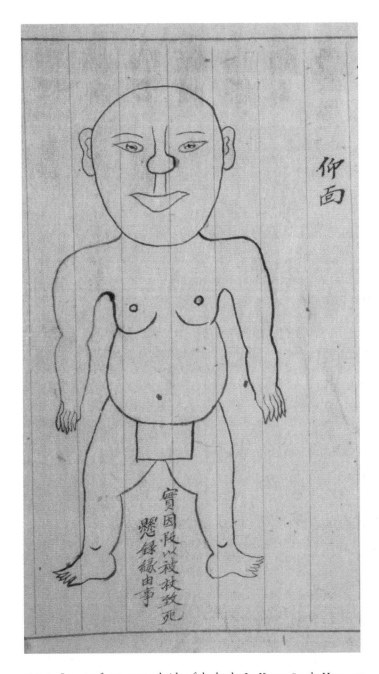

FIG. 5 Inquest form, ventral side of the body. In *Kangwŏn-do Hoeyang-gun Changyang-myŏn Hanch'i-ri ch'isa namin Kim Kap-san ch'ogŏman*, 35a (see fig. 2). Courtesy of Seoul National University, Kyujanggak Institute for Korean Studies.

Crown of the head (*chŏngsim*) Left side of the head (*p'yŏnjwa*)	Yellowish-white in color
Right side of the head (*p'yŏnu*)	Slightly red
Fontanel (*sinmun*) Cranium (*turo*) Forehead (*aekkak*) Both temples (*yangt'aeyanghyŏl*) Both eyebrows (*yangmi*) Corners of the eyebrows (*mich'ong*)	Normal color
Both eyelids (*yanganp'o*)	Closed
Pupils (*anjŏng*)	Normal
Both cheeks (*yangsihyŏp*)	Right side is slightly red while left is yellowish-white
Both ears (*yangi*) Ear flaps (*iryun*) Ear lobes (*isu*) Ear holes (*igyu*) Bridge of the nose (*piryang*) Tip of the nose (*pijun*)	Yellowish-white in color
Nostrils (*pigyu*)	Stench secretion present.
Philtrum (*injung*)	Normal
Upper and lower lips and around the lips (*sangha sunmun*)	Slightly open; the silver hairpin inserted [inside the mouth] did not change color
Mouth (*ku*)	Slightly open
Upper and lower molars (*sangha ach'i*)	Missing
Tongue (*sŏl*)	By lower teeth
Under the jaw (*hamhae*)	Blue in color
Throat (*inhu*) Esophagus (*sikkisang*)	Normal

Both depressed areas above the shoulder blades (*yanggyŏlbun'gol*) Both shoulders (*yanggyŏn'gap*) Both armpits (*yangaekchi*) Upper arms (*yanghŭppak*)	Normal in color
Inside the elbow (*yanggokch'u*)	Marks from binding; consistently purple in color
Both wrists (*yangsuwan*)	Normal
Palms (*susim*)	Normal
Fingers (*suji*)	Loosely held in fists
Fingertips (*sujidu*)	Normal
Underneath fingernails (*sujigappong*)	Right side is yellowish-white while the other side is blue
Chest (*hyungdang*) Both breasts (*yangyu*) Between chest and belly (*simgam*) Upper belly (*tubok*) Ribs (*yangnŭk*) Sides under arms (*yanghyŏp*) Lower belly (*chedu*)	Blue in color
Both groins (*yanggwa*)	Right side is yellowish-white and the skin is scraped; the left side is slightly red and swollen`
Penis (*kyŏngmul*) Scrotum (*sinnang*)	Normal
Both thighs (*yangt'oe*)	Lower inner part of right thigh has one purple-black spot, which is also slightly swollen. Inside is shallow while outer part is deeper. Its circumference is 9 *ch'on* with 3 *ch'on* in length and 1 *ch'on* 7 *p'un* in width. Left thigh is normal.
Both knees (*yangsŭl*)	Right knee is slightly swollen and purple-black in color; the left knee looks normal *continued*

Both shins (*yanggyŏmin*)	Upper part of the right shin has open wound with torn flesh. When pressed, blood comes out. Its circumference is 3 *ch'on*. Lower part of the right shin has a spot with sunken bone and dry skin. Its circumference is 3 *ch'on* 5 *p'un* and it is purple-black in color. A little below that, there is one scar with broken skin and bruises. It is in a willow-leaf shape and surrounded by bloodstains. There is one wound with sunken bone on the left shin. It is purple-black in color. Flesh is curled and contracted and its circumference is 9 *ch'on* 5 *p'un*.
Both ankles (*yanggagwan*)	Bloody traces on upper part caused by tying; extravasation all over
Both tops of the feet (*yanggangmyŏn*) Toes (*chokchi*) Toenails (*chokchigap*) Both legs are straight (*yanggak sinjik*)	Yellowish-white

Dorsal Side of the Body (*hammyŏn*)

[Illustration of the dorsal side of the body, with the following entry written in between the two legs.]

The true cause of death is recorded as torture.

Occipital (*noehu*) Neck hairline (*palje*)	Normal
Both roots of the ears (*yangigŭn*) Back of the neck (*hanggyŏng*)	Slightly red
Both backs of the shoulders (*yangbibu*)	Slightly red
Both elbows (*yanghŭlju*)	Marks from binding, extravasation all over

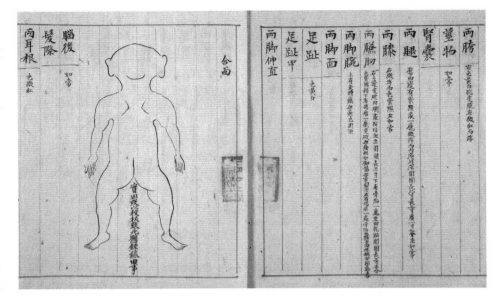

FIG. 6. Inquest form, dorsal side of the body (beginning on the left side). In *Kangwŏn-do Hoeyang-gun Changyang-myŏn Hanch'i-ri ch'isa namin Kim Kap-san ch'ogŏman*, 38a (see fig. 2). Courtesy of Seoul National University, Kyujanggak Institute for Korean Studies.

Wrists (*suwan*) Both backs of the hands (*yangsubae*) Fingers (*suji*) Fingernails (*sujigap*) Spine (*ch'ŏkpae*) Area along the spine (*ch'ŏngnyŏ*)	Slightly red in color
Back ribs (*yanghurŭk*) Sides under arms (*yanghuhyŏp*)	Blue
Waist (*yoan*)	Blue with two old moxibustion scars in the shape of a jujube leaf
Both buttocks (*yangdun*)	Yellowish-white in color

continued

Anus (*kokto*)	The silver hairpin inserted inside the anus did not change color
Both thighs (*yangt'oe*)	Yellowish-white in color
Both crooks of the knees (*yanggokch'u*)	Right side is purple-red but the left side is normal
Both calves (*yangt'oedu*)	Left calf is bruised all over. Right calf from the crook of the knee down to right above the ankle is bruised and purple in color.
Both ankles (*yanggakkwa*)	Upper part has marks from binding and bruises all over
Heels (*kakkŭn*)	Yellowish-white in color

Both soles of the feet (*yanggaksim*)
Toes (*chokchi*)
Toe tips (*chokchidu*)
Underneath toenails (*chokchigappong*)
Both legs are straight (*yanggak sinjik*)

The inquest has been held in the presence of relevant people, and it is clear beyond doubt that the true cause of death was torture.

Complainants and close relatives of the deceased	Ms. Ch'oe	All released
District administrator	Kim Kyŏng-hŭi	
Village headman	Yi Kyŏng-ch'an	
Close neighbors	Kim Chung-ok	
	Chŏng Tong-baek	
	Kim Tŏg-wŏn	
Eyewitness and an involved witness	Kim Mun-ho	Imprisoned
A related and involved witness	Ms. Yu	All imprisoned
Involved witnesses	Kim Ch'ae-wŏn	
	Kim Chŏng-hyŏn	
	Kim Yun-sŏp	

Accomplice	Kim P'yŏng-il	Fled
Principal offender	Kim Pyŏng-nyŏl	Imprisoned with cangue[31]

We hereby record and submit the condition of the wounds on the body of the deceased man Kim Kap-san. If it is later discovered that we added or omitted injuries of the aforementioned deceased man Kim Kap-san, or entered fabricated information on the record, or conducted the inquest examination in a corrupt way, we inquest officials shall submit ourselves for punishment.

Pak Yong-dŏk, the first inquest official and magistrate of Hoeyang

> Kim Ch'ŏl-gyu, head court clerk
> Song T'aeg-yŏng, court clerk
> Yi Tong-sik, herbalist
> Song Hwan-ik, legal clerk
> Pak Nae-ch'un, sheriff
> Kim Ch'ŏn-gil, coroner's assistant

* *

Illustration of the Kwangsan Kims' Cemetery

[Illustration of the cemetery with four entries of notes from top right in a clockwise direction]
Tomb of a Kwangsan Kim member with no descendant
Dug a hole on the left side of the mound and under the plaster encasing of the original coffin.
The depth of the hole is 6 *ch'ŏk* deep and 6 *ch'ŏk* 5 *ch'on* wide.
The tomb on the right is a couple's burial of the plaintiff Kim Pyŏng-nyŏl's ancestors ten generations before him.

[below the illustration]
Plaintiffs: Kim Pyŏng-nyŏl, Kim P'yŏng-il, Kim Ch'ae-wŏn, Kim Chŏng-hyŏn, and Kim Yun-sŏp
Defendants: Kim Mun-ho and Kim Kap-san
Village headman: Kim Chung-ok
Court clerk who examined the site: Kim Ch'ang-sŏng

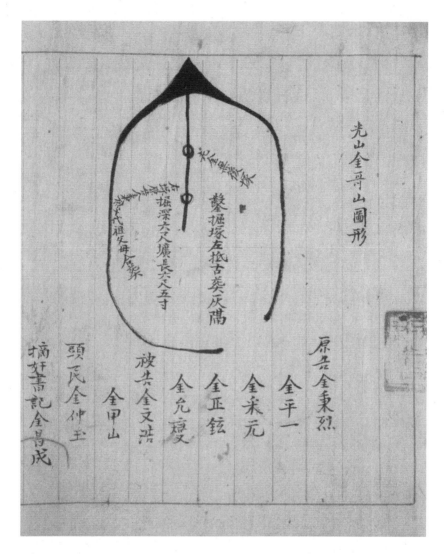

FIG. 7 Illustration of the Kwangsan Kims' cemetery. In *Kangwŏn-do Hoeyang-gun Changyang-myŏn Hanch'i-ri ch'isa namin Kim Kap-san ch'ogŏman*, 41a (see fig. 2). Courtesy of Seoul National University, Kyujanggak Institute for Korean Studies.

[cover page]

The fourth year of the Kwangmu reign (1900)

SPECIAL INVESTIGATION REPORT CONCERNING THE CRIMINAL CASE
INVOLVING THE DECEASED MALE KIM KAP-SAN FROM HANCH'I
SUBDISTRICT, CHANGYANG DISTRICT, HOEYANG LESSER COUNTY

· ·

[title page]

SPECIAL INVESTIGATION RECORD CONCERNING THE CRIMINAL CASE
INVOLVING DECEASED MALE KIM KAP-SAN FROM HANCH'I SUBDISTRICT,
CHANGYANG DISTRICT, HOEYANG LESSER COUNTY

· ·

REPORT

In the CONFIDENTIAL DIRECTIVE (*pihun*) that arrived around eight in the
evening (*sul-si*) on 1899.12.28 (1/28/1900), it was written: "[The magistrate of]
Hoeyang Lesser County had already conducted the inquest and reported on the
deceased male Kim Kap-san from Hanch'i Subdistrict, Changyang District of
said county.[32] Since there was no doubt about the true cause of death, the corpse
was released for burial. However, there were some incomplete aspects in clearly
determining the offender, and thus it was impossible to close the case with just
one inquest. Therefore, you, the magistrate [of Ch'ŏlwŏn Lesser County], have
been appointed as a special investigator. You should immediately go to said
county and carry out the investigation in accordance with the law. In terms of
the victim's last wish and the report of the close relative of the deceased, the
antagonist is Kim P'yŏng-il. But Kim Pyŏng-nyŏl, who is an eighty-some-year-
old, dull-eyed old lineage heir, was found to be the principal offender. Although
[what the Kwangsan Kims did] was on behalf of their ancestor, the law strictly
demands that the killer shall die. There are laws governing the [treatment of]
the chief organizer, the leaders, and the followers, depending on their degree
of involvement. In addition, one criminal matter may not have two primary
offenders. Only after thoroughly investigating the matter, there will be no
resentment either by Pyŏng-nyŏl or P'yŏng-il. Thus, make every effort in this
investigation so that we obtain the truth. Submit both reports to provide the
grounds to rectify this criminal matter. When county officials are ordered to
conduct official business like this, they make all sorts of excuses to try to avoid

having to take the job. Unless there is a particular formal reason, do not make an excuse. Go there immediately and carry out an investigation." Therefore, I immediately headed to said county and conducted the investigation in accordance with the regulations. On 1990.1.9 (2/8/1900), I interrogated:

Beginning with the first round of interrogation of Ms. Ch'oe, the dead man's wife, three rounds of interrogations of and testimonies by concerned people are recorded. Only newly revealed and contested information is translated here, with a summary of questions and testimonies in italics to help contextualize the translated part, so that the reader can follow the development of the case.

In the testimony of Ms. Ch'oe, after describing how the event unfolded after 10.13 (11/15), when many Kwangsan Kim members arrested her husband Kim Kap-san, she says:

"On 10.14 (11/16), when the Kwangsan Kims took my husband up to the Kwangsan Kims' cemetery . . . and tortured him again, a person named Kim P'yŏng-il talked to my husband, saying, 'If you pay me 100 *yang* of money, I will let you go home safely.' But my husband did not listen to him and thus was tortured further. I met my husband at Swae Pass when he was on his way to the county seat to attend the hearing. There, he told me, '. . . If I die, take revenge on Kim P'yŏng-il for my death.'"

After the interrogation of Kim Kyŏng-hŭi, Kim Chung-ok, Kim Ch'ang-sŏng, Chŏng Tong-baek, and Kim Tŏg-wŏn, the special investigator questions Kim Mun-ho, saying:

". . . Illegal burials, though prohibited, do often take place. Even so, they are not like what you did. You demolished another's tomb, dug into the plaster encasement, and dared to place your father's bones right by the plaster encasement, as if in a couple's burial. . . ." *After noting how extraordinarily immoral Mun-ho's crime was, the special investigator focuses on why Kim P'yŏng-il, among the many who tortured Kap-san, was identified in Kap-san's last words as the dying man's antagonist. In response, Kim Mun-ho says:* ". . . All the Kwangsan Kims tortured us at that time; how could [Kap-san] have picked out Kim P'yŏng-il as the culprit? I cannot remember everything that I had to go through. . . ."

The special investigator then asks Ms. Yu if she, in her capacity as a geomancer, picked the spot for Mun-ho's illegal burial, and also accuses her of leaking Mun-ho's secret and causing the entire incident. Ms. Yu responds:

"I am originally from Seoul, but settled here several years ago. I have one grown-up child. To find a marriage partner for this child, I visited Hanch'i Subdistrict. Because I was acquainted with Kim Mun-ho, I stayed at his home. While we were chatting at night, Mun-ho said, 'Before I had no son, but [now I] have one; this must be a blessing emanating from my ancestor's grave (sanŭm).' I chimed in, saying, 'That is so, of course.' Then he told me that very matter that he should not have uttered, saying, 'I placed an illegal burial at the gravesite of the Kwangsan Kims' apical ancestor. As a result I had a boy.' I just listened to this story and went back home.

"After several days, I was arrested by the county authorities because of the matters concerning the wedding. Because I had no way to meet various expenses, I sent someone to Kim Chung-ok's house and to ask for the 25 yang of money that I had left with him earlier in order to get out of the financial difficulty. Then he made an excuse, saying that he would send that money to Mr. T'ak, the teacher, and declined my request outright. I was so upset I blurted out, 'The Kims will be destroyed once I open my mouth!' Ms. Chang from Kaesŏng, my adopted older sister (suyanghyŏng), begged to know what I meant, but I resisted and did not tell her. Because she bothered me all night, I eventually told her about Kim Mun-ho's illegal burial at the Kwangsan Kims' cemetery. The story spread to other people and culminated in this crime involving a death. Whenever I think of it, I just want to die. I earned a name as a diviner in the countryside. I sometimes examined a patient's pulse, and some sick people were healed. I am not a geomancer at all, and so there is no way that I picked the spot [for an illegal burial]. . . ."

When questioning Kim Ch'ae-wŏn, the investigator suggests that while it was understandable to torture Kim Mun-ho, it was wrong to torture Kim Kapsan—all the more so because Kap-san came to die. After commenting that the Kwangsan Kims must have meant to kill Kap-san with such severe torture, the investigator states that there would have been no crime if a guilty person had died, but the death of an innocent person creates resentment. Kim Ch'ae-wŏn, after describing the development of events, says:

"... Mun-ho is lucky to be alive, and unfortunately Kap-san died. My grudge over his destruction of the tomb for an illegal burial has not yet been absolved, yet I am now implicated in this unexpected criminal investigation. My resentment is bone-deep. Speaking of the complainant Ms. Ch'oe, she designated all Kwangsan Kim members as the antagonist on the day she filed the complaint. Then, when she first testified after three days had passed, she picked out Kim P'yŏng-il as the antagonist. What was she thinking at first, and [what was she thinking] later? Something must have happened in between [filing the complaint and testifying], considering her sudden change of testimony. . . ."

The interrogation of Kim P'yŏng-il, who was not originally questioned because he "fled" at the time of the first inquest, follows the interrogations of Kim Chŏng-hyŏn and Kim Yun-sŏp. The investigator's questioning focuses on the reasons Kim Kap-san designated P'yŏng-il as his antagonist. Kim P'yŏng-il, after describing the unfolding of the incident, testifies to his whereabouts following the incident and voices his opinion, saying:

". . .After Mun-ho and Kap-san were carried to the county seat, I returned home to take care of lineage business. I left home on 10.20 (11/22) for a lineage senior's home at Port Hope, carrying 200 *yang* of money for the renovation of the lineage shrine dedicated to our ancestor Lord of Chŏlli P'ansŏ in Port Hope, P'ungdŏk.[33] After delivering the funds, I went directly to Seoul. On 11.14 (12/16), my cousin Kim Pyŏng-p'il unexpectedly came to Seoul, so I asked him the reason. In reply, he said, 'After you departed, Kim Kap-san died in prison. In the complaint filed by Ms. Ch'oe, the close relative of the deceased, she indicated you as the antagonist.' I was shocked to hear this and returned home immediately. I surrendered myself to the authorities and was imprisoned while waiting for the investigation. . . . Speaking of Kim Mun-ho and Kim Kap-san's crimes, they do not only concern the laws governing illegal burial. Their crime of digging up the tomb is worse. People sometimes carry out illegal burials, but no one would do it in such a perverse way. They dug the left side of my tenth-generation ancestor's tomb, created a space under the coffin, and secretly buried Mun-ho's father's bones. Wouldn't the affected descendants fume with indignation and tremble with rage? Even if I had beaten them to death on the spot, my grievance would not have been resolved. We only used torture to prevent possible trouble later on. Kap-san unfortunately died, and his death has led to these criminal proceedings. However, my rage would not completely disappear even if I chopped off his head thousands of times. . . . Over the last few years, there were more than forty lineage members who came to earn fame but were falsely charged by those young and cunning bastards and subsequently bled to death.[34] In addition, our grave guard also vomited blood and died. Now I begin to realize that these deaths had to do with Mun-ho's illegal burial. . . . [Ms. Ch'oe] insisted that she met her husband at Swae Pass on his way to the county seat, and there Kap-san indicated Kim P'yŏng-il as his antagonist. Please [check with] the court clerk and officers [who were escorting Kap-san as to] whether this couple really met there or not. . . ."

After questioning Kim Pyŏng-nyŏl, the special investigator interrogates Ms. Ch'oe a second time and asks why she submitted false testimonies about her encounter with her husband and her husband's last words, saying:

"I asked the escorting officials whether or not you met your husband at Swae Pass, and they reported, saying, 'Ms. Ch'oe's testimony is a lie. We did not see her coming on the day we escorted Kap-san. Thus, how could she have met him and [heard] Kap-san leave his [last] wish? This is a false charge.' Though you, a country bumpkin, must have felt like a wall was falling [because of your husband's death], how dare you make a skewed and arbitrary charge against P'yŏng-il as the antagonist when the law of avenging a death is strict and the designation of the principal offender should be most careful. . . ."

Despite the fact that her false testimony was revealed, Ms. Ch'oe acknowledges nothing in her reply and simply states that she has already said everything and that there is nothing more to add.

The second round of interrogation of the other people summoned to court does not produce any new information, except for Kim Ch'ang-sŏng, the court clerk, who testifies that he did not see Ms. Ch'oe's meeting with and talking to Kim Kap-san at the Swae Pass, confirming the previous testimonies by the escort officers.

In the second interrogation of Kim P'yŏng-il, the investigator focuses on why P'yŏng-il was designated as the antagonist and also on the 100 yang of money that he reportedly demanded from Kap-san, as mentioned by Ms. Ch'oe in her first testimony. In response, Kim P'yŏng-il says:

". . . As for the story of demanding 100 *yang* of money, no such thing ever happened. Our priority was resolving our resentment on behalf of our ancestors. How could I try to exact money at that point?! It is nothing but a lie from Ms. Ch'oe. As for designating me as the culprit, there is no reason. I stand out a bit [because of having held local positions], so people in the countryside call my name, Kim P'yŏng-il, like a catch-all identification. Even common folks have all heard about and know me. At this death incident, the deceased's wife

Ms. Ch'oe used my name, which she knows well, as if her dead husband had mentioned it in his last wish. This is absolutely unfair.

"Even though Kim Mun-ho's illegal burial had been removed, his act could not be let go. So, I came down from the cemetery to report the illegal burial to the authorities. On that night, Im Yŏ-gyŏng, who lives in Hanch'i Subdistrict and who is Kim Chung-ok's in-law, came to talk to me, saying, 'This is such a serious matter. Having this sort of incident is nothing like not having one. I will collect 1,000 *yang* in cash from the Kyŏngju Kims and give it to you. How about resolving the matter confidentially [without involving the authorities]?' I replied, 'The resentment over the illegal burial has not yet faded. Where could we use this 1,000 *yang* of money?' Then he blushed with shame and left. Considering this discussion, would I have taken 100 *yang* after declining 1,000? This single matter must be Ms. Ch'oe's false charge...."

Ms. Ch'oe is interrogated a third time about her charge that Kim P'yŏng-il attempted to extort 100 yang *from her husband, using the countercharge revealed by P'yŏng-il that the Kyŏngju Kims—Kim Kap-san and Kim Mun-ho's lineage—had offered 1,000* yang *to him to settle the matter. Again, Ms. Ch'oe does not add a word of explanation about the conflicting testimonies. The investigator then asks Kim Chung-ok whether he sent his in-law Im Yŏ-gyŏng to the Kwangsan Kims to offer 1,000* yang *to resolve the issue. Kim Chung-ok replies that he did ask Im to be a go-between to offer 1,000* yang *to the Kwangsan Kims, but he did not know that Im had talked to Kim P'yŏng-il. In the last entry of Kim P'yŏng-il's third interrogation, the investigator, puzzled by Ms. Ch'oe's consistent claim that P'yŏng-il is the antagonist and thinking that there must be a reason behind it, asks P'yŏng-il why. P'yŏng-il simply answers that he does not know what sort of grudge prompted Ms. Ch'oe to indicate him as the antagonist.*

[Concluding statement by the special investigator]
Each person's testimonies are as stated. Both Kim lineages are arguing against each other. As if "a multitude of men of Chu are strong; one man of Qi is weak," a myriad of ants assist and a swarm of bees rise up once a lonesome Yu wags her tongue.[35] This is the grounds for an in-depth investigation. Although the corpse has been buried, it is appropriate to investigate to the utmost to discern whether or not there is remaining resentment. How sad! This Kim Kap-san, who was originally from the north [Hamgyŏng Province] but happened

to come and reside in this eastern land [Kangwŏn Province], died unexpectedly. Though he most likely had a resentful death, how could he have avoided punishment for the illegal burial? Considering the facts of the incident, how could he have known that the disastrous act of Mun-ho's illegal burial would be disclosed and that calamity would fall upon him? After carrying out such a wrongful act, what use would there be if he were still alive? The death is really his own fault.

As for Kim Pyŏng-nyŏl, he is old but still healthy. He is almost ninety years in age. He could not suppress his anger and called in several hundred lineage members. Although he did not see with his own eyes the torture of Mun-ho and Kap-san, his close and remote relatives participated in it as if they were fighting for blood. He is a man of the leading branch and the lineage chief. He sat on a high seat and oversaw the entire matter. He issued the circular and called for a lineage meeting. All those relatives exercised violence en masse and killed Kap-san. Then who could be blamed? Though he did not kill him with his own hands, it is difficult for Pyŏng-nyŏl to avoid being designated as "the principal offender."

Ms. Ch'oe is only twenty-nine years in age. She was unlucky and in the flowering of her life has become a lonely widow. She asked to avenge her husband's death, and that is natural. Yet her designation of one person [as her husband's antagonist] out of many assailants occurred because of her small mind. Speaking of her husband's last wish [that P'yŏng-il be punished for his death], it is groundless, though it is possible. Nothing like that happened while officers were escorting Kap-san, so where did she meet him and what sort of conversation took place? I asked the officers, who said they did not see her. I queried the court clerk, who said he did not know. In addition, when a criminal is escorted, there is no quiet place for conversation because there are many eyes to watch. Isn't it deceiving that she testified as though she had met with him, yet no one saw or knew? It is not worth holding a foolish, small-minded woman responsible.

Kim Kyŏng-hŭi resided in another county, but rushed to come [to Kap-san's home] after hearing of Kap-san's death. He filed a complaint together with Ms. Ch'oe, his cousin's wife. Kim Chung-ok heard of Mun-ho's illegal burial and worried that something serious might happen. He reprimanded Mun-ho severely and had him dig up the illegal burial immediately and remove it. The court clerk Kim Ch'ang-sŏng upheld the order and went to the Kwangsan Kims' cemetery to make a drawing of the area. Because the torture of Kap-san took place before his arrival, he did not witness it.

Chŏng Tong-baek, on his way [to T'ongch'ŏn], listened to Chung-ok's begging [Tong-baek] to take care of meals for the numerous Kwangsan Kims. Kim Tŏg-wŏn learned [about the trouble] with Kap-san in the middle of the night. He felt scared and ran away for a while, but was [then] arrested as a close relative.

Kim Mun-ho initially carried out an illegal burial of his father's bones in order to obtain an auspicious burial site. He accidentally disclosed the secret to Ms. Yu; if not, would there have been this extreme incident [involving a death]? He was the primary culprit. Kap-san was an accomplice. But one is alive and the other is dead; a person's fate is just like that. When considering his crime, how can Mun-ho wish to live? Since he already knows his crime, he simply wishes to die.

Ms. Yu, discarding proper conduct as an acquaintance [of Mun-ho], disclosed the secret because of an insignificant grudge, which consequently led to this murder. The root cause of this criminal case, therefore, lies with her; if not her, then who else? She must be punished.

Kim Ch'ae-wŏn, together with other lineage members, went to the gravesite and examined the spot of the illegal burial. After that, he directed all of his relatives, [who] bound Mun-ho and Kap-san and tortured them. Kim Chŏng-hyŏn participated in the incident from the beginning to the end. Kim Yun-sŏp participated in everything from binding them to torturing them.

Kim P'yŏng-il honored the orders from the lineage chief and attended the lineage members' gathering. Although the story of extorting 100 *yang* of money came out of the mouth of the close relative of the deceased, declining 1,000 *yang* of money has been proved by Chung-ok's testimony. After Mun-ho and Kap-san went to the county seat [and were put under custody], P'yŏng-il went to Seoul to take care of some lineage business. After hearing the news [of Kap-san's death] from his younger cousin, he returned home without completing his business. Then he voluntarily showed up and was imprisoned until the opening of this interrogation. Thus, I interrogated him according to the regulations.

Yi Kyŏng-ch'an, the district administrator, was sick and in pain; therefore, I was not able to question him. Im Yŏ-gyŏng, who appeared in Kim P'yŏng-il's testimony, should have been interrogated once. But, according to Kim Chung-ok's testimony, it is clear that Yŏ-gyŏng's effort to mediate between the two [lineages of] Kims was because of Chung-ok's request. Therefore, he was not questioned.

Kim Pyŏng-nyŏl, principal offender; Kim P'yŏng-il, accomplice; Kim Mun-ho, eyewitness; Ms. Yu, a related witness; Kim Ch'ae-wŏn, Kim Chŏng-hyŏn, and Kim Yun-sŏp, involved witnesses—these people are under the custody of the court clerk of said county [and are] to be imprisoned securely. Ms. Ch'oe and Kim Kyŏng-hŭi, close relatives of the deceased; Kim Chung-ok, village headman; Kim Ch'ang-sŏng, court clerk; Chŏng Tong-baek and Kim Tŏg-wŏn, close neighbors—these people have been temporarily released because it is quite miserable to keep them in prison in such cold weather.

I have compiled two copies of the report to submit. Because the special investigation has been completed, I, the magistrate, am returning to my office.

I humbly submit this report for your review.

1900.2.13 (3/13/1900)

Ku Pong-jo, special investigator and magistrate of Ch'ŏlwŏn
[seal affixed]

To the honorable judge (*p'ansa*) at the court (*chaep'anso*)

REPORT NUMBER 11

As for the criminal case concerning the deceased Kim Kap-san of Hanch'i Subdistrict, Changyang District, in Hoeyang Lesser County, after reviewing the first inquest report by Pak Yŏng-dŏk, magistrate of Hoeyang, and the special investigation report by Ku Pong-jo, magistrate of Ch'ŏlwŏn, I securely imprisoned the following criminals and await orders from the MINISTRY: Kim Pyŏng-nyŏl, the principal offender; Kim P'yŏng-il, accomplice; and Ms. Yu, a related witness.[36] The rest have been released after proper warnings. I hereby submit both reports.

Please review them to make your judgment.

1900.4.9 (5/7/1900)

Chŏng Il-yŏng, judge, Kangwŏn Provincial Court [seal affixed]

To honorable Kwŏn Chae-hyŏng, minister, Ministry of Justice, and councilor (*ch'anjŏng*), State Council (Ŭijŏngbu)
[seal affixed]

REPORT NUMBER 3

After assuming the post of judge, I have now reviewed various criminal records from those counties under my jurisdiction.[37] The inquest reports concerning the deceased Kim Kap-san of Hoeyang had been forwarded to the ministry by the previous judge, and the relevant criminals have also been sentenced. Because the report has not yet been made, however, I examined the draft report [written by the previous judge], after confirming the seal. The report says: "Kim Pyŏng-nyŏl, as the lineage chief, issued the circular to gather lineage members in order to interrogate Kim Mun-ho and his assistant Kim Kap-san about facts concerning the illegal burial. He could not carry out the investigation because he was old and ill when Kim Kap-san was first caught and interrogated. But he ordered all lineage members to resolve the issue based on law by reporting to the authorities after hearing the confession. However, the members all became enraged and took turns torturing [Kap-san]. As a result Kap-san died. Although Kim Pyŏng-nyŏl did not intend to kill him, nor did he participate in the interrogation, he could not avoid his responsibility as the one in charge. He also confessed to his role in his testimony. [His crimes] fit with two articles in the *Great Ming Code*: the law that 'only the senior or older member [is] to be punished if the members of one family commit crimes jointly,' in chapter 1, 'Laws on Punishments and General Principles' (K: Myŏngnye; C: Mingli); and the law concerning the original conspirator in the article 'Killing Others in Affrays or by Intention' (K: T'ugu kŭp kosal in; C: Dou'ou ji gusha ren), in section 2, 'Homicide' (K: Inmyŏng; C: Renming).[38] However, his crime was downgraded one level because he did not conduct the interrogation. On account of the ORDER FROM THE MINISTRY (*pu chiryŏng*), he is designated as 'the accused' (*p'igo*), not the principal offender, and thus his crime can be downgraded an additional one level. He is also older than eighty years in age, and, thus, on account of the regulation concerning no judicial torture (*kosin*),[39] the punishment by beating was waived. He should have been sentenced to ten years in prison. However, he could not be arrested and sentenced because he was old and sick and might die any day. In addition, Kim Tae-hyŏn, a lineage member, submitted a petition again [for his release]. On account of the ORDER FROM THE MINISTRY to release him temporarily because imprisonment of an old and sick person goes against the spirit of legal prudence (*hyulchŏn*), he has been released for now.

"As for Kim P'yŏng-il, he simply participated in torturing Kim Kap-san out of the same anger as the other lineage members when they interrogated Kim Mun-ho, who had carried out an illegal burial, and Kim Kap-san, who had helped Mun-ho. There was no evidence that he was the ringleader at all. The story that he tried to exact 100 *yang* [from Kap-san] when he had refused to take 1,000 [from Im Yŏ-gyŏng] is absurd. It is also clear that the relative of the deceased had changed her testimony after submitting her complaint, in terms of indicating Kim P'yŏng-il as the antagonist. Therefore, it is understandable that Kim P'yŏng-il would call it a false charge and unjustifiable. In addition, Kim Pyŏng-nyŏl is now defined as the accused; thus, the category of 'accomplice' (*kanbŏm*) must be [changed to] 'an involved witness' (*kallyŏn*).

"As for Ms. Yu, she is liable for being careless about her words and spreading the story after she learned of the illegal burial by Kim Mun-ho. However, this criminal matter concerning Kim Kap-san's death originated from the Kwangsan Kims, not from what she had done. Therefore, she has been released along with Kim P'yŏng-il."

Now, this case absolutely contains some uncertainties. Kim P'yŏng-il commanded all the lineage members and had them take turns applying torture until they broke the legs of [Kim Kap-san and Kim Mun-ho]. Kim Pyŏng-nyŏl issued a circular [to convene lineage members], but meant to follow the law and not to harm a life. Im Yŏ-gyŏng, as an in-law of the Kyŏngju Kims, tried to mediate a peaceful resolution by offering 1,000 *yang* of money to Kim P'yŏng-il. Kim Pyŏng-nyŏl issued the circular, but [he] was older than eighty years in age and did not commit any crime from the outset. Kim P'yŏng-il, as a "fixer" of the lineage, led the entire clan and plotted to kill Kap-san. Ms. Ch'oe, the close relative of the deceased, indicated only P'yŏng-il as the antagonist against whom [her husband wished] to be avenged. Kim Mun-ho, an eyewitness who heard and saw the incident, also mentioned P'yŏng-il as being at the scene. At the time, P'yŏng-il was like a tiger or wolf with his fierce rage and imposing leadership, and no one was able to oppose him. How could the precarious Ms. Ch'oe and the fearful Kim Mun-ho have dared to accuse only Kim P'yŏng-il as the antagonist among the many powerful Kwangsan Kims [if P'yŏng-il had not truly been the culprit]?

When looking up the article "Plotting to Kill Others" (K: Mosal in; C: Mousha ren) in section 2, "Homicide," of the *Great Ming Code*, those who formulate the plan, even though they do not take part in carrying out the crime, shall be punished as principals.[40] In the article "Killing Others in Affrays or by Intention," in cases where several persons jointly plot to strike others collectively and death results, the fatal injury shall be considered to be the most serious blow, and the persons who strike [and cause the fatal injury] shall be punished by strangulation. The persons who formulate the plots shall be punished by one hundred strokes of beating with a heavy stick and exiled for life to [a distance of] 3,000 *li*.[41] The person who plotted was P'yŏng-il. The person who originally plotted [to kill Kap-san] was P'yŏng-il. Both the law and the evidence are very clear. So, it is correct and accords with the law to name P'yŏng-il as the principal offender. Even if it was for his ancestors, why did P'yŏng-il not follow the words of the lineage chief to resolve the matter by law, but [instead went forward with] the intent to kill and commit a murder? And after that, he turned around and fled, with the excuse of conducting a lineage matter at Port Hope. He showed up to be arrested only at the second inquest. His testimony was full of excuses. But both reports accepted his words in the same manner. If so, how could the dead Kap-san not be resentful? The release of P'yŏng-il is not right. However, I am not intelligent enough to make such a decision on my own and attach the said report to the end of this one. Please review it.

1900.9.9 (10/31/1900)

Chu Sŏng-myŏn, judge, Kangwŏn Provincial Court [seal affixed]

To honorable Kwŏn Chae-hyŏng, minister, Ministry of Justice, and councilor, State Council
[seal affixed]

[cover page]
First month of the fifth year of the Kwangmu reign (1901)

SPECIAL INVESTIGATION REPORT CONCERNING THE CRIMINAL CASE INVOLVING THE DECEASED MALE KIM KAP-SAN FROM HOEYANG LESSER COUNTY

. . . .

[title page]
The accused: Kim Pyŏng-nyŏl
                       Kim Mun-ho[42]

SPECIAL INVESTIGATION REPORT CONCERNING THE CRIMINAL CASE
INVOLVING THE DECEASED MALE KIM KAP-SAN FROM HOEYANG LESSER
COUNTY ON THE FIRST MONTH OF THE FIFTH YEAR OF THE KWANGMU
REIGN [SEAL]

Review completed[43]

. . . .

REPORT, UNNUMBERED

In the CONFIDENTIAL DIRECTIVE that just arrived, it is written:[44] "In the
Order (*hullyŏng*) Number 26 of the Ministry of Justice, it says: '[This office]
received Report Number 3, in which it says. . . .'[45]

'According to this report, it has been clearly proven that Kim Pyŏng-
nyŏl, as the lineage chief, issued a circular to all lineage members, and told
them to resolve the matter in accordance with the law and not to harm the
lives [of the perpetrators]. He had no ill intent in his original directive. It is
absolutely incorrect for both inquest and investigation reports to name him
as the principal offender on account of his issuing the circular on behalf of
the lineage. In the previous instruction, this is what was meant when it said
that there were things to be discussed and judged. He did not commit a real
crime and was older than eighty years in age. There is room for clemency
for him. Release Kim Pyŏng-nyŏl right away. Kim P'yŏng-il, though it was
in the name of his ancestors, became enraged and plotted to break the legs
[of the perpetrators] by commanding lineage members to take turns torturing them, not thinking of any lawful resolution to the matter. His intention
was extremely evil. There is no way to forgive him because he committed the
crime with his own hands. How could he avoid the punishment concerning
the original conspirator? Sentence him on account of this law and report
back immediately.

'The death of Kap-san originated from taking turns torturing him. When
a person ends up dying, there must be those who caused the death. Even if
many caused the death together and thus no single person could be picked
out, there must be distinctions between those who were heavily involved and
lightly involved. If an investigation was carried out to discern those involved,
the principal offender could naturally be found. Yet both the investigation
by [Hoeyang Lesser] County and the judgment by the [Provincial] Court did
not reach any such distinctions, and thus there is no easy way to wash away

the dead person's grudge. [Attempts to determine] the facts of this case had become extremely sloppy. Secure all those who committed a crime and interrogate every one of them in order to nail down one principal offender, and report which laws apply [to each crime].

'The original crime of Kim Mun-ho was an illegal burial at another person's gravesite, but there was no such precedent in terms of the extremely vicious nature of his crime. The disastrous troubles originated solely from him. He should not be left out because he had already fled. Arrest him as soon as possible and submit a sentencing recommendation after looking up the appropriate laws. Carry out this order in such a way.'

"Such an order [from the ministry] was received at the time of the previous provincial governor; however, it has not yet been carried out. Now, you, the magistrate [of Kŭmsŏng Lesser County], are appointed the special investigator. You should go to said county at once to arrest and interrogate each and every person related to this criminal incident. After finding and judging all those who took part in torture as well as the original conspirator, compile a list and report back. Kim Mun-ho was caught and imprisoned in said county during the term of the previous provincial governor. After thoroughly investigating his crimes, report as soon as possible, so that this office can relay the report [to the ministry]. Also report the date when this directive is delivered to your office at once."

Receiving this directive, I departed for said county immediately and carried out the investigation. On 1901.1.19, I interrogated:

Beginning with the first round of interrogation of Kim Chung-ok, two rounds of depositions by concerned people such as Ms. Yu, Kim Mun-ho, and Kim P'yŏng-il were recorded. Only newly revealed and contested information is translated here, with a summary of questions and testimonies in italics to help contextualize the translated parts, so that the reader can follow the development of the case.

In Ms. Yu's first round of testimony, she reports a different story as to how she came to know about the illegal burial. She also says that she was tortured when she was taken to the Kwangsan Kims' cemetery for a face-to-face meeting with Kim Mun-ho and Kim Kap-san. After saying that she sold yeast for a living and had some business with Kim Chung-ok, she states what she saw and learned on one of her visits to Hanch'i Subdistrict: "Kim Kap-san and Kim Kyŏng-hŭi [the close relative of Kap-san who filed the death complaint along with Kap-san's wife Ms. Ch'oe] fought with Kim Mun-ho for more than three days. So I asked why. They did not answer in the beginning and asked me to go away. Then Kap-san said to Mun-ho, 'Thanks to whom did you get to have your son? You received such an ancestral blessing after placing an illegal burial in the gravesite of the Kwangsan Kims' apical ancestor. Why didn't you pay me the 200 *yang* that you had promised me earlier? It is upsetting that you tried to avoid your responsibility by paying me only half.' So I heard, and that was that. I had known Mun-ho from before, so I asked him how he had [carried out] an illegal burial while I stayed there. He replied that he had dug up a Kwangsan Kim's tomb and placed his father there as though it were a couple's burial. . . . The Kwangsan Kims interrogated me, saying, 'With what grudge against the Kwangsan Kims did you divine the spot for an illegal burial for Kim Mun-ho at our ancestral gravesite?' I answered that that was not true. Then they tortured me by twisting my legs. Although the torture was severe, . . . I did not say a word. Then, they released me. . . ."

In Kim P'yŏng-il's first round of testimony, he states that he arrived only on 10.14 (11/16), after the torturing had already begun. Then, he describes the scene as follows: "When we investigated the place for the illegal burial, [we saw] they had dug a hole and placed the corpse together with existing ones, as if three bodies were buried together. How could I explain our bitterness that went bone-deep? The cries of the older members reached to Heaven; it is impossible to describe the boiling rage of the younger members. There was some discussion about killing them, and such a sentiment was overwhelming. I reminded them that Kim Mun-ho had committed a crime punishable by law and that we could be adversely affected if we arbitrarily killed Kim Mun-ho. And I announced to the lineage members that it was our proper duty to report the matter to the authorities and follow the law. . . . When I went to the cemetery . . . both men had already been tortured, so how could I have been in charge? . . . There were more than one hundred lineage elders who were my seniors at the scene. Even if I, a person younger than them, had proposed anything, who would have listened to me? . . . P'yŏng-il is my second name. Living in this narrow mountainous region, I have served as the chief local administrative official and also as a district administrator many times. That was how I got to earn this particular nickname [meaning "impartial"] in the town and country, near and far. Both Kim Mun-ho and Kim Kap-san are wicked men from Hamgyŏng Province and may have been implicated in troubles [earlier] because of tax collection matters. And they might have accumulated hatred against me from those experiences and thus submitted a false charge. How unfair it is. . . . If, indeed, I had committed a crime on that day, why wouldn't I have fled far away, rather than voluntarily appearing at the court?"

In her second deposition, Ms. Yu explains how she had become a godmother to Kim Mun-ho's son: "Mun-ho's wife, seeing my ring, told me that she had seen a silver ring in her precognitive dream about the birth of a child and asked me to be her son's godmother. So, I gave my ring to her. Mun-ho's wife wanted to give me one bolt of fine cotton in return, but I declined. However, she sent it to me later, so I took it. That was how I became the godmother. . . ."

While all other members of the Kwangsan Kims during the deposition denied their leading roles in the incident leading to the death of Kap-san, Kim Pyŏng-nyŏl in his second deposition states: "I sent out a circular to the lineage members and advised them to obtain the correct information even if they had to torture them. On account of that, they did torture them, which led to this disaster of killing a person. Therefore, in this criminal case, I am the one who was in charge of the incident and who talked about [torture]. It is your decision whether I shall be sentenced to capital punishment or banishment. Because of Mun-ho's illegal burial, numerous deaths occurred within the lineage. Please punish Mun-ho according to the law concerning the illegal burial, so that our resentment shall be resolved."

[Concluding statement by the special investigator]
After stating how prudent the court needed to be, the investigator tries to analyze the incident, writing: ". . . The deceased Kim Kap-san was originally from Hamgyŏng Province, but came to live in Kangwŏn Province. His assistance with his nephew's illegal burial was almost like riding the billowing waves. His receiving severe torture by numerous Kwangsan Kims was more like being a toad pressed under a rock. He ended up losing his life after [committing] an illegal act. Though the results of his deeds were lamentable, his death is appalling.

"As for Kim Pyŏng-nyŏl, he is over eighty years old and the most senior [member] of the entire lineage. He issued a circular to gather lineage members after unexpectedly hearing about the illegal burial. He sent out the order to torture in order to get the facts. But he did not take part because he was not able to climb there with his weak legs. The circular was issued by the lineage chief. Lineage members gathered because of the circular. Torture took place because lineage members gathered. A person died because of the torture. A judgment for this case can be drawn from this reasoning. However, [even though] there is no evidence for his direct participation [in torture], it is proper to put him in the category of the accused (p'igo).

"Kim P'yŏng-il is a descendant of one branch of the lineage, among several hundred lineage members. He was out of town for lineage business and arrived at the scene later. Seeing that the grave had been destroyed for an illegal burial, his eyeballs almost popped out. He proceeded to the court and called for justice. That is out of his true integrity. In honor of the DIRECTIVE, I interrogated him and others repeatedly, but no trace of his wrongdoing has been revealed.

"Kim Yun-sŏp, Kim Chŏng-hyŏn, and Kim Ch'ae-wŏn are members of the Kwangsan Kims. At the time of the lineage gathering at Swae Pass, one was present when Kap-san and Mun-ho were tortured while the others arrived after the torturing was over. They reported that the lineage gathering and torturing were on account of the circular issued by the lineage chief. They said they were unable to distinguish conspirators and leaders because all took part together.

"Kim Mun-ho heard popular sayings about illegal burials. Not thinking of destroying another's [gravesite], he dug a hole and placed an illegal burial there. That is punishable by the Ming laws. . . . He named P'yŏng-il as a participant in the incident, but was not able to report who the primary conspirator was. It is truly a pity.

"When considering her composition and listening to her words, Ms. Yu is deceptive. When asking her about the incident and examining its causes, she is absolutely horrendous. She spoke of a matter that she should not have talked about. She went to a place she should not have approached. That was how this homicide took place. Therefore she must be punished, though she had already been sentenced in accordance with the official report.

"Chŏng Tong-baek was passing by the gathering place of the Kwangsan Kims and took on the role of feeding them. Kim Chung-ok is an eleven ch'on relative of Kap-san in the rank of granduncle to him, and the second uncle to Mun-ho. After he heard the rumor about Mun-ho's illegal burial, he summoned Mun-ho and ordered him to remove it. He testified as to why he would not identify the antagonist [if he knew who that was] on behalf of his grandson [Kap-san]. Such an amicable testimony seems to be out of his naive nature as an old country man.

"Close neighbor Kim Tŏg-wŏn and district administrator Yi Kyŏng-ch'an did not appear at court because of illness. Ms. Ch'oe and Kim Kyŏng-hŭi, close relatives of the deceased, returned to Hamgyŏng Province, and thus I was not able to interrogate them. I cannot overcome my regret regarding this. Kim Ŭng-gŭn and a woman from Kaesŏng who appeared in peoples' testimonies must have been questioned once. However, I was not able to get hold of them because one went back home and the other was out of town.

"On the day I arrived in said county to carry out the investigation, all those summoned to appear at court did not come forward right away, so I had to waste several days there. The accused Kim Pyŏng-nyŏl, mentioned earlier, was put under the charge of the court recorder for his imprisonment at said county. As for Kim P'yŏng-il, Kim Yun-sŏp, Kim Chŏng-hyŏn, Kim Ch'ae-wŏn, Kim Mun-ho, and Ms. Yu, it is inconvenient to keep them in the freezing prison, so I put each under the charge of a custodian. I ordered the others to be released. I have compiled and submitted a list of prisoners. The investigation has been completed, so I, the magistrate, am returning to my office.

I humbly submit this report for your review."

1901.1.27 (3/17/1901)

Cho Ch'ŏl-ha, special investigator and magistrate
of Kŭmsŏng Lesser County
[seal affixed]

To the honorable judge at the Kangwŏn Provincial Court
[seal affixed]

REPORT NUMBER 7

In accordance with ORDER Number 26, which was a response to the report made by previous judge Chu Sŏng-myŏn on the criminal case concerning Kim Kap-san of Hoeyang, I appointed Kŭmsŏng magistrate Cho Ch'ŏl-ha as the special investigator, and had him report back to me after carrying out the investigation.[46] Meanwhile, in ORDER Number 36, it was written: "Sentence criminal Kim P'yŏng-il in the criminal case concerning Kim Kap-san of Hoeyang, after consulting the relevant laws from your court, and then report back. Find one principal offender among those criminals in accordance with the laws. Arrest the fugitive Kim Mun-ho and interrogate him properly.

Report all at once. In addition, review and make judgments about all other cases and send reports on them."

I reviewed the case based on all available reports since the special investigation report just arrived today. The deceased Kim Kap-san dug a hole to carry out an illegal burial, though he followed Mun-ho's lead. Even demolishing the mound and breaking the margins of the tomb is unlawful. How much more so is placing a burial as if it were a couple's? He was killed by many beatings and rounds of torture, the result of the deep resentment [felt by] many of the Kwangsan Kims. The facts are cruel, but he caused his own death.

Kim Pyŏng-nyŏl, the accused, issued a circular to gather lineage members as the lineage chief. When Kap-san was first caught and interrogated, Pyŏng-nyŏl was not present because he was sick. And he ordered his lineage members to follow the law. However, the members gathered there were all so outraged that they took turns to torture him to death. Though Pyŏng-nyŏl did not intend to kill anyone and was not present, he confessed that he was the leader. Therefore, his crime likely fits into the code: "only the senior or older member [is] to be punished if the members of one family commit crimes jointly" in the chapter "Laws on Punishments and General Principles" in the *Great Ming Code*. Yet, it was natural for him to issue a circular to gather lineage members because the matter concerned their ancestor. He is older than eighty years in age and he himself did not participate in the torture. These circumstances are something to consider.

Why, one could wonder, did the dead man single out Kim P'yŏng-il as the antagonist? He has been found to be the accomplice (*ch'abŏm*), and it is impossible to forgive him. Yet he followed orders from the lineage chief with the same outrage as the other lineage members. He did not lead the torture because he [only] arrived at the site of the incident after some rounds of torture. He was not the original conspirator, either. Also, he cried [that the accusations were] unfair and argued for a false charge on the basis that the testimony indicating him as the antagonist surfaced three days after the initial complaint. Considering all these circumstances, [since] his crime fits the code concerning "the other persons shall be punished by one hundred strokes of beating with a heavy stick" in the article "Killing Others in Affrays or by Intention" of the *Great Ming Code*, I sentence him to one hundred strokes of beating with a light stick.[47]

Ms. Yu heard the story of the illegal burial on her visit to collect a payment for yeast, and spread the story by forgetting to watch her mouth when talking to her adopted sister. However, she did not make up the story.

Kim Mun-ho, the eyewitness, falsely believing in the divined spot, plotted together with Kap-san and dug a hole at the Kwangsan Kims' apical ancestor's tomb [in which] to place the illegal burial like a couple's burial. This crime falls under the code "Replacing the Corpse" in the article "Uncovering Graves" (K: Palch'ong; C: Fazhong) in the chapter "Violence and Robbery" (K: Chŏkto; C: Zeidao) in the *Great Ming Code*.[48] However, he listened to [another's] advice and removed the illegal burial before the incident took place. He was also cruelly tortured when the incident unexpectedly broke out. Furthermore, he repented his own crimes. Considering all these circumstances, I downgrade his punishments and sentence him to eighty strokes of beating with a light stick and two years in prison.

After sentencing, I compiled two sets of the punishment record for the criminals Kim P'yŏng-il and Kim Mun-ho and [hereby] forward them to the ministry along with the special investigation report. Because I am not intelligent enough, I was not able to find the principal offender in this criminal case. I hereby submit this report.

Please review it.

1901.2.6 (3/25/1901)

Kim Chŏng-gŭn, judge, Kangwŏn Provincial Court [seal affixed]

To the honorable Kim Yŏng-jun, minister, Ministry of Justice, councilor, State Council, acting chief justice (*chaep'anjang*) of the Supreme Court (P'yŏngniwŏn), and general (*ch'amjang*) of the Army (Yukkun) [seal affixed]

REPORT NUMBER 19

In Order Number 8, it is written: "The principal offender of the criminal case concerning Kim Kap-san of Hoeyang shall be determined without delay.[49] Kim P'yŏng-il and Kim Mun-ho shall be questioned at the same court in order to uncover the truth. Report everything, including whether or not Kim Pyŏng-nyŏl has been released. As for the code pertaining to Kim Mun-ho's crimes, apply the code 'Persons who place an illegal burial shall be punished the same as persons who steal another's house,' but downgrade it two levels.[50] Thus, revise the sentencing report to two years in prison."

The former judge, on account of ORDER Number 26, immediately released Kim Pyŏng-nyŏl on 1900.9.29 (11/20/1900). Kim P'yŏng-il and Kim Mun-ho are under the custody of Hoeyang. I just sent a directive to the county to escort them to this court. On account of your ORDER, I shall question them and review the pertaining codes to make a judgment. After that, I shall submit a report. Hereby, I submit this report.

Please review it.

1901.3.18 (5/6/1901)

Pak Chu-hŏn, acting judge of Kangwŏn Provincial Court and magistrate of Hoengsŏng [seal affixed]

To honorable Kim Kŏn-ha, minister, Ministry of Justice, councilor, State Council, and acting minister, Ministry of the Interior
[seal affixed]

INQUIRY (*CHILP'UMSŎ*) NUMBER 3

In ORDER Number 8 from the Ministry of Justice, which arrived during the term of the acting judge and Hoengsŏng magistrate Pak Chu-hŏn, it is written: "Investigate and report the crimes committed by Kim P'yŏng-il and Kim Mun-ho, as well as the legal codes pertaining to those crimes in the case concerning Kim Kap-san of Hoeyang."[51] Thus, I brought them over to this court and rigorously interrogated them face-to-face for three rounds over the course of two days.

The judge then transcribes the testimonies of the two people. Kim P'yŏng-il repeats his previous points: that he arrived on the scene after torture had already taken place, so he was not the leader, and that the original complaint submitted by Kap-san's wife did not mention him as the antagonist. Kim Mun-ho also does not say anything new and repeats his point, asking why he would protect Kim P'yŏng-il if he were the primary culprit.

Reviewing these testimonies along with the other original inquest reports again and again, it is indeed impossible to know who the leader was and who committed the heavier crime in this incident involving many assailants. It is really difficult to designate the primary offender. Kim P'yŏng-il simply followed orders from the lineage chief with the same kind of collective rage as the other members. He arrived at the scene after the torture was over and thus was neither the leader nor the original conspirator. There is no doubt on these [points] when taking Kim Mun-ho's testimony into consideration. I will make a judgment after receiving your ORDER.

As for Kim Mun-ho, on account of the ORDER, his crime likely fits into the code "Persons who place an illegal burial shall be punished the same as persons who steal another's house" in the "Hearing" (Ch'ŏngni) section, and the code concerning "Persons who steal and live in another's house" in the "Prohibitions" (Kŭmje) section in the *Comprehensive Collection of Dynastic Codes*.[52] However, he removed the illegal burial before the incident took place. He was also cruelly tortured when the incident unexpectedly broke out. Considering all these circumstances, I shall downgrade his punishment and sentence him to two years in prison. After sentencing and carrying out this punishment, I shall compile the sentencing document and report it to you. Illegal burial is not one of the six offences (*yukpŏm*).[53] And the ruling is made only now, after his serving as a prisoner for three years.[54] And I wonder if he deserves clemency. Hereby, I inquire about this.

Please review.

1901.5.15 (6/30/1901)

Kim Chŏng-gŭn, judge, Kangwŏn Provincial Court [seal affixed]

To the honorable acting minister, Ministry of Justice, councilor, State Council, and senior councilor, State Council
[seal affixed]

REPORT NUMBER 31

Concerning the case of Kim Kap-san of Hoeyang, I had submitted an inquiry after interrogating criminals Kim P'yŏng-il and Kim Mun-ho face-to-face.[55] In ORDER Number 13, it is written: "At the time of the face-to-face interrogation, because Mun-ho said that his very first testimony [where he testified that P'yŏng-il was at the torture scene] was a false one, P'yŏng-il was proven innocent. Thus, release P'yŏng-il. It is lamentable that this case has dragged on for years because of Kim Mun-ho's changing testimonies. The previous order sought the information whether Kim Pyŏng-nyŏl had been released, but your report did not mention this. This is very suspicious, so file a report regarding this [matter]."

After receiving this order, I released Kim P'yŏng-il at once. As for filing a report concerning Kim Pyŏng-nyŏl's release, I examined the filed documents and found that the previous judge Chu Sŏng-myŏn, on account of the Order Number 26 from the Ministry of Justice, had released him on 1900.9.29 (11/20/1900). Hoengsŏng magistrate Pak Chu-hŏn, as the acting judge at the time, recorded this in Report Number 19. This was the reason I did not mention this in my previous report. I regret not reporting it again after receiving your order. I hereby submit this report.

Please review.

1901.5.27 (7/12/1901)

      Kim Chŏng-gŭn, judge, Kangwŏn Provincial Court [seal affixed]

To the honorable Yi Chae-gon, acting minister, Ministry of Justice, councilor, State Council, and associate judge (*hyŏpp'an*), Ministry of Justice [seal affixed]

NOTES

TRANSLATORS' NOTES

1   *Sinju Muwŏllok*, 74–79.

2   For more detailed discussion of historical changes in measurements, see Pak Hŭng-su, "Toryanghyŏng chedo"; and "Toryanghyŏng," Online EncyKorea, www.encykorea.com.

3   See Sun Joo Kim, *Marginality and Subversion in Korea*, 237, n28.

INTRODUCTION

1   For representative studies along this line of thinking, see Palais, *Politics and Policy in Traditional Korea* and "Political Leadership and the Yangban in the Chosŏn Dynasty."

2   One of the most representative studies along this line of thinking is Kim Yong-sŏp, "The Two Courses of Agrarian Reform in Korea's Modernization."

3   For the most representative studies, see Ko Sŏk-kyu, *19-segi Chosŏn ŭi hyangch'on sahoe yŏn'gu*; and Paek Sŭng-jong, *Han'guk sahoesa yŏn'gu*. *Yangban* in general refers to the social and political elites of late Chosŏn Korea. For a specific definition of *yangban*, see Sun Joo Kim, *Marginality and Subversion in Korea*, 194–95n9.

4   Pak Ki-ju, "19.20 segi ch'o chaech'on yangban chiju kyŏngyŏng ŭi tonghyang"; and Yi Yŏng-hun, "Ch'ongsŏl," 382–89.

5   Sun Joo Kim, *Marginality and Subversion in Korea* and "Taxes, the Local Elite, and the Rural Populace in the Chinju Uprising of 1862."

6   Sun Joo Kim, "Chosŏn hugi P'yŏngan-do Chŏngju ŭi hyangan unyŏng kwa yangban munhwa."

7   Karlsson, "Famine Relief, Social Order, and State Performance in Late Chosŏn Korea" and "Royal Compassion and Disaster Relief in Chosŏn Korea."

8   Such volumes are titled or labeled as *kŏmbalsa* (concluding statements of inquest hearings), *munan palsa* (concluding statements of inquest examinations), *songan* (litigation records), *ogan* (criminal investigation records), and *kŏmje* (trial adjudications).

9   *T'ŭkkyo chŏngsik*, 111a–112a; *Sŭngjŏngwŏn ilgi*, 1779.1.20; *Ch'ugwanji*, 1:531.

10 For the use of torture in interrogation, see the section "Judicial Administrative Structure: Investigation and Criminal Procedure" later in this chapter.

11 *T'ŭkkyo chŏngsik*, 112a–113a.

12 Although *Hŭmhŭm sinsŏ* was compiled in 1822 by Chŏng Yag-yong (1762–1836), it

contains cases from King Chŏngjo's reign between 1776 and 1800. Therefore, many of the cases in the three compilations naturally overlap. For studies based on these three sources, see Shaw, *Legal Norms in a Confucian State*; Sim Chae-u, *Chosŏn hugi kukka kwŏllyŏk kwa pŏmjoe t'ongje*; Kwŏn Yŏn-ung, "*Simnirok* ŭi kich'ojŏk kŏmt'o"; Kim Sŏngyŏng, "Chosŏn hugi yŏsŏng ŭi sŏng, kamsi wa ch'ŏbŏl"; and Kim Ho, "*Hŭmhŭm sinsŏ* ŭi ilgoch'al."

13 *Yusŏ p'ilchi,* though its author and exact compilation date are unknown, was an essential manual for local people—not only officials and yangban, but ordinary people—who wanted to file a complaint or petition about various problems. Though it introduces no standard form for an inquest record, a form for joint interrogation under torture (*tongch'u*) is included as an appendix. Scholars assume that the first availability or circulation of *Yusŏ p'ilchi* may have been sometime in the late eighteenth or early nineteenth century.

14 Robert E. Hegel also points out the impossibility of recording various dialects in legal documents, which are drafted in a uniform language. The impossibility of transcribing local dialects is found in Korean inquest records, too, indicating the limitation of these sources to transmit the vernacular rhetorical power of ordinary men and women. Hegel, *True Crimes in Eighteenth-Century China*, 18–19; Sommer, *Sex, Law, and Society in Late Imperial China*, 26–28.

15 Davis, *Fiction in the Archives*; Ginzburg, *The Night Battles*.

16 Hegel, *True Crimes in Eighteenth-Century China*, x.

17 Chosŏn bureaucracy was structured into the eighteen-rank system, ranging from the highest senior first (Sr. 1) followed by junior first (Jr. 1) down to junior eighth (Jr. 8). Each bureaucratic post corresponded to a rank. For example, the chief state councilor (*yŏngŭijŏng*) was a post of senior first rank. An official was promoted or demoted depending on his (de)merit, and could theoretically hold only a post corresponding to his attained rank or lower. In practice, however, an official often held posts lower than his rank because there were fewer posts available the higher one advanced.

18 According to one study, the average length of magistracy in seven select counties between 1800 and 1863 was about 17 months. Yun Chŏng-ae, "Chosŏn hugi suryŏng taech'aek kwa kŭ insa silt'ae," 242.

19 For a study of local clerks in Chosŏn period, see Hwang, *Beyond the Birth*, 161–207; and Sun Joo Kim, "Fragmented," 138–44. For a study of military officials in Chosŏn Korea, see Park, *Between Dreams and Reality*.

20 For a study of local yangban associations (*hyangan*), see Kawashima, "A Study of Hyangan"; and Sun Joo Kim, "Chosŏn hugi P'yŏngan-do Chŏngju ŭi hyangan unyŏng kwa yangban munhwa."

21 Shaw, *Legal Norms in a Confucian State*, 43–69. More recent works that we consulted are Cho Chi-man, *Chosŏn sidae ŭi hyŏngsabŏp*; Cho Yun-sŏn, *Chosŏn hugi sosong yŏn'gu*; Han Sang-gwŏn, *Chosŏn hugi sahoe wa sowŏn chedo*; Sim Chae-u, *Chosŏn hugi kukka kwŏllyŏk kwa pŏmjoe t'ongje*, 31–72; and Yi Myŏng-bok, *Chosŏn sidae hyŏngsa chedo*.

22 Henceforth, when both the Chinese and Korean terms are given, they will be indicated respectively by C and K.

23 Chǒng Kǔng-sik and Cho Chi-man, "Chosŏn chŏn'gi *Taemyŏngyul* ǔi suyong kwa pyŏnyong"; Shaw, *Legal Norms in a Confucian State.*

24 While the *Great Ming Code* remained as "ancestral instructions," the drastic social changes in the late Ming entailed rather malleable translation of the *Great Ming Code* in local adjudication even before the collapse of the dynasty. With the arrival of the Manchu Qing dynasty, the *Great Ming Code* was subsequently inherited, yet was selectively adopted by the Manchu government to effectively rule the vast and diverse population. The Qing government had revised the *Great Ming Code* more than 30 times by 1912, expanding its several hundred statutes and sub-statutes to 1,907 statutes.

25 There were five different levels of punishment: beating with a light stick (*t'aehyŏng*), beating with a heavy stick (*changhyŏng*), penal servitude (*tohyŏng*), banishment (*yuhyŏng*), and the death penalty (*sahyŏng*). Each penalty ranged from light to heavy, and a criminal often received a combination of different punishments. For example, there were three levels of banishment depending on the distance between the capital and the banished place. And the punishment of banishment was always combined with one hundred blows with a heavy stick. Sim Chae-u, *Chosŏn hugi kukka kwŏllyŏk kwa pomjoe t'ongje*, 44–49.

26 The five human relations (*oryun*) are the relations between sovereign and minister, father and son, husband and wife, elder and younger, and friend and friend. The moral values governing the first three of these relations were designated as the three cardinal values (*samgang*).

27 McKnight, "Introduction," 19–21.

28 *The Washing Away of Wrongs* was drafted by Sung Tz'u (1186–1249) during the Song dynasty. Hegel, *True Crimes in Eighteenth-Century China*, 15. For Brian E. McKnight's English translation and study of this manual, see Sung Tz'u, *The Washing Away of Wrongs.*

29 The *Muwŏllok* was compiled by Wang Yü in 1308 (or 1335). It was based on previous forensic science handbooks, including *The Washing Away of Wrongs*. Though it is not clear when and how *Muwŏllok* began to be used by the Chosŏn court, the annotated edition *Sinju muwŏllok* (Newly annotated coroner's guide for the elimination of grievances) was completed in 1438. A revised edition, *Chŭngsu muwŏllok* (Amplified and corrected coroner's guide for the elimination of grievances), and its Korean version, *Chŭngsu muwŏllok ŏnhae* (Amplified and corrected coroner's guide for the elimination of grievances in vernacular Korean), were published in 1796. All references to *Muwŏllok* in this book are from Kim Ho's modern Korean translation titled *Sinju muwŏllok.*

30 *Sinju muwŏllok,* 303.

31 Ibid., 81.

32 Ibid., 461.

33 Ibid., 461.

34 Ibid., 173–81, 207–9, and 235.

35 *T'ŭkkyo chŏngsik,* 50b–51b.

36 *Sinju muwŏllok,* 322–27.

37 *T'ŭkkyo chŏngsik,* 13b.

38 *Sinju muwŏllok,* 461. For examples of a routine use of a silver hairpin during the examination of the body, see cases 1, 3, 5, and 8. See case 2 for how a test result could complicate the adjudication of the case.

39 *T'ŭkkyo chŏngsik,* 22a.

40 Ibid., 26a–b.

41 Ibid., 32a–33a.

42 We would like to thank Robert E. Hegel, who suggested the English translations for these three terms. Edward J. Baker also gave us useful advice on explaining these legal terms.

43 Two representative studies based on the *Simnirok* are Shaw, *Legal Norms in a Confucian State,* and Sim Chae-u, *Chosŏn hugi kukka kwŏllyŏk kwa pŏmjoe t'ongje.*

44 This order was made in 1784. *T'ŭkkyo chŏngsik,* 47a–b.

45 The following discussion of legal reforms after 1894 relies on To Myŏn-hoe, "Kabo kaehyŏk ihu kŭndaejŏk pŏmnyŏng chejŏng kwajŏng."

46 Unlike inquest records, petitions have been examined by a number of scholars. A well-known Korean journal, *Munhŏn kwa haesŏk* (Documents and interpretations), has introduced and translated valuable petitions over the years. For representative studies on late Chosŏn litigation and petition systems, see Han Sang-gwŏn, *Chosŏn hugi sahoe wa sowŏn chedo,* and Cho Yun-sŏn, *Chosŏn hugi sosong yŏn'gu.* For works on women's petitioning practice in the Chosŏn, see Kim Kyŏng-suk, "Chosŏn hugi yŏsŏng ŭi chŏngso hwaldong"; Haboush, "Gender and the Politics of Language in Chosŏn Korea"; and Jisoo Kim, "Voices Heard."

47 Han Sang-gwŏn, *Chosŏn hugi sahoe wa sowŏn chedo,* 10. Han's extensive study on the petition system is based on the 4,000 petition cases filed during King Chŏngjo's reign.

48 Studies show how the patriarchal Chosŏn society recognized women as legal subjects on equal footing with their male counterparts. Unlike imperial China, where a woman had to rely on a male proxy to enter the legal space, a Chosŏn woman had the legal capacity to establish herself as a legal agent for and defender of her family without being required to have male representation. Kim Kyŏng-suk, "Chosŏn hugi yŏsŏng ŭi chŏngso hwaldong"; Haboush, "Gender and the Politics of Language in Chosŏn Korea"; and Jisoo Kim, "Voices Heard."

CASE 1

1 Chapter 6, Section 2, Article 308 in *The Great Ming Code / Da Ming lü,* 171.

2 Chapter 6, Section 8, Article 390 in *The Great Ming Code,* 214.

3 Chang Pyŏng-in, "Chosŏn chung-hugi kant'ong e taehan kyuje ŭi kanghwa," 88–95, and Sim Chae-u, *Chosŏn hugi kukka kwŏllyŏk kwa pŏmjoe t'ongje,* 54–55. See also *Taejŏn hoet'ong* (Comprehensive collection of dynastic codes), 735–36.

4   Shaw, *Legal Norms in a Confucian State*, 99–106. For specific cases that reveal the state's control over female sexuality, see Kim Sŏn-gyŏng, "Chosŏn hugi yŏsŏng ŭi sŏng," 83–96. For various legal revisions concerning adultery and fornication during the Chosŏn period, see Chŏng Kŭng-sik, "Urinara kant'ongjoe ŭi popchesajŏk koch'al," 211–42.

5   Chang Pyŏng-in, "Chosŏn chung-hugi kant'ong e taehan kyuje ŭi kanghwa," 107; Kim Sŏn-gyŏng, "Chosŏn hugi yŏsŏng ŭi sŏng," 83–90; and Jungwon Kim, "Negotiating Virtue and the Lives of Women in Late Chosŏn Korea," 58–105.

6   It is not clear what constituted "one round of beating." According to the *Taejŏn hoet'ong* compiled in 1865, one round of beating with a heavy stick (*chang*) should not exceed 30 strokes when used for torture, and beating with a heavy stick should not exceed 100 strokes total in one day. See *Taejŏn hoet'ong*, 653 and 668.

7   Shaw, *Legal Norms in a Confucian State*, 119.

8   Shaw, *Legal Norms in a Confucian State*, 119. See also Sim Chae-u, *Chosŏn hugi kukka kwŏllyŏk kwa pŏmjoe t'ongje*, 138–41.

9   McKnight, "Introduction," 19.

10 Chunghwa-bu ogan (Inquest records of Chunghwa County), Harvard-Yenching Library collection TK 4899 4352. This source does not carry page numbers. We assigned numeric page numbers to each folio page beginning with the first page of the book after the cover page.

11 *Kojong sillok*, 1865.11.28; and *Sŭngjŏngwŏn ilgi* (Records of the Royal Secretariat), 1866.11.29.

12 This case is from *Chunghwa-bu ogan*, 81–113.

The magistracy of a county (tohobu) was a senior third-rank post. There were eighteen ranks in Chosŏn bureaucracy—nine ranks divided by junior and senior—and each bureaucratic post was ranked. See note 17 and table 1 in the introduction of this book. When an official's rank was higher than the rank prescribed for his post, the character *haeng* preceded the title of his post, which is translated "brevetted" in this book. It was popular practice in the late Chosŏn for an official to serve in a lower-ranking post, for the king frequently upgraded the ranks held by his officials in recognition of their meritorious service. For more details on this topic, see Ch'oe Sŭng-hŭi, "Chosŏn sidae yangban ŭi taegaje," 1–32.

13 See the translators' notes for the meaning of all capital letters in the translations throughout this book.

14 Here, *yi* means "second" and *sam* means "third." Thus, although the two brothers did not live in the same subdistrict, they were not far from each other.

15 Regarding the use of a silver hairpin, see the introduction to this book, between note numbers 30 and 33.

16 See the introduction (before note 42 in the text) for an explanation of this term.

17 This means simply that they met when they were very young. Before marriage, both boys and girls would have pigtails. Upon marriage, a man began to have a topknot while a woman wore her hair in a bun.

18 These are the concluding remarks of the magistrate of Chunghwa County, the official in charge of this first inquest investigation.

19 See *Sinju muwŏllok*, 432–33.

20 The inquest form was preprinted to record the result of the inquest report, including the examination of the corpse. Each form bears a unique serial mark, which was assigned in accordance with the sequence of Chinese characters appearing in the *Ch'ŏnjamun* (Thousand-character classic); *un* is one of those characters.

21 The original text says all murders "do not" derive from the three things. I have dropped the negative here because it is apparent that this is an error, probably introduced during transcribing.

22 This refers to article 308 of the *Great Ming Code*.

23 According to *Taejŏn hoet'ong*, a son should not be interrogated to testify against his father, a younger brother against his older brother, a wife against her husband, or slaves against their owners. See *Taejŏn hoet'ong*, 660.

24 In the original text, the entire provincial governor's adjudication statement is indented.

CASE 2

1 According to Sim Chae-u's analysis of 1,112 criminal cases in the *Simnirok*, 4.4 percent of 1,004 cases involving murder or suicide were caused by gravesite litigation. Sim Chae-u, *Chosŏn hugi kukka kwŏllyŏk kwa pŏmjoe t'ongje*, 153. In addition, analysis of various petitions recorded in the *Ilsŏngnok* (Record of daily reflections; one of the major court records of the late Chosŏn) during the reign of King Chŏngjo (r. 1776–1800) shows that 574 cases out of 4,304 (about 13 percent) concerned gravesite litigation. Among those cases, about 70 percent concerned illegal burials. See Han Sang-gwŏn, "Chosŏn hugi sansong ŭi silt'ae wa sŏnggyŏk," 779 and 791.

2 For more detailed discussion of geomancy, see Sun Joo Kim, *Marginality and Subversion*, 89–95, and Skinner, *The Living Earth Manual of Feng-Shui*, 14–23.

3 For more discussion of this subject, see Kim Sŏn-gyŏng, "Chosŏn hugi sansong," and Sun Joo Kim, *Marginality and Subversion in Korea*, 89–91.

4 *Kyŏngguk taejŏn*, 3:36b.

5 Han Sang-gwŏn, "Chosŏn hugi sansong ŭi silt'ae wa sŏnggyŏk," 784–85.

6 Han Sang-gwŏn, "Chosŏn hugi sansong ŭi silt'ae wa sŏnggyŏk," 824. See also *Sok taejŏn*, 5:32b–34a.

7 Han Sang-gwŏn, "Chosŏn hugi sansong ŭi silt'ae wa sŏnggyŏk," 793–94 and 824.

8 For various ways in which the non-yangban population was involved in gravesite litigations, see Han Sang-gwŏn, "Chosŏn hugi sansong ŭi silt'ae wa sŏnggyŏk," 782–91.

9 Yi Chae-hŭi, "Kukka ka kyŏnjehan yangbandŭl ŭi hwaryŏhan chugŏ munhwa," 204–5.

10 See Cho Yun-sŏn, *Chosŏn hugi sosong yŏn'gu*, 131, and Jisoo Kim, "Voices Heard."

11 See Han Sang-gwŏn, "Chosŏn hugi sansong ŭi silt'ae wa sŏnggyŏk," 794–97, and Cho Yun-sŏn, *Chosŏn hugi sosong yŏn'gu*, 128–30.

12 Ms. Pak was not unique in acting this way. There were other similar cases where the enraged complainant dug up the illegal burial. See Han Sang-gwŏn, "Chosŏn hugi san-song ŭi silt'ae wa sŏnggyŏk," 816–19.

13 According to Sim Chae-u's analysis of *Simnirok*, out of 1,112 offenders whose crimes warranted capital punishment, only thirty-six (3.2 percent) received a death sentence, while out of 1,004 murder or suicide cases, only twenty (2 percent) received a death sentence. See Sim Chae-u, *Chosŏn hugi kukka kwŏllyŏk kwa pŏmjoe t'ongje*, 138–41 and 234–35. See also Shaw, *Legal Norms in a Confucian State*, 118–20.

14 The *Kŏman (Inquest Records)* is in the collection of the Kungnip Chungang Tosŏgwan (National Library of Korea), han kojo 34–51. The entire book is available as images through the library's database, and the present translated case is found on pp. 14–18 (page numbers assigned by the library).

15 There are at least five different editions of *Simnirok* according to Sim Chae-u. See his *Chosŏn hugi kukka kwŏllyŏk kwa pŏmjoe t'ongje*, 95–103.

16 The *Simnirok* is available in Korean translation, and both original texts and transla-tions are also available online, which enables a search function for these twelve cases. All twelve cases in the *Kŏman* were filed with the county-level authorities between approximately 1775 and 1786, and the first royal judgment came between 1778 and 1787.

17 *Kugyŏk Simnirok*, 2:285–91. The text is also online athttp://db.itkc.or.kr.

18 This particular method of appeal, by presenting a petition directly to the king or local officials, was rather popular throughout the Chosŏn dynasty. See Shaw, *Legal Norms in a Confucian State*, 85–92.

19 For statistical information on the length of a trial in the late eighteenth century, see Sim Chae-u, *Chosŏn hugi kukka kwŏllyŏk kwa pŏmjoe t'ongje*, 212–13.

20 *Sinju muwŏllok*, 461. See the introduction to the present volume regarding the use of a silver hairpin during an autopsy.

21 This case is from *Kŏman*, 14–18.

22 "Incoming dragon vein" refers to the mountain range stemming from the main moun-tain of black tortoise to the north of the ideal burial site, and forming the azure dragon hill to the east.

23 The original text says "her," but this must be a scribal error for "her brother," consider-ing the context.

24 The character *ko* in the text refers to *kohan*. The article "Pogo han'gi" (= *kohan*, C: Baogu hanqi; Period of responsibility for crimes) in the *Da Ming lü* (Great Ming code) specifies as follows: "In cases of striking and injuring others with hands, feet, or other objects, the period of responsibility for the offense shall be limited to 20 days; in cases of injuring others with the blade of a metal implement, boiling liquid, or fire, the period shall be limited to 30 days; and in all cases of breaking limbs, dislocating joints, breaking bones, or causing miscarriages, regardless of whether the injuries are caused by use of hands, feet, or other objects, the period shall be limited to 50 days." See *The Great Ming Code*, 179–80, for more details on this law.

25 This is Ŏ Sa-p'il, mentioned in the latter part of the text.

26 Chŏm-hwa was a female slave of Ŏ Sa-p'il, as revealed in the latter part of this text.

27 Ŏ Sa-p'il of the Hamjong Ŏ descent group was born in 1711 and passed the higher civil service examination (*munkwa*) in 1744.

28 In the original text, this line starts one space above other lines because all direct references to the king and his official pronouncements are raised above the text in traditional writings, as indicated here in the translation by the use of all capital letters. There are also other ways to mark the royal voice in traditional writings: leaving one or two letter spaces blank, or changing a line and starting at the top of the next line.

29 In the provincial governor's concluding statement, Kim Wŏn-ch'ŏl used a hoe to attack Ms. Pak.

CASE 3

1 Shaw, *Legal Norms in a Confucian State*, 106–15. See case 7, n1 for the four main status groups in the late Chosŏn and the eight occupations of those in the lowborn group, and the introductory paragraphs of case 7 for more on slaves.

2 For the social status of sons and daughters by a yangban father and his commoner or slave concubine, see Deuchler, "Heaven Does Not Discriminate."

3 For the tripartite relationship among state, elite, and non-elite producers in their effort to get hold of local resources, and resultant conflicts in various forms, including open uprisings, see Sun Joo Kim, "Taxes, the Local Elite, and the Rural Populace in the Chinju Uprising of 1862."

4 *Kŏman ch'o (Selected Inquest Records)* is in the collection of the Kungnip Chungang Tosŏgwan (National Library of Korea). It consists of two volumes, "kŏn" and "kon." This case is in kon 24–37 (pagination by the library).

5 Min Ch'i-sŏ appears once in the *sillok* on 1842.8.26 (9/30/1842), as the magistrate of Anŭi. Therefore, the *imin* year in this text is 1842. See *Hŏnjong sillok*, 1842.8.26.

   This case is from *Kŏman ch'o*, kon 24–37.

6 The elbows belong to the dorsal side of the body according to the *Muwŏllok* (Coroner's guide for the elimination of grievances).

7 *Ch'ŏmji* is a contraction of *ch'ŏmjijungch'ubusa*, a senior third-rank military position. However, it does not seem that Yi Pong-un held a real bureaucratic post; he probably purchased this title.

8 *Pan* was an appellation reserved for yangban; "Sin *pan*" (Yangban Sin) refers to the accused Sin P'il-ho, who was a yangban.

9 See the introduction (before note 42 in the text) for an explanation of the terms *saryŏn* and *kallyŏn*.

10 In the original text, this statement is indented.

11 Ch'oe U-hyŏng of the Sangnyŏng Ch'oe descent group earned a literary licentiate degree (*chinsa*) in 1837 and passed the higher civil service examination in 1850. Later in life, his bureaucratic service included ministerial posts.

12 In the original text, this statement is indented.

13 See case 1, n6 for the variations in the number of blows in a round of beating.

CASE 4

1 Out of about 165 biographies of chaste widows (*yŏllyŏjŏn*) compiled during the Chosŏn dynasty, only six were produced during the early Chosŏn. Publication of chaste women's biographies thrived from the seventeenth century on, reaching its peak during the eighteenth and nineteenth centuries.

2 This legal code articulates that "those who had guilt, sons of corrupt officials, sons and grandsons of remarried or unfaithful women, and sons of concubines are not permitted to take the civil service exam." *Kyŏngguk taejŏn* (Great code of administration), 3:1b.

3 In the original text, Madam Chang is written "Chang *ssi*," and Ms. Ŭn is written "Ŭn *nyŏ*." Chosŏn legal testimonies record one's social status, and *ssi* (translated here as "Madam") usually refers to yangban women, whereas *choi* (or *sosa*) indicates commoner women. It is clear that Madam Chang was a yangban widow in this case. As for Ms. Ŭn, *nyŏ* literally means "a woman" (not a yangban woman, but not necessarily a commoner, either), which distinguishes her status from that of Madam Chang. The fact that she is not recorded as "Ŭn *choi*," however, makes it difficult to determine her exact social status. If she was not a non-yangban commoner woman, what status did she have? We assume she may have been the daughter of a yangban's concubine. In this case, we simply translate *nyŏ* as "Ms." For more on such appellations, see the Translators' Notes.

4 Capp, *When Gossips Meet*, 189. Bernard Capp, in analyzing court records on female disputes in early modern England, points out that "whore" was the most common verbal insult for women because "sexual 'honesty' was so fundamental to female reputation that its language was often transferred to other forms of misconduct, plausibly enough in a culture that saw women's sexual and non-sexual honesty as indivisible."

5 Chapter 6, article 347, "Maein" (C: Maren; Cursing others), in *The Great Ming Code*, 190.

6 Local communities during the Chosŏn were closely connected through marriage, and it was quite common that people with the same surname gathered and lived either in the same village or neighboring districts. As seen throughout the testimonies, the witness Mr. Yi was related to both the victim and defendant in this case, as a remote nephew of Madam Chang and a cousin-in-law of Ms. Ŭn.

7 Barahona, *Sex Crimes, Honour, and the Law in Early Modern Spain*, 119.

8 It is not clear when Kim Ki-hyŏn was appointed a magistrate of Yech'ŏn Lesser County, yet later records show that he served in various posts for more than thirty years and was praised for his exceptional governing skills by kings who continued to promote him to several important positions. *Ch'ŏlchong sillok*, 1854.7.30; and *Sŭngjŏngwŏn ilgi* (Records of the royal secretariat), 1864.10.22 and 1865.5.10.

This case is from *Kŏman ch'o*, kon 85–96. See case 3 for more information on this collection of inquest records.

9 The two volumes in which this case is included do not give us exact dates of the cases,

except for the year of *imin*, which could be either 1842 or 1902 by the sixty-year cycle. However, it is clear from the intercalary third month (*yun samwŏl*) in this document that the volumes carry cases of 1842 because 1842 included an intercalary month, whereas there was no intercalary month in 1902.

10 The original text reads "though Ms. Ŭn has yangban title." Yet as discussed in note 3, her social status is not clear since she is also recorded as *nyŏ* ("woman") throughout the document. It seems best to assume that she was the daughter of a yangban's concubine. Though born to a yangban father, she was therefore supposed to carry her mother's social status and would never have been considered to be a genuine yangban.

11 This phrase comes from the biography of a Chinese general, Yuan Jingan, included in the *Bei Qi shu* (K: *Pukchesŏ*; Book of Northern Qi, 550–77). Literally translated as "To rather be a jade broken than a tile intact," it implies that one would rather die with honor than survive with dishonor.

12 In the original text, this statement is indented.

13 Having obtained his literary licentiate degree (*chinsa*) in 1822 at the age of thirty-five, Sŏng Kyo-muk (1788–?) was appointed the magistrate of Yonggung Lesser County in the first month of 1841. By 1914, Yonggung had been merged into Yech'ŏn under Japanese colonial rule (1910–45).

14 In the original text, this statement is indented.

15 The currency is recorded as a different character—*min* (a string of coins)—in the original text. However, *yang* is still used in translation because both currencies had the same cash value and *yang* is used earlier in the document. For a study of how to translate currency units of the Chosŏn dynasty, see Pak Hye-suk, "18 segi–19 segi e poinŭn hwap'ye tanwi pŏnyŏk ŭi munje."

16 See case 1, n6 for the variations in the number of blows in a round of beating.

CASE 5

1 This is the well-known story of the filial daughter Sim Ch'ŏng, who sacrifices her life for the sake of her blind father's miraculous restoration of vision. In the tale, Blindman Sim falls into a drainage ditch and almost dies, but is saved by a Buddhist monk who tells him he can "open" Sim's eyes with a hefty sacrificial rice offering to the Buddha. Blindman Sim's spontaneous pledge leads to his daughter Sim Ch'ŏng's determination to sell herself as prey to the fierce dragon king of the sea for the sum needed to make the rice offering. For a study and English translation of the "Song of Sim Ch'ŏng," see Pihl, *The Korean Singer of Tales*.

2 Yi Sŭng-gyŏng was from the Hansan Yi descent group. He passed the lower civil service examination in 1837 and obtained a classics licentiate degree (*saengwŏn*). Some of his writings are available in his collected works in draft form, entitled *Yŏsa nanjip* (Collected works on miscellaneous matters). He is also the author of *Kyŏngjo puji* (Gazetteer of Seoul), compiled in 1851.

3 A traditional woman's skirt is usually long, covering her upper body, including the

breasts, down to her feet. It is a wrap-around skirt with a long sash attached to the top part of the skirt, which actually wraps around her breasts and upper back rather than her waist, before being tied together to avoid the skirt from opening and slipping down.

4   *Sinju muwŏllok,* 365; Sung Tz'u, *The Washing Away of Wrongs,* 108.

5   From the names of two brothers, Kyŏng-sam was the third and Kyŏng-o was the fifth among an unknown number of siblings. There may have been sisters in between the two, but it is not too much to assume that Kyŏng-o was at most only several years younger than Kyŏng-sam.

6   This summary of the entire case investigation is indented in the original text.
    This case is from *Chunghwabu ogan,* 1–46.

7   Mun Yu-mok, the dead boy's father, previously stated that the boy had a pockmark a little behind the left side of the head, not the right.

8   See this volume's introduction (just before note numbers 31 and 32 in the text) for the use of a silver hairpin to test for death by poison.

9   In the original text, this is recorded as the third deposition (*samch'u*), which we take to be a mistake for the second deposition, considering the entire sequential format of this inquest record, and especially because Ko Kyŏng-sam's testimony is followed by the second, not third, deposition of Ms. Cho.

10 These are the concluding remarks of the magistrate of Chunghwa County, the official in charge of this first inquest investigation.

11 As seen in case 1, Chosŏn law in principle prohibited a wife's testimony against her husband (see case 1, n23). The same law seems to have applied to close relatives such as brother-in-law and niece.

12 Chosŏn elites as well as ordinary people believed in the existence of spirits and ghosts. See Walraven, "Popular Religion in a Confucianized Society," 163–71. It was probably a popular belief that the fingernails of a person killed by a ghost turn blue.

13 The old proverb "A pear falls off a tree as soon as a crow flies away" means that two things can happen coincidentally. That is, the pear falls naturally, not because the crow picks at it and damages it. In this case, the death of the baby may have happened coincidentally and not necessarily as the result of Ms. Kim's choking.

14 The text says Ko Kyŏng-o is the "father" of the principal offender, but this must have been a scribal error springing from the fact that "husband" and "father" are homonyms in literary Chinese.

15 This sentence seems to have been added later on and stands out because its line begins far above the other lines of writing and is also written in lighter ink and a different calligraphic style. Yet this piece of information is crucial in identifying the year when this investigation was carried out. Yi Sŭng-gyŏng was born in 1815 and earned a classics licentiate degree (*saengwŏn*) in 1837. From other inquest reports collated in *Chunghwa-bu ogan* (Inquest records of Chunghwa County), where this particular report is found, we know that these crimes took place in a *pyŏngin* year, which should then be 1866.

16 This particular article in the *Da Ming lü* (Great Ming code) is called "T'ugu" (C: Dou'ou;

Affrays and batteries). See *The Great Ming Code*, 177–79, for details on this article. For more details on the article called "Pogo han'gi" (= *kohan*, C: Baogu hanqi; Period of responsibility for crimes), see the *Great Ming Code*, 179–80, and case 2, n24.

17 In the original text, the entire provincial governor's adjudication statement is indented. The provincial governor at the time was Pak Kyu-su. For more on Pak, see the last introductory paragraph of case 1.

CASE 6

1 To avoid a corpse's decay, the *Muwŏllok* (Coroner's manual for elimination of grievances) emphasizes a timely autopsy process. *Sinju muwŏllok*, 139–53.

2 Cho Yun-sŏn, *Chosŏn hugi sosong yŏn'gu*, 251–59. According to Mark A. Allee, Qing legal authorities concluded that "there was no explicit concept of civil as distinct from criminal law." He explains that complaints that were "minor (e.g., disputes over household matters, real property, and marriage)" and "serious (e.g., crimes involving force, violence, personal injury)" in traditional Chinese law "can only be approximated by the labels 'civil' and 'criminal' as used in Western law." As in China, the sharp distinction drawn between criminal and civil legal cases was not clear in Chosŏn Korea. Allee, *Law and Local Society in Late Imperial China*, 10–12.

3 An Chŏng-bok (1712–91), an eighteenth-century scholar who produced volumes on governing locals, points out that "the expense for an autopsy is quite heavy for people. Therefore, [people] tend to settle matters privately even with their enemies by accepting bribes. . . . Only when the government provides a victim's family with material support for the funeral will such evil practice of private settlement disappear." An Chŏng-bok, *Imgwan chŏngyo*, sokp'yŏn, 116. We used a version from Kungnip Chungang Tosŏgwan (National Library of Korea), cho 31–65.

4 The year *kich'uk* in the original source could be either 1829 or 1889. However, it is safe to assume that *kich'uk* in this case is 1889 since the first inquest official, Sim Chŏngt'aek, was appointed a magistrate of Hayang Lesser County in the first month of 1889. *Sŭngjŏngwŏn ilgi* (Records of the Royal Secretariat), 1889.1.30.

5 It was common for a victim's family to request the costs of medical treatment or of the settlement of a death. If successful, such settlements not only avoided complicated and expensive legal procedures but secured some financial support for the victim's family. For an example, see Cho Yun-sŏn, *Chosŏn hugi sosong yŏn'gu*, 276.

6 This is usually based on the principle of the "period of responsibility for crimes" (*pogo* or *pogo han'gi*), which mandates that the court suspend judgment until the beaten victim either recovers or dies. See *Taejŏn hoet'ong* (Comprehensive collection of dynastic codes), 720. Also see chapter 6, section 2, article 326 in *The Great Ming Code*, 179.

7 The law continues, "although [the miscarriage] is caused by the affray and battery, if the child dies beyond the period of responsibility, or if the fetus is less than ninety days old and the child is not formed, in each case the offenders shall be punished in accordance

with specific provisions on striking and injuring. They shall not be punished for 'causing a miscarriage.'" Chapter 6, section 3, article 325 [1] in *The Great Ming Code*, 178.

8 Ibid.

9 Although peddlers were mainly merchants, to make a living many of them also had side jobs, such as a craft or farming. Yi Hŏn-ch'ang, "Chosŏn malgi pobusang kwa pobusangdan," 146–47.

10 Yŏn Chŏng-yŏl, *Han'guk pŏpche sasangsa*, 514–16.

11 Various peddlers' associations appear in official documents, particularly from the early nineteenth century, asking for the public acknowledgment of their existence. At the beginning, it was usually the local magistrate who approved the associations, but later the central government came to be in charge of them. Yi Hŏn-ch'ang, "Chosŏn malgi pobusang kwa pobusangdan," 150–56.

12 This article is included in the "Posangch'ŏng chŏlmok" (Principles of peddlers' associations) created by peddlers of several regions in Ch'ungch'ŏng Province in 1870. Quoted from Yi Hŏn-ch'ang, "Chosŏn malgi pobusang kwa pobusangdan," 154.

13 The 1876 Kanghwa Treaty was the first modern-style international treaty signed between Chosŏn and Japan. As this unequal treaty forced the Chosŏn government to open three ports for trade, it was obvious that the native merchants had to compete with foreign merchants. There are quite a number of homicide cases dealing with deaths of Chinese or Japanese merchants due to conflicts with native merchants and local people after 1876.

14 This case is from *Ogan ch'ogae*, 2:61–69.

15 Since the deceased was a pregnant woman, the postmortem must have been carried out by an old woman. Sung Tz'u, *The Washing Away of Wrongs*, 83.

16 "If she was carrying a child, then when the area from below the heart to the navel is palpated, it will be firm like iron or stone." Ibid.

17 See the introduction and case 2 for a more detailed discussion of the use of a silver hairpin to determine whether poison was the cause of death.

18 A *toe* is a Korean unit of measure in volume; 1 *toe* is approximately 1.8 liters.

19 A *turak* is a measure of land; 1 *turak* is the amount of land where 1 *mal* (4.765 U.S. gallons) of rice seed is sewn.

20 This practice of heaving a wounded person to an offender's house and asking for money was regarded as an immoral custom. See the death case of Sundŭk, a temple slave of Andong, Kyŏngsang Province in 1785, in *Kugyŏk Simnirok* 3:134–36.

21 In the early Chosŏn period, *yuhak* was one of the yangban titles in various official documents, such as household registers and state service examination rosters. However, from about seventeenth century on, many quasi-yangban began to use this title as a way to avoid military tax obligations, and it was no longer possible to identify persons with the *yuhak* designation as authentic yangban. See Shin, "The Social Structure of Kŭmhwa County in the Late Seventeenth Century," and Palais, *Confucian Statecraft and Korean Institutions*, 361.

22 Yi Sŏk-chin was appointed magistrate of Ŭihŭng Lesser Prefecture in 1888, after briefly serving in the same position in Yangsŏng. In 1889 he was replaced by a magistrate of Nangch'ŏn in Kangwŏn Province. Although he resigned from his post due to illness by the end of 1891, he was questioned for his inability to deal with a small peasant revolt in that area during his tenure and was also punished in 1892 for not carrying out an investigation of a corpse in a timely way. *Sŭngjŏngwŏn ilgi*, 1888.6.27; 1889.7.27; 1892.6.29; 1892.9.3.

23 This well-known phrase, found in the *Sanguozhi* (K: *Samgukchi*; Record of the Three Kingdoms), means that if parents are not safe, children cannot be protected either.

24 See case 1, n6, for the variations in the number of blows in a round of beating.

CASE 7

1 In the late Chosŏn the population was composed largely of four status groups: the elite (*yangban*), the "middle people" (*chungin*), commoners (*yangin*), and the lowborn (*ch'ŏnmin*). As the term the "eight meanest groups of people" (*p'alch'ŏn*) indicates, people in the lowborn status group were slaves, monks, shamans, clowns, butchers, bier carriers, and various craftsmen such as basket-weavers and tanners.

2 The *Kyŏngguk taejŏn* (Great code of administration) clearly outlines that butchers and entertainers (or clowns) must register and reside within a designated area. The births, deaths, and runaways among these people had to be reported to the authorities, and those who escaped from the designated area were to be punished. *Kyŏngguk taejŏn*, 5:4b. Butchers (*paekchŏng*) in particular were regarded as "a stigmatized minority, comparable to the *burakumin* in Japan, and as inferior even to slaves and female entertainers (*kisaeng*)." Joong-Seop Kim, "In Search of Human Rights," 312–15.

3 *Kyŏngguk taejŏn*, 6:4a–38a; *Taejŏn hoet'ong* (Comprehensive collection of dynastic codes), 775–81.

4 Although slaves themselves were illiterate and did not produce their own writing, studies on slaves during the Chosŏn dynasty are abundant because a large number of both official and unofficial documents such as legal codes, litigations, private contracts, inheritance records, and yangban's diaries deal with slave issues.

5 Most government-owned public slaves were freed in 1801.

6 Choi et al., eds., *Sources of Korean Tradition*, 2:275.

7 According to the *Great Ming Code*, "In all cases where a wife or concubine commits adultery with another, if [her own husband] himself catches the adulterer and the adulterous wife at the place of adultery and immediately kills them, he shall not be punished. If he only kills the adulterous lover, the adulterous wife shall be punished in accordance with the Code [Art. 390] and be remarried or sold by her husband." See chapter 6, section 2, article 308 [1] in *The Great Ming Code*, 171.

8 See chapter 3 of Jungwon Kim, "Negotiating Virtue and Lives of Women in Late Chosŏn Korea."

9 Torture was a crucial method in obtaining confessions. Although inquest records never

document the use and degree of torture employed throughout the testimonies, we can assume that "the importance of confession encouraged aggressive interrogation as standard judicial practice." For a detailed discussion of the role of torture in imperial China, see Brook et al., *Death by a Thousand Cuts*, 43.

10   Chapter 6, section 2, article 305 [1] in *The Great Ming Code*, 169.

11   We checked other sources, such as *Sabŏp p'umbo* (Provincial reports concerning legal matters), to see if Kim Kyŏng-un was ultimately arrested and further investigations were conducted, but no information was available.

12   Legal edicts on the punishment of a magistrate who could not catch a criminal within a certain period had changed over time—from expulsion from his position to demotion of his performance in evaluation. Yet the last edict on this subject, promulgated in 1838, shifted again and stopped degrading the administrative performance. *Sugyo tŭngnok* (Compilation of received edicts), 12:a–13:a.

13   Jungwon Kim, "Negotiating Virtue and Lives of Women in Late Chosŏn Korea," chapter 3.

14   Chapter 6, section 2, article 308 [2] in *The Great Ming Code*, 171.

15   *Taejŏn hoet'ong*, 650. The heaviest criminal cases, for punishment by death, should be concluded in 30 days; the medium, for exile, in 20 days; and the small, for flogging, in 10 days. If the time period has been exceeded, written grounds should be submitted to the king.

16   Kim Ho's brief introduction to the document, available in the Kyujanggak Archive, notes that the case began in the tenth month of 1896 and ended in the first month of 1897. It seems that he calculated dates based on the title of this case—the second year of Kŏnyang (1897)—while missing *ŭlmi*, the two-character combination that indicates the year 1895, which appears only once in the beginning of the document. Kŏnyang is one of the two reign titles of King Kojong, the other being Kwangmu, as appears in case 8.

17   For a detailed discussion of troubles in tax administration in the area by disguised Tonghak believers or Catholics, see Yumi Moon, "The Populist Contest," 53–68.

18   This case is from *Anak-kun oksu Paek choi ch'ogŏm kŭp myŏngsa munan*, kyu 21560.
        Although this is the death report of the tanner Cho P'al-bok, it is unusually titled with the name of Cho's wife, Ms. Paek, who was imprisoned for committing adultery and being involved in her husband's death. A few lines of writing on the title page that includes the judicial decisions are written in a different calligraphic style and are distinguishable from the title line.

19   The arrest of Yi Haeng-mun took place only after the first inquest investigation was held, so this particular one-sentence report seems to be misplaced here at the beginning of the inquest record.

20   According to *Muwŏllok* (Coroner's manual on the elimination of grievances), the eyes and mouth of those who have died from beating are open, the hair rumpled, and both legs untidy. *Sinju Muwŏllok*, 439.

21   Due to the quality of the original text, several characters are not visible in this sentence.

22   Again, some characters are not readable.

23 A *p'yŏngnip* (bamboo hat) was also known as a mourner's hat because a mourner wore this particular hat during the mourning period. Besides such use, only people of low status, such as the lowborn, post-station attendants, and peddlers, wore this hat. See the later testimony, which establishes the fact that the hat was worn not by Yi as he fled but by the man who stood by.

24 Yu Ki-dae was appointed a magistrate of Anak in the third month of 1895. However, he was dismissed from the position the next year (1896) because he failed to collect and submit local taxes on time while making a personal profit. *Sŭngjŏngwŏn ilgi* (Records of the royal secretariat), 1895.3.1 and 1896.6.16.

25 The Jiuyi Mountains are located in Hunan Province, China. The mountain range in Anak where this incident took place is called the Kuwŏl Mountains by local people, and "Kuŭi," the Korean pronunciation of "Jiuyi," is quite close to "Kuwŏl." In the *Shi Ji* (K: *Sagi*; Records of the grand historian), Sima Qian notes that Emperor Shun was buried in the Jiuyi Mountains. Sima Qian, *Shi Ji*, 1:28b. The inquest official's comparison of the Jiuyi Mountains and the Kuwŏl Mountains was probably a way to display his classical knowledge.

26 Yi Myŏng-sŏn was appointed provincial governor of Hwanghae Province in the fifth month of 1895. Being criticized for his inability to put down Tonghak insurgencies in the area, in which local yangban participated, he submitted a memorial to resign from his post, which was accepted by the king in the second month of the following year (1896). *Sŭngjŏngwŏn ilgi*, 1895.5.30; 1896.2.15; and 1896.2.18. He is titled a "former" provincial governor in this report since the report was drafted in the ninth month of 1897, after he had already left his position.

27 We do not know who made this report.

28 This *myŏngsagwan* (special investigator) was a temporary official sent by a provincial governor for an important legal case.

29 According to *Muwŏllok*, the corpse should be wrapped in a straw mat and buried in a hole with a mark to be ready for a possible second autopsy. *Sinju Muwŏllok*, 319. Because the identity of the corpse was unknown and no one claimed it as a family member, Cho's body was still kept by the court, not being handed over to either his village or to relatives for a permanent burial.

30 In the Korean kinship system, this is called *o-ch'on*, and it is written in that way in the original text.

31 This must be the Namwŏl Pass that Yi Ik-ch'ŏl mentions in his first inquest investigation.

32 For information on the title *yuhak* (youthful student), see case 6, n20.

33 This must be the same Namwŏl Pass as mentioned during his first inquest interrogations.

34 Nam Hyo-wŏn was appointed to the junior fifth rank post of governor's aide (*p'an'gwan*) of Hwanghae Province in the fourth month of 1895, and then was promoted to a junior fourth rank post of magistrate of Sinch'ŏn in the ninth month of the same year. However, he was dismissed from his position in the fifth month of 1897. In 1899, he was submitted to a disciplinary measure because of failure in collecting local taxes—especially for the

year 1895—when he was serving as the Sinch'ŏn magistrate. *Sŭngjŏngwŏn ilgi*, 1895.4.19; 1895.9.1; 1897.5.29; and 1899.12.17.

35 The provincial governor made this sentence of "something comparable to thirty strokes of beating with a heavy stick," rather than simply thirty strokes of beating with a heavy stick, because four of the five different levels of punishments—beating with a heavy stick (*changhyŏng*), penal servitude (*tohyŏng*), banishment (*yuhyŏng*), and the death penalty (*sahyŏng*)—had been abolished with the reform of penal affairs during the Kabo Reform period (1894–96). Only beating with a light stick (*t'aehyŏng*) had not been abolished.

A cangue was the large wooden neck board that was put on a suspect who had committed a crime so heavy that it warranted the punishment above flogging. For a criminal who received the death penalty, shackles and leg irons were also imposed in addition to a cangue. However, even in death penalty cases, some groups of people—such as merit subjects, officials, and women of yangban as well as commoner status—were exempted from wearing the cangue except when they had committed treason. *Kyŏngguk taejŏn*, 5:1b. It is apparent that women were sometimes put in a cangue, although a regulation in 1747 strictly prohibited such punishment. *T'ŭkkyo chŏngsik* (Special edicts deciding legal codes), 37b. It may be that the cangue practice was eliminated by the nineteenth century, especially after the Kabo Reform. Yet, as To Myŏn-hoe points out, although the reforms introduced radical changes in penal codes, they also created a great confusion, as well as a long delay in actual practice. To Myŏn-hoe, "Kabo kaeyŏkki ŭi hyŏngsa pŏpkyu ŭi kaehyŏk," 103–22.

CASE 8

1 For discussion of the northern region of Korea and the development of regional discrimination against it, see Sun Joo Kim, *Marginality and Subversion in Korea*, 35–65; and Sun Joo Kim, ed., *The Northern Region of Korea*, 3–17 and 93–115.

2 *Churi* is the colloquial form of *churoe*. The term *roehyŏng* in the text also refers to the same punishment.

3 Article 337 [5] in *The Great Ming Code*, 185.

4 Deuchler, "The Practice of Confucianism," 312–23; and Sim Chae-u, *Chosŏn hugi kukka kwŏllyŏk kwa pŏmjoe t'ongje*, 36–38.

5 Sim Chae-u, *Chosŏn hugi kukka kwŏllyŏk kwa pŏmjoe t'ongje*, 168.

6 Ibid., 276–77.

7 For Kim Yun-bo's painting of *churi*, see his *Hyŏngjŏng toch'ŏp* (Painting album of penal affairs).

8 These reports are found in the *Sabŏp p'umbo* (Provincial reports concerning legal matters). What is missing are orders and directives sent from the Ministry of Justice, among other documents.

9 For more detailed regulations, see chapter 1, article 21 in *The Great Ming Code*, 30.

10 For the Chosŏn Confucian elites' general attitude against female shamans and shamanism, see Walraven, "Popular Religion in a Confucianized Society."

11 These few lines of writing, from upper right to left on the title page, including one big character on the bottom right, are in a different calligraphic style and are distinguishable from the title line on the left (see fig. 3). We assume that these were written by the office that received this report, most likely the Ministry of Justice, because the first inquest official seems to have submitted the report to the ministry.

This case is from *Kangwŏn-do Hoeyang-gun Changyang-myŏn Hanch'i-ri ch'isa namin Kim Kap-san ch'ogŏman.*

12 The title page generally has the number assigned for the report, but from the fact that this title of the report says "unnumbered," we gather the number must have been assigned after the report was filed with the Provincial Governor's Office.

13 A community funeral home seems to have been a storage place where funeral materials (including funeral biers) were stored. Community members collectively owned, tended, and used funeral goods. See one such example in case 7.

14 Unlike earlier inquest reports, this one specifies which types of rulers were used so that possible confusion could be prevented. The *chi-ch'ŏk* supposedly was for measuring distance over the ground, and might refer to the *yangjŏn-ch'ŏk,* which was used for land survey and registration. One *yangjŏn-ch'ŏk* for first-grade land during the fifteenth century was 99.296 cm in length. See Pak Hŭng-su, "Toryanghyŏng chedo," 617.

15 Chinese cotton (*tangmok*) was a product of the Western world but was called "Chinese" because it was imported through China. It became very popular because of its high quality.

16 For the use of a silver hairpin in autopsies, see the introduction (just before note numbers 30 and 31).

17 For the practices of adoption in late Chosŏn Korea, see Peterson, *Korean Adoption and Inheritance.*

18 *Ch'on* is the marker that shows the remoteness or closeness of relatives to oneself. For example, an uncle is three *ch'on* apart from oneself; a cousin is one's four *ch'on* relative; and a second cousin is one's six *ch'on* relative.

19 This *yŏ myŏngin* (enlightened woman) refers to Ms. Yu, whose name appears in earlier testimonies. In the testimony of Kim Tŏg-wŏn, the person who invited Ms. Yu was Pak Tŏg-yun, not Pak Tae-gyŏng. It is possible that Tae-gyŏng is Tŏg-yun's courtesy name.

20 Yuan Tiangang lived in China during the Tang dynasty (618–907) and was known to have specialized in various occult arts such as physiognomy.

21 From the above deposition of Kim Tŏg-wŏn, it is apparent that the first deposition of Ms. Yu took place before his. Yet in this report, her deposition is recorded after his. The same recording practice is witnessed in the second deposition.

22 On *kohan* (K: *pogo han'gi*; the period of responsibility for crimes), see case 5, n16.

23 The title "Sŏnjŏn" refers to the military post of royal messenger. Mr. Yu may have previously served as a royal messenger or he may have purchased this post.

24 In the second round of questioning, the specific age of each person was not recorded. Instead, just the character for "age" was entered, probably because this information was already provided in the first round.

25 In the first interrogation, Kim Ch'ae-wŏn is recorded as an involved witness rather than an accomplice.

26 See the translators' notes for the meaning of words in all capital letters.

27 This quote is from the conversation between King Xuan of Qi and Mencius about royal compassion in *Mencius*, book 1, part 1, chapter 7. In Legge's translation, the anecdote goes, "The king [Xuan of Qi] was sitting aloft in the hall, when a man appeared, leading an ox past the lower part of it. The king saw him, and asked, Where is the ox going? The man replied, We are going to consecrate a bell with its blood. The king said, Let it go. I cannot bear its frightened appearance, as if it were an innocent person going to the place of death. The man answered, Shall we then omit the consecration of the bell? The king said, How can that be omitted? Change it for a sheep. . . . The heart seen in this is sufficient to carry you [king Xuan of Qi] to the royal sway. The people all supposed that your Majesty grudged the animal, but your servant knows surely, that it was your Majesty's not being able to bear the sight, which made you do as you did. . . . Your conduct was an artifice of benevolence. You saw the ox, and had not seen the sheep. So is the superior man affected towards animals, that, having seen them alive, he cannot bear to see them die. . . . Now here is kindness sufficient to reach to animals, and no benefits are extended from it to the people. . . . Your majesty's not exercising the royal sway, is because you do not do it, not because you are not able to do it." Legge, *The Work of Mencius*, 137–42. The context in which this quote is used here—the victim Kap-san allegedly accusing P'yŏng-il as the principal offender because he saw P'yŏng-il directing the torture, though the order to torture him in fact came down from Kim Pyŏng-nyŏl, who had to stay home because of old age—deviates from the apparent lesson of this anecdote: namely, that the kingly Way is to treat one's people with the compassion that the king displayed toward the trembling sacrificial ox.

28 The inquest was held on 1899.11.1 (12/3/1899) but the report was completed and submitted 1899.12.14 (1/14/1900), meaning that the reporting process took almost a month and a half.

29 Two seal impressions on this page are unidentifiable.

30 The autopsy forms, according to the *Muwŏllok* (Coroner's guide for the elimination of grievances), were to be preprinted in great numbers and used by their serial marks, but as the illustration of the form here shows (fig. 5), this one was handwritten with lines drawn around the entries.

31 See case 7, n36 for the use of a cangue as a penal instrument.

32 This report is from *Hoeyang-gun Changyang-myŏn Hanch'i-ri ch'isa namin Kim Kap-san oksa saan*.

33 Chŏlli p'ansŏ was minister of the Ministry of Personnel and Rites, a late Koryŏ (918–1392) bureaucratic post. The "Lord of Chŏlli P'ansŏ" refers to Kim Kwang-ni, one of the recognized late Koryŏ ancestors of the Kwangsan Kim lineage. See the online lineage homepage at: www.kwangsankim.co.kr.

34 It is unknown what specific incidents had caused many deaths in the Kwangsan Kim lineage at the time.

35 This quote is from *Mencius*, book 3, part 2, chapter 6, where Mencius, in a conversation

with Dai Busheng about how to make a virtuous king, uses the following anecdote: "'Suppose that there is a great officer of Ch'ŭ [Chu] here, who wishes his son to learn the speech of Ch'î [Qi]. Will he in that case employ a man of Ch'î as his tutor, or a man of Ch'ŭ?' 'He will employ a man of Ch'î to teach him,' said Pŭ-shăng [Busheng]. Mencius went on, 'If but one man of Ch'î be teaching him, and there be a multitude of men of Ch'ŭ continually shouting out about him, although his father beat him every day, wishing him to learn the speech of Ch'î, it will be impossible for him to do so. But in the same way, if he were to be taken and placed for several years in Chwang or Yo, though his father should beat him, wishing him to speak the language of Ch'ŭ, it would be impossible for him to do so." This passage discusses the influence of example and association and the importance of having the ruler be a virtuous man. For the entire passage in *Mencius*, see Legge, *The Works of Mencius*, 275–76.

36 This report is from *Sabŏp p'umbo*, 5:457.

37 This report is from *Sabŏp p'umbo*, 6:54–55.

38 The former is chapter 1, article 29 [2] in *The Great Ming Code*, 40; the latter is chapter 6, section 2, article 313 [3] in *The Great Ming Code*, 173.

39 In chapter 6 "Laws on Penal Affairs," section 11 "Judgment and Imprisonment," article 428 "Old and Young Persons Are Not Put to Judicial Torture": "In all cases involving persons who . . . are 70 years of age or more . . . , judicial torture shall not be allowed." *The Great Ming Code*, 230.

40 This is chapter 6, section 2, article 305 [4] in *The Great Ming Code*, 170.

41 This is chapter 6, section 2, article 313 [3] in *The Great Ming Code*, 173.

42 Though Kim Mun-ho's name is written side by side with Kim Pyŏng-nyŏl's and under the category of the accused, Kim Mun-ho was not one of the accused.

43 The first two lines and one big character on this title page are written in a different calligraphic style in the original text.

44 The author of this confidential directive seems to be the court at the provincial government level.

    This report is from *Hoeyang-gun ch'isa namin Kim Kap-san oksa saan.*

45 Report No. 3 refers to the report translated just before this one, written on 1900.9.9 by Chu Sŏng-myŏn, a judge for the Kangwŏn Provincial Court and submitted to the Ministry of Justice. In this document, only a summary of Report No. 3 is recorded, which has not been translated here.

46 This report is from *Sabŏp p'umbo*, 6:433–34.

47 With the reforms in penal affairs introduced after 1894, beating with a heavy stick (*changhyŏng*) was abolished. See To Myŏn-hoe, "Kabo kaehyŏk ihu kŭndaejŏk pŏmnyŏng chejŏng kwajŏng," 330. This explains the discrepancy here between the punishment indicated in *The Great Ming Code* and the sentence that Kim P'yŏng-il received, which was for 100 strokes of beating with a light stick rather than a heavy one.

48 *The Great Ming Code*, 165.

49 This report is from *Sabŏp p'umbo*, 6:529

50 This is not from the *Great Ming Code*, but rather the *Taejŏn hoet'ong* (Comprehensive collection of dynastic codes). See *Taejŏn hoet'ong*, 745–47.

51 This report is from *Sabŏp p'umbo*, 6:640.

52 Both codes are in the chapter "Hyŏngjŏn" (Laws on penal affairs). According to these codes, persons who steal and live in another person's house shall be punished by three years of penal servitude. See *Taejŏn hoet'ong*, 695 and 745–47.

53 The six offenses refer to the following: treason, murder, larceny, robbery, adultery, and fraud. They were categorized as the major offenses and excluded from pardon. Many more crimes belonged to this category in Chosŏn Korea. See To Myŏn-hoe, "1894–1905 nyŏn'gan hyŏngsa chaep'an chedo yŏn'gu," 66, 183, and 288.

54 It was less than two years from the first inquest date of 1899.11.1 to the date of this report 1901.5.15, and Kim Mun-ho had been in and out of prison during this time. Counting the number of years in traditional Korea includes the starting as well as the ending year—in this case 1899, 1900, and 1901, thus three years.

55 This report is from *Sabŏp p'umbo*, 7:5.

GLOSSARY

PERSONAL NAMES

An Yŏng-dŭk 安永得
An Yu-jong 安有宗

Chang Mun-wŏn 張文元
Cho Ch'ŏl-ha 趙哲夏
Cho Hyŏng-suk 趙兄叔
Cho Kuk-po 趙國甫
Cho Kyŏng-sin 曺京信
Cho P'al-bok 趙八卜
Cho Tae-rim 趙大林
Ch'oe Chun-ak 崔峻岳
Ch'oe Pong-nip 崔奉立
Ch'oe U-hyŏng 崔遇亨
Chŏm-hwa 占化
Chŏng Ho-in 鄭好仁
Chŏng Hwan-sŏp 鄭煥涉
Chŏng Il-yŏng 鄭日永
Chŏng Kwŏn 鄭權
Chŏng Nan-yŏl 鄭蘭悅
Chŏng Tong-baek 鄭東伯
Chu Sŏng-myŏn 朱錫冕

Han Chae-hyŏp 韓在協
Han Ho-ban 韓好班
Han Yong-sŏn 韓用善
Hong Chae-u 洪在愚
Hong Chin-o 洪珍五
Hong Hae-bung 洪海鵬
Hong Myŏng-ha 洪明河
Hyŏn Sa-ch'ŏl 玄四喆
Hyŏng-ch'ŏl 亨哲

I-ch'ŏl 利哲
Im Ch'ang-nin 林昌獜

Im Si-jŏng 林時鼎
Im Yŏ-gyŏng 任汝京
Ing-sim 芿心

Kang Chae-yŏl 姜在烈
Kim Ch'ae-wŏn 金采元
Kim Ch'ang-sŏng 金昌成
Kim Ch'i-gŏl 金致杰
Kim Ch'i-muk 金致默
Kim Ch'i-su 金致水
Kim Ch'ŏl-gyu 金哲珪
Kim Ch'ŏn-gil 金千吉
Kim Chong-ch'ŏl 金宗哲
Kim Chŏng-gŭn 金禎根
Kim Chŏng-hyŏn 金正鉉
Kim Chun-gŭn 金俊根
Kim Chung-ok 金仲玉
Kim Hag-in 金學仁
Kim Hyŏng-un 金兄云
Kim I-hyŏn 金利鉉
Kim Il-un 金日云
Kim Ing-no 金益魯
Kim Kap-san 金甲山
Kim Ki-hyŏn 金箕絢
Kim Ku-sim 金久心
Kim Kwang-ni 金光利
Kim Kyŏng-hŭi 金景希
Kim Kyŏng-un 金京云
Kim Mun-ho 金文浩
Kim Myŏng-sin 金明信
Kim Nak-ki 金樂騏
Kim P'yŏng-il 金平一
Kim Pyŏng-nyŏl 金秉烈
Kim Pyŏng-p'il 金秉弼

Kim Tae-hyŏn 金大鉉
Kim Tŏg-wŏn 金德源
Kim Tŭg-ŭm 金得音
Kim Wŏn-ch'ŏl 金元哲
Kim Yŏng-jun 金永準
Kim Yun-bo 金允輔
Kim Yun-o 金潤五
Kim Yun-sŏp 金允燮
Ko Kyŏng-o 高京五
Ko Kyŏng-sam 高京三
Ko Pok-chi 高卜只
Ku Pong-jo 具鳳祖

Min Ch'i-sŏ 閔致敍
Mun Chong-ji 文種之
Mun Yu-mok 文柳木

Nam Hyo-wŏn 南孝源

O Ch'ang-jo 吳昌祚
Ŏ Sa-p'il 魚史弼
O Tae-ryŏn 吳大鍊

Pak Chu-hŏn 朴周憲
Pak Kun-hae 朴君海
Pak Kyŏm-ch'oe 朴謙最
Pak Kyŏng-ju 朴慶州
Pak Kyu-su 朴珪壽
Pak Nae-ch'un 朴來春
Pak Sŏk-hwan 朴石煥
Pak Tae-gyŏng 朴大京
Pak Tŏg-yong 朴德用
Pak Tŏg-yun 朴德允
Pak Yong-dŏk 朴用悳
Pak Yun-sŏk 朴允石
Pong-nok 奉祿
Pong-sam 奉三

Sim Chŏng-t'aek 沈定澤
Sin Chong-han 辛宗漢
Sin Chong-su 辛宗洙
Sin Kab-yŏn 辛甲連
Sin Kyŏng-sŏp 申京涉
Sin P'il-ho 愼必浩

Sŏ Yong-gŭn 徐用根
Sŏ Yu-dŏk 徐有德
Song Chi-hyŏp 宋之協
Song Hwan-ik 宋煥翊
Sŏng Kyo-muk 成敎默
Song Sŏn-yŏ 宋先汝
Song T'aeg-yŏng 宋宅英
Sŭng-mun 承文

Yang Hak-pŏm 楊學凡
Yang Hang-nyŏn [Hak-ryŏn] 楊學連
Yang Su-gŭn 楊守根
Yi Chae-gon 李載崑
Yi Chŏng-gon 李貞坤
Yi Ch'un-gŭn 李春根
Yi Haeng-mun 李行文
Yi Hang-nok 李學录
Yi Hun 李薰
Yi Hŭng-guk 李興國
Yi Hyang-hŏn 李香憲
Yi Hyŏng-sŏk 李亨錫
Yi Ik-ch'ŏl 李益哲
Yi In-myŏng 李仁明
Yi Kŏn-ha 李乾夏
Yi Kun-sŏ 李君西
Yi Kyŏng-ch'an 李京讚
Yi Kyŏng-jae 李景在
Yi Myŏng-sŏn 李鳴善
Yi Nak-to 李洛道
Yi Pong-dol 李奉乭
Yi Pong-un 李奉云
Yi Pyŏng-ch'ŏl 李丙哲
Yi Sŏk-chin 李奭鎭
Yi Sŭng-gyŏng 李承敬
Yi Sŭng-o 李升五
Yi Tong-sik 李東植
Yu Chin-ch'ŏl 柳辰哲
Yu Ki-dae 柳冀大
Yu Myŏng-han 柳明漢
Yu Si-jong 劉時宗
Yuan Tiangang 袁天綱
Yun Mi-ryŏk 尹未力
Yun-sam 允三

PLACE NAMES AND GENERAL TERMS

aekkak 額角 forehead

ajŏn 衙前 local clerks

amhaeng ŏsa 暗行御史 secret royal inspector

angmyŏn 仰面 ventral side of the body

anjŏng 眼睛 pupils

chaaek 自縊 suicide by hanging

ch'abŏm 次犯 accomplice

chaep'anjang 裁判長 chief justice

chaep'anso 裁判所 court

chaik 自溺 suicide by drowning

chajahyŏng 刺字刑 punishment of tattooing a letter on a criminal's face or arm

Chakch'ŏng 作廳 Bureau of Public Administration

ch'amjang 參將 general

ch'amjŏng 參政 senior councilor

chang 杖 heavy stick, or a beating with a heavy stick

Chang *ssi* 張氏 Madam Chang

Changdong 長洞 Chang Village

ch'anggam 倉監 granary supervisor

changgyo 掌校 head officer

changhyŏng 杖刑 punishment by beating with a heavy stick

Changyang 長陽 place name

changyang purhyo 將養不效 nursing [of the injury] did not work

ch'anjŏng 贊政 councilor

cha-si 子時 around midnight

chedu 臍肚 lower belly

chesa 題辭 adjudication

chi 地 a particular serial mark or an entry in *Ch'ŏnjamun* (Thousand-character classic)

chi-ch'ŏk 地尺 land-measuring ruler

chigwan 地官 geomancer

chiji 地支 the twelve Earthly branches

chilp'umsŏ 質稟書 inquiry

chin 辰 a particular serial mark or an entry in *Ch'ŏnjamun* (Thousand-character classic)

chinsa 進士 literary licentiate degree or one who holds such a degree

chipkang 執綱 subdistrict administrator

Cho *choi* 曹召史 Ms. Cho

Choch'u-am 滌湫巖 Choch'u Rock

Ch'oe *choi* 崔召史 Ms. Ch'oe

ch'ogŏm 初檢 first inquest investigation

ch'ogŏmgwan 初檢官 first inquest official

choi or *sasa* 조이 or 召史 Ms., or title for a commoner woman

ch'ŏk 尺 unit of length = 10 *ch'on*

chokchi 足趾 toes

chokchidu 足趾肚 toe tips

chokchigap 足趾胛 toenails

chokchigappong 足趾甲縫 underneath the toenails

ch'ŏkpae 脊背 spine

"Chŏkto" (C: Zeidao) 賊盜 "Violence and Robbery," a chapter in the *Great Ming Code*

chŏlli p'ansŏ 典理判書 minister in the Ministry of Personnel and Rites

chŏllin 切隣 close neighbor

Ch'ŏlwŏn 鐵原 place name

ch'ŏmji 僉知 a senior third-rank military post (abbreviated title)

ch'ŏmjijungch'ubusa 僉知中樞府事 a senior third-rank military post

chŏn 錢 monetary unit, 10 *chŏn* = 1 *yang*

ch'on 寸 a marker that shows the remoteness or closeness of relatives to oneself

ch'on 寸 unit of length, 10 *p'un*

ch'on 村 village or hamlet

chŏnan 奠雁 a ceremony where the groom brings a pair of wild geese to the bride's house

Chŏn-ch'ŏn 前川 Chŏn Stream

Chŏng *choi* 鄭召史 Ms. Chŏng

ch'ŏn'gan 天干 ten Heavenly stems

chŏngbŏm 正犯 the principal offender

chŏngni 情理 sentiment and reason

"Ch'ŏngni" 聽理 "Hearing," a section in *Taejŏn hoet'ong* (Comprehensive collection of dynastic codes)

ch'ŏngnyŏ 脊膂 area along the spine

chŏngsim 頂心 crown of the head

chŏngŭi 情誼 proper sentiment and sense of justice

chŏngyu 丁酉 name of a year in the sixty-year cycle or 1877

Ch'ŏnjamun 千字文 *Thousand-Character Classic*

ch'ŏnmin 賤民 a lowborn person

chonwi 尊位 subdistrict administrator

chŏnyo 纏繞 a binding coil knot

ch'ŏpchŏng 牒呈 an official report submitted by a lower-level administrative unit to a higher one

Chosŏn hyŏngsaryŏng 朝鮮刑事令 *Chosŏn Penal Order*

ch'ugo 推考 deposition

Ch'ugwanji 秋官誌 *Treatise on the Ministry of Penal Affairs*

ch'uk-si 丑時 around two in the morning

chunggun 中軍 deputy commander (of the Provincial Military Commander's Office) or chief military officer in the county government

Chunghwa-bu ogan 中和府獄案 *Inquest Records of Chunghwa County*

Chŭngsu muwŏllok 增修無冤錄 *Amplified and Corrected Coroner's Guide for the Elimination of Grievances*

Chŭngsu muwŏllok ŏnhae 增修無冤錄諺解 *Amplified and Corrected Coroner's Guide for the Elimination of Grievances in Vernacular Korean*

churoe 周牢 method of torture or punishment where wooden sticks are inserted between bound legs and twisted; also known as *churi* or *chyuli*

chwajang 座長 village elder

chwasu 座首 director of the Hyangch'ŏng (Bureau of Local Yangban)

chyuli t'ŭlgo 쥬이틀고 "Twisting the Legs by Inserting Wooden Sticks"

Da Ming lü (K: *Taemyŏngnyul*) 大明律 *Great Ming Code*

haeng 行 brevetted

haengsagwan 行查官 special investigator

hamhae 頷頦 under the jaw

hammyŏn 合面 dorsal side of the body

han 漢 "that bastard," "brute," or derogatory suffix for a man

Hanch'i 翰峙 place name

hanggyŏng 項頸 back of the neck

Hansŏng-bu 漢城府 Seoul Magistracy

hoebong 灰封 preserving the corpse with ashes

Hoengsŏng 橫城 place name

Hoeyang 淮陽 place name

hojang 戶長 head clerk

hooe 號外 unnumbered

hullyŏng 訓令 order

Hŭmhŭm sinsŏ 欽欽新書 *New Writings on Circumspection in Judicial Decisions*

hŭmhyul chi ŭi 欽恤之義 meaning of legal prudence

Hŭpkok 歙谷 place name

hyangan 鄉安 local yangban association

hyangban 鄉班 local yangban

Hyangch'ŏng 鄉廳 Bureau of Local Yangban

hyangim 鄉任 quasi-bureaucratic posts at the Hyangch'ŏng (Bureau of Local Yangban)

hyangjang 鄉長 village elder

hyangni 鄉吏 local clerks

hyangso 鄉所 assistant director of the

Hyangch'ŏng (Bureau of Local Yangban)

hyŏllyŏng 縣令 prefectural magistrate

hyŏmae 嫌碍 procedural avoidance

hyŏn 縣 lesser prefecture or prefecture

hyŏn'gam 縣監 lesser prefectural magistrate

Hyŏngbang 刑房 Bureau of Penal Affairs

Hyŏngbŏp taejŏn 刑法大全 *Comprehensive Collection of Penal Codes*

Hyŏngjo 刑曹 Ministry of Penal Affairs

"Hyŏngjŏn" 刑典 "Laws on Penal Affairs," a chapter in *Taejŏn hoet'ong* (Comprehensive collection of dynastic codes)

Hyŏngjŏng toch'ŏp 刑政圖帖 *Painting Album of Penal Affairs*

hyŏngni 刑吏 a jailer or clerk at the Hyŏngbang (Bureau of Penal Affairs)

hyŏpp'an 協辦 associate judge

hyulchŏn 恤典 legal prudence

hyungdang 胸膛 chest (of the body)

idu 吏讀 "clerk's writing," which borrows either the reading or the meaning of Chinese characters to express colloquial Korean

igyu 耳竅 ear holes

ihŏn 里憲 subdistrict administrator

iim 里任 subdistrict administrator

ijŏng 里正 subdistrict administrator

Ilsŏngnok 日省錄 *Record of Daily Reflections*

imin 壬寅 name of a year in the sixty-year cycle or 1842

in'gi 印記 securing [the place where the corpse is placed] with seals

inhu 咽喉 throat

injung 人中 philtrum

"Inmyŏng" (C: Renming) 人命 "Homicide," a section in the *Great Ming Code*

iryun 耳輪 ear flaps

isu 耳垂 ear lobes

ka or *ga* 哥 Mr., or a somewhat derogatory suffix for a man

kaengch'u 更推 second-round deposition

kakkŭn 脚跟 heels

kallyŏn 干連 an involved witness

kamgyŏl 甘結 a directive issued by a higher-level administrative unit to a lower one

kamsa 監司 provincial governor

Kamyŏng 監營 Provincial Governor's Office

kan 間 unit of measuring the size of a house; 1 *kan* refers to the width between two bearing poles, or 10 *ch'ŏk*

kanbŏm 干犯 accomplice

kanjŭng 看證 eyewitness

kanso ch'inhoek 奸所親獲 when the husband catches an adulterous wife and her lover in the act

Kansŏng 杆城 place name

kanŭm 奸淫 adultery

katbach'i 갓바치 tanner

kigwan 記官 court recorder

Kim *choi* 金召史 Ms. Kim

Kim *nyŏ* 金女 Ms. Kim

kimaek 氣脈 inner energy and pulse

kohan 辜限 death limit, or the period of responsibility for crimes

Koho 庫湖 place name

koju 苦主 accuser

kokto 穀道 anus

kŏman 檢案 inquest record

Kŏman ch'o 檢案抄 *Selected Inquest Records*

kŏmbalsa 檢跋辭 concluding statements of inquest hearings

kŏmgwan 檢官 inquest official

kŏmje 檢題 trial adjudications

kŏmsi 檢屍 physical examination of the body

kŏmsi munan 檢屍文案 a legal report written after examining a dead body

kong nobi 公奴婢 public slave

kongjŭng 公證 official witness

kongsano 公私奴 public and private slave

kosin 拷訊 corporal punishment or torture

Kosŏng 高城 place name

ku 口 mouth

kuae chi hyŏm 狗碍之嫌 procedural avoidance

kuch'ŏk 毆踢 striking others with the hands or feet

kulch'ong 掘塚 digging out a tomb

"Kŭmje" 禁制 "Prohibitions," a section in *Taejŏn hoet'ong* (Comprehensive collection of dynastic codes)

Kŭmsŏng 金城 place name

kun 郡 lesser county

kungnae 局內 perimeter of a tomb

kun'gwan 軍官 military officers

kunsu 郡守 lesser county magistrate

kŭnyu 根由 root cause

kwanch'alsa 觀察使 provincial governor

kwan-ch'ŏk 官尺 official (measuring) ruler

Kwangmu 光武 reign title of the Great Han Empire (Taehan Cheguk) from 1897 to 1906

Kwangsan Kim 光山金 Kim family whose clan seat is Kwangsan

kwanno 官奴 public slave

kyŏkchaeng 擊錚 to petition by striking a gong

kyŏl 決 case review completed

kyŏlsa 結辭 concluding statement

Kyŏngguk taejŏn 經國大典 *Great Code of Administration*

Kyŏngjo puji 京兆府誌 *Gazetteer of Seoul*

Kyŏngju Kim 慶州金 Kim family whose clan seat is Kyŏngju

kyŏngmul 莖物 penis

li 里 unit of distance, equal to 2,100 *ch'ŏk* (from 430.08 to 453.6 meters according to the late Chosŏn *zhou-ch'ŏk*)

li or *ri* 里 subdistrict

"Maein" (C: Maren) 罵人 "Cursing Others," an article in the *Great Ming Code*

mich'ong 眉叢 corners of the eyebrows

min 緡 a string of coins; 1 *min* = 1 *yang*

misi 未時 around two in the afternoon

mok 牧 special county

moksa 牧使 special county magistrate

"Mosal in" (C: Mousha ren) 謀殺人 "Plotting to Kill Others," an article in the *Great Ming Code*

Much'ŏng 武廳 Bureau of Military Administration

mun 文 monetary unit; 100 *mun* = 10 *chŏn* = 1 *yang*

munan 文案 inquest report

munan palsa 文案跋辭 concluding statements of inquest examinations

munjang 門長 lineage chief

munkwa 文科 higher civil service examination, or its degree or degree-holder

munyŏ 巫女 female shaman

Muwŏllok 無寃錄 *Coroner's Guide for the Elimination of Grievances*

muyŏk 無役 no military obligation

myŏn 面 district

"Myŏngnye" (C: Mingli) 名例 "Laws on Punishments and General Principles," a chapter in the *Great Ming Code*

myŏngsagwan 明查官 a special investigator

myŏnim 面任 district administrator

Naebu 內部 Ministry of the Interior

naejaejŏk palchŏn non 내재적발전론 internal development theory

naeryong 來龍 incoming dragon vein (in geomancy)

nakhyŏng 烙刑 a punishment where a hot iron is placed on the soles of a criminal's feet

nanjanghyŏng 亂杖刑 a punishment where the soles of a criminal's feet are beaten indiscriminately

nobi 奴婢 slave

noehu 腦後 occipital

nŭksa 勒死 strangled to death

nyŏn 年 "years in age," or years old

nyŏn samsip 年三十 thirty years in age, or thirty years old

o-ch'on 五寸 a father's or mother's cousin

ogan 獄案 criminal investigation records

ojak (C: *wuzuo*) 仵作 coroner's assistant

ojak no 仵作奴 slave coroner's assistant

ojak saryŏng 仵作使令 coroner's assistant

okchaegwan 獄在官 jailer

okchŏng 獄情 facts of the case

ŏmhyŏng ilch'a 嚴刑壹次 one round of beating

ongmuyangbŏm 獄無兩犯 one crime shall not have two offenders

Paek *choi* 白召史 Ms. Paek

paekkwal or *palgwal* 白活 complaint petition

Pak *choi* 朴召史 Ms. Pak

p'alch'ŏn 八賤 eight meanest groups of people

"Palch'ong" (C: *Fazhong*) 發塚 "Uncovering Graves," an article in the *Great Ming Code*

palgo 發告 to file a complaint, or complainant

palgwal or *paekkwal* 白活 complaint petition

palje 髮際 neck hairline

palsa 跋辭 concluding statement

p'anbu 判府 royal judgment

pang 坊 district, also transliterated *bang*

pangim 坊任 subdistrict administrator

p'an'gwan 判官 governor's aide

pangye 坊隸 district servant

p'ansa 判事 judge

pansu 班首 yangban village headman

p'anyun 判尹 chief magistrate of Seoul Magistracy

Pibyŏnsa 備邊司 Border Defense Command

p'ich'ŏk 被踢 kicked to death

p'igo 被告 defendant, or the accused

pigyu 鼻竅 nostrils

pihun 秘訓 confidential directive

p'iin nŭksa 被人勒死 strangled to death

p'iin salsa 被人殺死 murder

p'ija 被刺 stabbed to death

p'ijang 皮匠 tanner

p'ijang ch'isa 被杖致死 death as a result of torture

p'ijang nyŏ 皮匠女 female tanner

pijun 鼻准 tip of the nose

piryang 鼻梁 bridge of the nose

pobusang 褓負商 peddlers

pogo han'gi 保辜限期 period of responsibility for crimes

"Pogo han'gi" (C: *Baogu hanqi*) 保辜限期 "The Period of Responsibility for Crimes," an article in the *Great Ming Code*, also known as *kohan*

pogosŏ 報告書 report

p'ok 幅 unit of fabric by width

pokkŏm 覆檢 second inquest investigation

Pŏmmu Amun 法務衙門 Ministry of Justice

pŏmmul 法物 investigation tools used for the examination of the corpse

Pŏppu 法部 Ministry of Justice

posang 褓商 wrapping merchant

"Posangch'ŏng chŏlmok" 褓商廳節目 "Principles of peddlers' associations"

posangdan 褓商團 peddlers' association

pu 府 special city

Pu chiryŏng 部指令 order from the
Ministry of Justice

Pukkwan han'ak 北關悍惡 wicked
person from Hamgyŏng Province

p'um 品 a Chinese character used to
describe the way an illegal burial was
carried out

p'un 分 monetary unit; 100 p'un = 10
chŏn = 1 yang

p'un 分 unit of length; 10 p'un = 1 ch'on

P'ungdŏk 豊德 place name

p'unghŏn 風憲 district administrator

p'ungsu (C: fengshui) 風水 geomancy or
geomancer

punŭi 分義 propriety

pusa 府使 county magistrate

pusang 負商 pack-peddler

puyun 府尹 special city magistrate

Pyŏlgam 別監 assistant director of
the Hyangch'ŏng (Bureau of Local
Yangban)

pyŏlji 別紙 addendum

Pyŏngjo 兵曹 Ministry of Military
Affairs

p'yŏngmun 平問 interrogation without
torture

p'yŏngnip 平笠 coarse bamboo hat

P'yŏngniwŏn 平理院 Supreme Court

P'yŏngyang-bu 平壤府 P'yŏngyang
Special City

Pyŏngyŏng 兵營 Provincial Military
Commander's Office

p'yŏnjwa 偏左 left side of the head

p'yŏnu 偏右 right side of the head

roehyŏng 牢刑 method of torture or
punishment where wooden sticks
are inserted between bound legs
and twisted; also known as churi or
chyuli

saan 查安 special investigation report

sabi 私婢 private female slave

sabu 士夫 scholar-official

saengwŏn 生員 classics licentiate degree
or its degree-holder

Sahŏnbu 司憲府 Office of the
Inspector-General

sahwa 私和 private settlement

sahyŏng 死刑 capital punishment

sahyŏng 私刑 private punishment or
torture

sal 煞 death on the spot

samch'u 三推 third deposition

samsip se 三十歲 thirty years old

san 山 grave, gravesite, graveyard, or
mountain

sangha ach'i 上下牙齒 upper and lower
molars

sangha sunmun 上下脣吻 upper and
lower lips, around the lips

sangmyŏng 償命 requital for a life

sangyŏga 喪輿家 community funeral
home

sano 私奴 private male slave

sansong 山訟 dispute over a gravesite,
gravesite litigation

sanŭm 山陰 blessing emanating from
an ancestor's grave

saryŏn 詞連 a related witness

sasi 巳時 around ten in the morning

se 歲 years in age, years old

sich'in 屍親 a close relative of the
deceased

sijang 屍帳 autopsy or inquest form

sije 時祭 anniversary ancestor ritual

sikkisang 食氣顙 esophagus

"Sim Ch'ŏng ka" 심청가 "Song of Sim
Ch'ŏng"

simgam 心坎 between the chest and
belly

Simnirok 審理錄 Records of Royal
Reviews

Sin pan 愼班 Yangban Sin

Sinju muwŏllok 新註無冤錄 Newly
Annotated Coroner's Guide for the
Elimination of Grievances

sinmun 顋門 fontanel
sinnang 腎囊 scrotum
sin-si 申時 around four in the afternoon
sirin 實因 true cause of death
sisan 始山 tomb of the apical ancestor
siwigwan 侍衛官 escort
sŏgi 書記 court clerk
sŏjae 書齋 study hall
sojang 訴狀 petition
Sŏjin-gang 西津江 Sŏjin River
sŏl 舌 tongue
sŏng 姓 surname
songan 訟案 litigation records
songbyŏn 訟卞 hearing
Sŏnjŏn or Sŏnjŏn'gwan 宣傳官 royal
    messenger
sŏnsan 先山 lineage cemetery
ssi 氏 Madam, or title for a yangban
    woman
suji 手指 fingers
sujidu 手指肚 fingertips
sujigap 手指甲 fingernails
sujigappong 手指甲縫 underneath the
    fingernails
sujikkun 守直軍 watchman
sujok 首族 lineage leaders
sujong chi yul 隨從之律 the law
    concerning accomplices
sul-si 戌時 around eight in the evening
Sŭngjŏngwŏn 承政院 Royal Secretariat
Sŭngjŏngwŏn ilgi 承政院日記 *Records of
    the Royal Secretariat*
sun'gyo 巡校 sheriff
Sunyŏng 巡營 Provincial Governor's
    Office
susim 手心 palms
susŏgi 首書記 head court clerk
suwan 手腕 wrists
suyanghyŏng 收養兄 adopted older
    sister or brother
suyangje 收養弟 adopted younger
    brother
suyangmo 收養母 godmother
Swae-ryŏng 灑嶺 or 洒嶺 Swae Pass

taebangsulgaek 大方術客 master ascetic
taedohobu 大都護府 greater county
taedohobusa 大都護府使 greater county
    magistrate
Taehan Cheguk 大韓帝國 Great Han
    Empire
t'aehyŏng 笞刑 method of punishment
    that consists of being beaten with a
    light stick
Taejŏn hoet'ong 大典會通 *Comprehen-
    sive Collection of Dynastic Codes*
t'aesang 胎傷 injury to a fetus
taesin 大臣 minister
Taewŏn'gun 大院君 the father of King
    Kojong
tangbogun 塘報軍 scout soldier
tangjil 堂姪 a son of a male cousin or a
    second nephew
tangmok 唐木 Chinese cotton
to 道 province
togwa 道科 provincial examination
tohobu 都護府 county
tohobusa 都護府使 county magistrate
tohyŏng 徒刑 method of punishment
    consisting of penal servitude
tong 洞 village, also transliterated *dong*
T'ongch'ŏn 通川 place name
tongch'u 同推 joint interrogation under
    torture
tongim 洞任 village administrator
tongjang 洞長 village headman or
    village elder
tongmong 童蒙 young student
t'ongmun 通文 circular (i.e., newsletter)
tongsu 洞首 village headman or village
    elder
tubok 肚腹 upper belly
"T'ugu" (C: Dou'ou) 鬪毆 "Affrays and
    Batteries," an article in the *Great
    Ming Code*
"T'ugu kŭp kosal in" (C: Dou'ou ji gusha
    ren) 鬪毆及故殺人 "Killing Others
    in Affrays or by Intention," an article
    in the *Great Ming Code*

t'ujang 偷葬 "to steal a tomb site," meaning to carry out an illegal burial

tumin 頭民 village headman

tŭngsi salsa 登時殺死 the immediate killing of an adulterer and adulterous wife

turak 斗落 a measure of land where 1 *mal* (4.765 U.S. gallons) of rice seed is sown

turo 頭顱 cranium

Ŭigŭmbu 義禁府 State Tribunal

Ŭijŏngbu 議政府 State Council

ŭisaeng 醫生 herbalist or medical specialist

ŭlmi 乙未 name of a year in the sixty-year cycle

ŭm 陰 protection privilege

un 雲 a particular serial mark or an entry in *Ch'ŏnjamun* (Thousand-character classic)

Ŭn nyŏ 殷女 Ms. Ŭn

wŏn'go 原告 plaintiff

Xiyuan lu (K: *Sewŏllok*) 洗冤錄 *The Washing Away of Wrongs*

yakchŏng 約正 district administrator

yang 兩 monetary unit; 1 *yang* = 10 *chŏn* = 100 *p'un* or *mun*

yangaekchi 兩腋肢 both armpits

yanganp'o 兩眼胞 both eyelids

yangbibu 兩臂膊 both shoulders (back side)

yangdun 兩臀 both buttocks

yanggagwan 兩脚腕 both ankles

yanggak sinjik 兩脚伸直 both legs are straight

yanggakkwa 兩脚踝 both ankles

yanggaksim 兩脚心 both soles of the feet

yanggangmyŏn 兩脚面 both tops of the feet

yanggokch'u 兩曲瞅 both crooks of the knees

yanggokch'u 兩腆瞅 inside the elbow

yanggwa 兩胯 both groins (i.e., right and left sides)

yanggyŏlbun'gol 兩缺盆骨 both depressed areas above the shoulder blades

yanggyŏmin 兩臁朒 both shins

yanggyŏn'gap 兩肩胛 both shoulders

yanghuhyŏp 兩後脇 sides under the arms (back)

yanghŭlju 兩肐肘 both elbows

yanghŭppak 兩臂膊 upper arms

yanghuruk 兩後肋 back ribs

yanghyŏp 兩脇 sides under the arms (front)

yangi 兩耳 both ears

yangigŭn 兩耳根 both roots of the ears

yangjŏn-ch'ŏk 量田尺 a land-survey ruler

yangmi 兩眉 both eyebrows

yangnŭk 兩肋 ribs

yangnyŏ 良女 commoner woman

yangsihyŏp 兩腮脇 both cheeks

yangsubae 兩手背 both backs of the hands

yangsŭl 兩膝 both knees

yangsuwan 兩手腕 both wrists

yangt'aeyanghyŏl 兩太陽穴 both temples

yangt'oe 兩腿 both thighs

yangt'oedu 兩腿肚 both calves

yangyu 兩乳 both breasts

Yech'on 醴泉 place name

Yi Ch'ŏmji 李僉知 Mr. Yi, who has a senior third-rank military post

Yihwa-ch'on 李花村 Pear Blossom Hamlet

yŏ myŏngin 女明人 enlightened woman

yoan 腰眼 waist

yŏllyŏjŏn 烈女傳 biography of a chaste woman

Yŏngch'ŏn 永川 place name

Yongin 龍仁 place name

yŏngŭijŏng 領議政 chief state councilor
Yŏsa nanjip 餘事亂集 *Collected Works on Miscellaneous Matters*
Yu *choi* 柳召史 Ms. Yu
Yu *nyŏ* 柳女 Ms. Yu
Yu Sŏnjŏn 劉宣傳 Mr. Yu, who has the military post of royal messenger
yuae 有碍 procedural difficulty
yuhak 幼學 "youthful student" (a title)
yuhyŏng 流刑 punishment by banishment
yuhyŏp 乳脇 area between the breast and side (of the body)

Yukkun 陸軍 the Army
yukpŏm 六犯 six crimes
yulsaeng 律生 legal clerk
yun 閏 intercalary month
yun samwŏl 閏三月 intercalary third month
yu-si 酉時 around six in the evening
Yusŏ p'ilchi 儒胥必知 *Essential Knowledge for Scholar-Officials and Clerks*
yusu 留守 municipal chief magistrate
yusubu 留守府 municipality

BIBLIOGRAPHY

PRIMARY SOURCES

An Chŏng-bok. *Imgwan chŏngyo* (Essentials for officials). Seoul: Kungnip Chungang Tosŏgwan (National Library of Korea) Collection, cho 31–65.

Anak-kun oksu Paek choi ch'ogŏm kŭp myŏngsa munan (First inquest and special investigation reports concerning prisoner Ms. Paek from Anak Lesser County). Seoul: Kyujanggak Collection, kyu 21560.

Ch'ugwanji (Treatise of the Ministry of Penal Affairs). Compiled by Par Ir-wŏn in 1791. Reprint in 3 vols. by Seoul Taehakkyo Kyujanggak. Seoul: Seoul Taehakkyo Kyujanggak, 2004.

Chunghwa-bu ogan (Inquest records of Chunghwa County). Harvard-Yenching Library Collection, TK 4899 4352.

Chŭngsu muwŏllok onhae (Amplified and corrected coroner's manual for the elimination of grievances in vernacular Korean). Originally compiled by Wang Yü, edited by Ku T'aekkyu, and translated by Sŏ Yurin. Yŏngyŏng sin'gan, 1797. Harvard-Yenching Library Collection, TK 4899 7834.

The Great Ming Code / Da Ming lü. Translated by Jiang Yonglin. Seattle: University of Washington Press, 2005.

Hoeyang-gun Changyang-myŏn Hanch'i-ri ch'isa namin Kim Kap-san oksa saan (Special investigation report concerning the criminal case involving deceased male Kim Kap-san from Hanch'i Subdistrict, Changyang District, Hoeyang Lesser County). Seoul: Kyujanggak Collection, kyu 21062.

Hoeyang-gun ch'isa namin Kim Kap-san oksa saan (Special investigation report concerning the criminal case involving deceased male Kim Kap-san from Hoeyang Lesser County). Seoul: Kyujanggak Collection, kyu 21060.

Ilsŏngnok (Record of daily reflections). 86 vols. Edited by Seoul Taehakkyo Kyujanggak. Seoul: Seoul Taehakkyo Kyujanggak, 1982–1996.

Kangwŏn-do Hoeyang-gun Changyang-myŏn Hanch'i-ri ch'isa namin Kim Kap-san ch'ogŏman (First inquest record of the deceased male Kim Kap-san from Hanch'i Subdistrict, Changyang District, Hoeyang Lesser County, in Kangwŏn Province). Seoul: Kyujanggak Collection, kyu 21061.

Kim Yun-bo. *Hyŏngjŏng toch'ŏp* (Painting album of penal affairs). Reprint in *Kyegan misul* 39 (Fall 1986): 113–22.

Kŏman (Inquest Records). Seoul: Kungnip Chungang Tosŏgwan (National Library of Korea) Collection, han kojo 34–51.

Kŏman ch'o (Selected Inquest Records). 2 vols. Seoul: Kungnip Chungang Tosŏgwan (National Library of Korea) Collection, han kojo 34–37.

Kugyŏk simnirok (Records of Royal Reviews in Korean translation). 6 vols. Original text compiled by royal order of King Chŏngjo. Translated by Pak Ch'an-su and Kim Ki-bin. Seoul: Minjok Munhwa Ch'ujinhoe, 1998–2007.

Kyŏngguk taejŏn (Great code of administration). Compiled in 1485. Reprinted and edited by Han'gukhak Munhŏn Yŏn'guso. Seoul: Asea Munhwasa, 1983.

Legge, James. *The Works of Mencius*. Vol. 2 in *The Chinese Classics with a Translation, Critical and Exegetical Notes, Prolegomena, and Copious Indexes*. Oxford: Clarendon Press, 1895.

Ogan ch'ogae (Summary of inquest records). 2 vols. Seoul: Kungnip Chungang Tosŏgwan (National Library of Korea) Collection, han kojo 34–39.

Sabŏp p'umbo (Provincial reports concerning legal matters). Kyujanggak Collection, kyu 17278–v.1–128 (1894–1907). Reprinted and edited by Sin Yong-ha, 10 vols. Seoul: Asea munhwasa, 1988–90.

Sima Qian. *Shi Ji* (Records of the grand historian). Harvard-Yenching Library. http://pds.lib.harvard.edu/pds/view/19140085.

Sinju muwŏllok (Newly annotated coroner's guide for the elimination of grievances). Compiled by Ch'oe Chi-un et al. in 1438. Translated by Kim Ho. Seoul: Sagyejŏl, 2003.

Sok taejŏn (Supplement to the great code). Compiled in 1744. Reprinted and edited by Han'gukhak Munhŏn Yon'guso. Seoul: Asea munhwasa, 1983.

Sugyo tŭngnok (Compilation of received edicts). Seoul: Kyujanggak Collection, kyu 15412.

Sung Tz'u. *The Washing Away of Wrongs*. Translated by Brian E. McKnight. Ann Arbor: Center for Chinese Studies, University of Michigan, 1981.

Sŭngjŏngwŏn ilgi (Records of the Royal Secretariat). 126 vols. Edited by Kuksa P'yŏnch'an Wiwŏnhoe (National Institute of Korean History). Seoul: T'amgudang, 1961–1977.

Taejŏn hoet'ong (Comprehensive collection of dynastic codes). Compiled in 1865. Reprint, Seoul: Pogyŏng munhwawa, 1990.

T'ŭkkyo chŏngsik (Special edicts deciding legal codes). Seoul: Kyujanggak Collection, kyu, K0951.009 T296.

Yi Sŭng-gyŏng (1815–?). *Kyŏngjo puji* (Gazetteer of Seoul). Compiled in 1851. Seoul: Kyujanggak Collection, 6599.

———. *Yŏsa nanjip* (Collected works on miscellaneous matters). Sŏngnam: Changsŏgak Collection, K4–6266.

Yusŏ p'ilchi (Essential knowledge for scholar-officials and clerks). 1872 edition. Seoul: Kyujanggak Collection, kyu no. 6700 (1872).

SECONDARY SOURCES

Allee, Mark A. *Law and Local Society in Late Imperial China: Northern Taiwan in the Nineteenth Century*. Stanford: Stanford University Press, 1994.

Barahona, Renato. *Sex Crimes, Honour, and the Law in Early Modern Spain: Vizcaya, 1528–1735*. Toronto: University of Toronto Press, 2003.

Brook, Timothy, Jérôme Bourgon, and Gregory Blue. *Death by a Thousand Cuts*. Cambridge: Harvard University Press, 2008.

Capp, Bernard. *When Gossips Meet: Women, Family, and Neighbourhood in Early Modern England*. Oxford: Oxford University Press, 2003.

Chang Pyŏng-in. "Chosŏn chung-hugi kant'ong e taehan kyuje ŭi kanghwa" (A reinforcement of adultery regulations in the middle and late Chosŏn period). *Han'guksa yŏn'gu* 121 (June 2003): 83–116.

Cho Chi-man. *Chosŏn sidae ŭi hyŏngsabŏp: Taemyŏngnyul kwa kukchŏn* (Criminal law in Chosŏn: The *Great Ming Code* and Chosŏn law codes). Seoul: Kyŏngin munhwasa, 2007.

Cho Yun-sŏn. *Chosŏn hugi sosong yŏn'gu* (Study of late Chosŏn litigations). Seoul: Kukhak charyowŏn, 2002.

Ch'oe Sŭng-hŭi. "Chosŏn sidae yangban ŭi taegaje" (The rank transfer system for yangban during the Chosŏn period). *Chindan hakpo* 60 (1985): 1–32.

Choi, Yŏngho, Peter H. Lee, and Wm. Theodore de Bary, eds. *Sources of Korean Tradition, Vol. 2*. New York: Columbia University Press, 2000.

Chŏng Kŭng-sik. "Urinara kant'ongjoe ŭi popchesajŏk koch'al" (A study of adultery from the viewpoint of legal history in Korea). In *Hyŏngbŏp kaejŏng kwa kwallyŏnhayŏ pon nakt'aejoe mit kant'ongjoe e kwanhan yŏn'gu* (A study of adultery and abortion from the viewpoint of criminal law reform in Korea), edited by Sin Tong-un et al., 211–42. Seoul: Han'guk hyŏngsa chŏngch'aek yŏn'guwŏn yŏn'gu ch'ongsŏ, 1990.

Chŏng Kŭng-sik and Cho Chi-man. "Chosŏn chŏn'gi *Taemyŏngyul* ŭi suyong kwa pyŏnyong" (The reception and transformation of the *Great Ming Code* in the early Chosŏn). *Chindan hakpo* 96 (2003): 205–41.

Davis, Natalie Zemon. *Fiction in the Archives: Pardon Tales and Their Tellers in Sixteenth-Century France*. Stanford: Stanford University Press, 1987.

Deuchler, Martina. "'Heaven Does Not Discriminate': A Study of Secondary Sons in Chosŏn Korea." *Journal of Korean Studies* 6 (1988–89): 121–64.

———. "The Practice of Confucianism: Ritual and Order in Chosŏn Dynasty Korea." In *Rethinking Confucianism: Past and Present in China, Japan, Korea, and Vietnam*, edited by Benjamin A. Elman, John B. Duncan, and Herman Ooms, 292–334. Los Angeles: UCLA Asian Pacific Monograph Series, 2002.

Ginzburg, Carlo. *The Night Battles: Witchcraft and Agrarian Cults in the Sixteenth and Seventeenth Centuries*. Baltimore: The Johns Hopkins University Press, 1992.

Haboush, JaHyun Kim. "Gender and the Politics of Language in Chosŏn Korea." In *Rethinking Confucianism: Past and Present in China, Japan, Korea, and Vietnam*, edited by Benjamin A. Elman, John B. Duncan, and Herman Ooms, 220–57. Los Angeles: UCLA Asian Pacific Monograph Series, 2002.

Han Sang-gwŏn. *Chosŏn hugi sahoe wa sowŏn chedo* (The petition system and society in the late Chosŏn). Seoul: Ilchogak, 1996.

———. "Chosŏn hugi sansong ŭi silt'ae wa sŏnggyŏk—Chŏngjo-dae sangŏn kyŏkchaeng ŭl chungsimŭro" (The realities and nature of gravesite litigations in the late Chosŏn—An analysis of written petitions and petitions by striking a gong during the reign of King Chŏngjo). *Sŏnggok nonch'ong* 27, no. 4 (1996): 775–830.

Hegel, Robert E., comp. and trans. *True Crimes in Eighteenth-Century China: Twenty Case Histories.* Seattle: University of Washington Press, 2009.

Hwang, Kyung Moon. *Beyond Birth: Social Status in the Emergence of Modern Korea.* Cambridge: Harvard University Press, 2004.

Karlsson, Anders. "Famine Relief, Social Order, and State Performance in Late Chosŏn Korea." *Journal of Korean Studies* 12, no. 1 (Fall 2007): 113–42.

———. "Royal Compassion and Disaster Relief in Chosŏn Korea." *Seoul Journal of Korean Studies* 20, no. 1 (June 2007): 71–98.

Kawashima, Fujiya. "A Study of *Hyangan*: Kin Groups and Aristocratic Localism in the Seventeenth and Eighteenth Century Korean Countryside." *Journal of Korean Studies* 5 (1984): 3–38.

Kim Ho. "*Hŭmhŭm sinsŏ* ŭi ilgoch'al" (A study of *New Writings on Circumspection in Judicial Decisions). Chosŏn sidaesa hakpo* 54 (2010): 233–65.

Kim, Jisoo. "Voices Heard: Women's Right to Petition in Late Chosŏn Korea." PhD diss., Columbia University, 2010.

Kim, Joong-Seop. "In Search of Human Rights: The *Paekchŏng* Movement in Colonial Korea." In *Colonial Modernity in Korea*, edited by Gi-Wook Shin and Michael Robinson, 311–35. Cambridge: Harvard University Asia Center, 1999.

Kim, Jungwon. "Negotiating Virtue and the Lives of Women in Late Chosŏn Korea." PhD diss., Harvard University, 2007.

Kim Kyŏng-suk. "Chosŏn hugi yŏsŏng ŭi chŏngso hwaldong" (Women's petitioning activity in the late Chosŏn). *Han'guk munhwa* 36 (December 2005): 89–123.

Kim Sŏn-gyŏng. "Chosŏn hugi sansong kwa sallim soyugwŏn ŭi silt'ae" (Legal disputes over forest lands and the realities of forest land ownership in the late Chosŏn). *Tongbang hakchi* 77/78/79 (June 1993): 497–535.

———. "Chosŏn hugi yŏsŏng ŭi sŏng, kamsi wa ch'ŏbŏl" (Female sexuality in the late Chosŏn, control and punishment). *Yŏksa yŏn'gu* 8 (2000): 57–100.

Kim, Sun Joo. "Chosŏn hugi P'yŏngan-do Chŏngju ŭi hyangan unyŏng kwa yangban munhwa" (The management of the local yangban roster and elite culture in Chŏngju, P'yŏngan Province, in the late Chosŏn period). *Yŏksa hakpo* 185 (March 2005): 65–105.

———. "Fragmented: The *T'ongch'ŏng* Movements by Marginalized Status Groups in Late Chosŏn Korea." *Harvard Journal of Asiatic Studies* 68, no. 1 (June 2008): 135–68.

———. *Marginality and Subversion in Korea: The Hong Kyŏngnae Rebellion of 1812.* Seattle: University of Washington Press, 2007.

———. *The Northern Region of Korea: History, Identity, and Culture.* Seattle: Center for Korean Studies, University of Washington, 2010.

———. "Taxes, the Local Elite, and the Rural Populace in the Chinju Uprising of 1862." *Journal of Asian Studies* 64, no. 4 (November 2007): 993–1027.

Kim Yong-sŏp. "The Two Courses of Agrarian Reform in Korea's Modernization." In *Landlords, Peasants and Intellectuals in Modern Korea*, edited by Pang Kie-chung and Michael D. Shin, 21–52. Ithaca, NY: East Asia Program, Cornell University Press, 2005.

Ko Sŏk-kyu. *19-segi Chosŏn ŭi hyangch'on sahoe yon'gu, chibae wa chŏhang ŭi kujo* (A study of local society in nineteenth-century Chosŏn: The structure of control and resistance). Seoul: Seoul Taehakkyo Chu'lp'anbu, 1998.

Kwŏn Yŏn-ung. "*Simnirok* ŭi kich'ojŏk kŏmt'o" (Basic studies of the *Records of Royal Reviews*). In *Yi Ki-baek sŏnsaeng kohŭi kinyŏm Han'guk sahak nonch'ong* (Collection of papers on Korean history in commemoration of Professor Yi Ki-baek's seventieth birthday), edited by Yi Ki-baek Sŏnsaeng Kohŭi Kinyŏm Han'guk Sahak Nonch'ong Kanhaeng Wiwŏnhoe, vol. 2:1320–38. Seoul: Ilchogak, 1994.

Macauley, Melissa. *Social Power and Legal Culture: Litigation Masters in Late Imperial China*. Stanford: Stanford University Press, 1998.

McKnight, Brian E. "Introduction: Forensic Practice in Thirteenth-Century China." In Sung Tz'u, *The Washing Away of Wrongs*, translated by McKnight, 1–34. Ann Arbor: Center for Chinese Studies, University of Michigan, 1981.

Moon, Yumi. "The Populist Contest: The Ilchinhoe Movement and the Japanese Colonization of Korea, 1896–1910." PhD diss., Harvard University, 2006.

Paek Sŭng-jong. *Han'guk sahoesa yŏn'gu* (A study of the social history of Korea). Seoul: Ilchogak, 1996.

Pak Hŭng-su. "Toryanghyŏng chedo" (Weights and measures). In *Han'guksa* (History of Korea), edited by Kuksa P'yŏnch'an Wiwŏnhoe, vol. 24:599–625. Seoul: Kuksa P'yŏnch'an Wiwŏnhoe, 1994.

Pak Hye-suk. "18 segi–19 segi e poinŭn hwap'ye tanwi pŏnyŏk ŭi munje" (Translation of currency units in literature from the eighteenth and nineteenth centuries). *Minjok munhaksa yŏn'gu* 38 (2008): 203–33.

Pak Ki-ju. "19.20 segi ch'o chaech'on yangban chiju kyŏngyŏng ŭi tonghyang" (The trend of landlordism of landed yangban in the nineteenth and early twentieth centuries). In *Matchil ŭi nongmindŭl* (Peasants of Matchil), edited by An Pyŏng-jik and Yi Yŏng-hun, 205–41. Seoul: Ilchogak, 2001.

Palais, James B. *Confucian Statecraft and Korean Institutions: Yu Hyŏngwŏn and the Late Chosŏn Dynasty*. Seattle: University of Washington Press, 1996.

———. "Political Leadership and the Yangban in the Choson Dynasty." *Etudes thématiques: La société civile face à l'Etat dans les traditions chinoise, japonaise, coréenne et vietnamiennne* 3 (1994): 391–408.

———. *Politics and Policy in Traditional Korea*. Cambridge: Harvard University Press, 1975.

Park, Eugene Y. *Between Dreams and Reality: The Military Examination in Late Chosŏn Korea, 1600–1894*. Cambridge: Harvard University Asia Center, 2007.

Peterson, Mark A. *Korean Adoption and Inheritance: Case Studies in the Creation of a Classic Confucian Society*. Ithaca, NY: East Asia Program, Cornell University Press, 1996.

Pihl, Marshall R. *The Korean Singer of Tales.* Cambridge: Harvard University Asia Center, 1994.

Shaw, William. *Legal Norms in a Confucian State.* Berkeley: Institute of East Asian Studies, University of California, 1981.

Shin, Susan. "The Social Structure of Kŭmhwa County in the Late Seventeenth Century." *Occasional Papers on Korea* 1 (1974): 9–35.

Sim Chae-u. "Chŏngjo tae hŭmhyul chŏnch'ik ŭi panp'o wa hyŏnggu chŏngbi" (Promulgating grand principles of legal reasoning and restructuring punishing tools during Chŏngjo's reign). *Kyujanggak* 22 (1999): 135–53.

———. *Chosŏn hugi kukka kwŏllyŏk kwa pŏmjoe t'ongje*—Simnirok *yŏn'gu* (State power and crime control in the late Chosŏn period—A study of the *Records of Royal Reviews*). Seoul: T'aehaksa, 2009.

Skinner, Stephen. *The Living Earth Manual of Feng-Shui: Chinese Geomancy.* London: Routledge & Kegan Paul, 1982.

Sommer, Mathew. *Sex, Law, and Society in Late Imperial China.* Stanford: Stanford University Press, 2000.

Theiss, Janet. "Explaining the Shrew: Narratives of Spousal Violence and the Critique of Masculinity in 18th-Century Criminal Cases." In *Writing and Law in Late Imperial China: Crime, Conflict, and Judgment,* edited by Robert E. Hegel and Katherine Carlitz, 44–63. Seattle: University of Washington Press, 2007.

To Myŏn-hoe. "1894–1905 nyŏn'gan hyŏngsa chaep'an chedo yŏn'gu" (A study of the criminal trial system between 1894 and 1905). PhD diss., Seoul National University, 1998.

———. "Kabo kaehyŏkki hyŏngsa pŏpkyu ŭi kaehyŏk" (Reforms of penal regulations during the Kabo Reform). *Kyujanggak* 21 (1998): 103–22.

———. "Kabo kaehyŏk ihu kŭndaejŏk pŏmnyŏng chejŏng kwajŏng—hyŏngsabop ŭl chungsimŭro" (The legislative process of modern laws after the Kabo Reform—Criminal laws). *Han'guk munhwa* 27 (2001): 325–62.

Walraven, Boudewijn. "Popular Religion in a Confucianized Society." In *Culture and the State in Late Chosŏn Korea,* edited by JaHyun Kim Haboush and Martina Deuchler, 160–98. Cambridge: Harvard University Press, 1999.

Yi Chae-hŭi. "Kukka ka kyŏnjehan yangbandŭl ŭi hwaryŏhan chugŏ munhwa" (Luxurious residential culture of yangban that the state tried to regulate). In *Chosŏn yangban ŭi ilsaeng* (A life of yangban during the Chosŏn dynasty), edited by Kyujanggak Han'gukhak Yŏn'guwŏn, 177–208. Seoul: Kŭlhangari, 2009.

Yi Hŏn-ch'ang. "Chosŏn malgi pobusang kwa pobusangdan" (Late Chosŏn peddlers and peddler organizations). *Kuksagwan nonch'ong* 38 (1992): 143–75.

Yi Myŏng-bok. *Chosŏn sidae hyŏngsa chedo* (The criminal judicial system during the Chosŏn dynasty). Seoul: Tongguk University Press, 2007.

Yi Yŏng-hun. "Ch'ongsŏl: Chosŏn hugi kyŏngjesa yŏn'gu ŭi saeroun tonghyang kwa kwaje" (New perspectives and tasks in the study of economic history of the late Chosŏn). In *Suryang kyŏngjesa ro tasi pon Chosŏn hugi* (An examination of the late Chosŏn from the perspective of economic history), edited by Yi Yŏng-hun, 367–91. Seoul: Seoul taehakkyo ch'ulp'anbu, 2004.

Yŏn Chŏng-yŏl. *Han'guk pŏpche sasangsa* (The history of legal thought in Korea). Seoul: Hansŏng University Press, 2007.

Yun Chŏng-ae. "Chosŏn hugi suryŏng taech'aek kwa kŭ insa silt'ae" (Personnel policies over magistrate posts and their realities in the late Chosŏn). *Kuksagwan nonch'ong* 17 (1990): 227–44.

INDEX

ho). *See also* Kim Kap-san; Kim
Mun-ho
Kyŏngguk taejŏn (Great code of adminis-
tration), 13, 48, 62, 218n2
Kyujanggak Archive, 8, 135

law and society in 19th century, as
inscribed in inquest records, 20–22
"Laws on Punishments and General
Principles" (K: Myŏngnye; C: Mingli)
(chapter in *Great Ming Code*), 190
litigation and petition systems, 208n46

"Maein" (C: Maren; cursing others), 64
magistrates, county, 14, 15
marriage: local communities connected
through, 213n6; and remarriage, 62
measuring units, xii, xiii
Mencius, 222n27, 223n35
Min Ch'i-sŏ, 57
Ministry of Penal Affairs (Hyŏngjo), 14
miscarriage, causing a, 100, 216n7
modernization, 4
Mosal in (C: Mousha ren) ("Plotting to
Kill Others"; article in *Great Ming
Code*), 191
Mun Chong-ji, 75, 76, 81, 90, 92; concluding statement of first inquest investigation, 90–92; concluding statement
of second inquest investigation, 92–
94; concluding statement to special
investigation report, 94–98; corpse,
73–74, 77–79; inquest report, 75–90;
overview, 72
Mun Yu-mok, 89, 91, 93, 95, 96–98; depositions, 83, 86; finances, 79, 88, 89, 95;
Im Ch'ang-nin and, 95; interrogation, 76; Ko Kyŏng-sam and, 77, 79,
83; marriage, 74–76, 88; Ms. Cho and,
77, 79, 81, 83; Ms. Kim and, 72, 74–77,
79, 80, 82–86, 88, 89, 95, 98; oral
report, 76; overview, 76; Sŭng-mun
and, 76–77, 79, 81, 83, 85; testimony,
76–77, 79, 83, 86

murder, motives for, 42
*Muwŏllok (Coroner's Guide for the
Elimination of Grievances)*, 7, 15–18,
73, 207n29
Myŏngnye (C: Mingli) ("Laws on Punishments and General Principles";
chapter in *Great Ming Code*), 190

Nam Hyo-wŏn, 127, 220n34
northern provinces, prejudice against
people of the, 130

O Ch'ang-jo, 32–33
O Tae-ryŏn, 33

Paek, Ms., 128; accusations against Kim
Kyŏng-un and, 110, 124; adultery
with Kim Kyŏng-un, 109, 110, 124,
126, 128; Cho Kuk-po and, 126; Cho
Kwang-p'il and, 121; inquest report
of first inquest concerning, 112–28;
overview, 109; testimony, 110–11,
124–26
Pak, Ms., xiv, 49–54; corpse, 52–53;
death, 49, 50; dug up illegal burial,
49; overview, 49, 51–52
Pak Chu-hŏn, 201, 203
Pak Kun-hae, 158–60, 165
Pak Kyŏm-ch'oe, 52
Pak Kyŏng-ju, 100–106
Pak Kyu-su, 26
Pak Yong-dŏk, 172, 179
Pak Yun-sŏk, 146
Palch'ong (C: Fazhong) ("Uncovering
Graves"; article in *Great Ming Code*),
200
peddlers *(pobusang)*, 101
Penal Affairs, Ministry of (Hyŏngjo), 14
"Plotting to Kill Others" ("K: Mosal
in; C: Mousha ren) (article in *Great
Ming Code*), 191
pobusang (peddlers), 101
posang (wrapping merchant), 101
private settlement *(sahwa)*, 99–103, 106